the
confessing
Baptist

*Essays on the Use of Creeds
in Baptist Faith & Life*

the confessing Baptist

Essays on the Use of Creeds in Baptist Faith & Life

EDITED BY

· ROBERT GONZALES JR. ·

FREE GRACE PRESS

Cover design by Scott Schaller

Printed in the United States of America.

Free Grace Press
1076 Harkrider
Conway, AR 72032
freegracepress.com

ISBN: 978-1-952599-36-1

Dedicated to

Samuel E. Waldron and Gregory G. Nichols,
two of my theological mentors who encouraged in me
a deep appreciation for the Second London Baptist
Confession of Faith

Contents

Contributors

Nicolas Alford is an ordained minister of the gospel and graduate of Reformed Baptist Seminary (master of theological studies), where he is a guest lecturer. He has served in various pastoral ministries, taught theology in both domestic and international contexts, and served on several overseeing boards and committees for Christian organizations. He has authored or contributed to several books, most recently *Further Up and Further In: Experiencing the Inexhaustible Gospel of Jesus Christ* (Wrath & Grace, 2021). Nick is passionate about Christ-centered life and ministry, spending time with his wife and three children, and despairing over the Seattle Mariners. A native of the Pacific Northwest, Nick can often be found on a mountain trail or floating in a boat, soaking in the glory of God. He and his family are members of Olympic Evangelical Free Church in Poulsbo, Washington.

Thomas K. Ascol has been in pastoral ministry since 1978 and senior pastor of Grace Baptist Church in Cape Coral, Florida, since 1986. Tom earned a BS in sociology from Texas A&M University, and an MDiv and PhD from Southwestern Baptist Theological Seminary. Along with numerous articles in journals and periodicals, he has edited and written nine books, including *Dear Timothy: Letters on Pastoral Ministry, From the Protestant Reformation to the Southern Baptist Convention, Traditional Theology and the SBC, Truth and Grace Memory Books* (3 vols.), and *Strong and Courageous: Following Jesus Amid the Rise of America's New Religion*. He is a former teaching fellow at the Nicole Institute of Reformed Theological Seminary and has taught theology in numerous seminaries and colleges throughout North and South America and Africa. He is also the president of Founders Ministries and the president of the Institute of Public Theology. Tom and his wife, Donna, have six children and fourteen grandchildren.

Brian Borgman is founding pastor of Grace Community Church. He earned a BA in biblical studies from Biola University (La Mirada, CA), a master of divinity from Western Conservative Baptist Seminary (Portland, OR), a ThM in historical theology from Puritan Reformed Theological Seminary (Grand Rapids, MI) and a doctor of ministry from Westminster Seminary (Escondido, CA). Brian has written numerous books, including *Feelings and Faith* (Crossway) and *An Exile's Guide to Walking with God* (Free Grace Press). He is married to Ariel, and they have three grown children and three grandchildren.

Vadim Chepurny serves as assistant to the dean at Reformed Baptist Seminary. Vadim is a graduate of UC Davis (electrical engineering) and The Master's Seminary (MDiv). He and his wife, Anna, along with their daughter, Leah, are currently residing in Sacramento, where Vadim serves as a pastoral intern at Immanuel Baptist Church and is pursuing future ministry in Ukraine.

Robert Gonzales Jr. holds an MA in theology and a PhD in Old Testament interpretation from Bob Jones University. He is the author of *Where Sin Abounds: The Spread of Sin and the Curse in Genesis with Special Focus on the Patriarchal Narratives* (Wipf & Stock) and has contributed to *Reformed Baptist Theological Review*, *Founders Journal*, and *Westminster Theological Journal*. When he is not serving as a dean or professor, Bob is riding dirt bikes, playing softball, or hiking. He and his wife, Becky, have five children and, at the time of editing this volume, one grandchild.

Michael A. G. Haykin was born in England of Irish and Kurdish parents. He serves as chair and professor of church history at The Southern Baptist Theological Seminary. He is also the director of the Andrew Fuller Center for Baptist Studies, located on the Southern campus. He also teaches in the core faculty of Heritage Theological Seminary in Cambridge, Ontario, as professor of church history. Dr. Haykin has a BA in philosophy from the University of Toronto (1974), a master of religion from Wycliffe College at the University of Toronto (1977), and a ThD in church history from Wycliffe College at the University of Toronto (1982). Dr. Haykin and his wife, Alison, have two married children: Victoria (married to Mischa) and Nigel (married to Sharon).

Jeffrey D. Johnson is the teaching pastor of Grace Bible Church in Conway, Arkansas. He has a MRel and DMin from Veritas Theological Seminary and is the director of academics at Grace Bible Theological Seminary in Conway, Arkansas. He is also the author of a number of books, including *The Fatal Flaw of the Theology Behind Infant Baptism*, *Behind the Bible: A Primer on Textual Criticism*, *The Church: Why Bother?*, *The Kingdom of God: A Baptist Expression of Covenant & Biblical Theology*, and *The Absurdity of Unbelief*, and the founder of Free Grace Press.

Thomas J. Nettles has taught and written about Baptist history since 1976. He has taught on the faculty of four theological seminaries and served as visiting professor at several others. Along with numerous journal articles and scholarly papers, Dr. Nettles is the author and editor of sixteen books. Among his books are *By His Grace and for His Glory*; *Baptists and the Bible*, which he co-authored with L. Russ Bush; *Teaching Truth, Training Hearts,* a study on the use and text of catechisms in Baptist life; *Living by Revealed Truth,* a biography of Charles H. Spurgeon; and *James Petigru Boyce: A Southern Baptist Statesman.*

Samuel E. Waldron began serving as a pastor in 1977. He is a graduate and former professor of Trinity Ministerial Academy. Sam holds a ThM from Grand Rapids Baptist Seminary and a PhD in systematic theology at The Southern Baptist Theological Seminary. He has authored such books as *A Modern Exposition of the 1689 Confession of Faith* (Evangelical Press), *Baptist Roots in America* (Simpson), *The End Times Made Simple* (Calvary Press), and *A Reformed Baptist Manifesto* (Reformed Baptist Academic Press). He is currently the president of and a professor for Covenant Baptist Theological Seminary in Owensboro, Kentucky.

Luke Walker is the preaching pastor of Redeeming Cross Community Church in Minneapolis where he has served since 2012. He is also the founding author of Wrath and Grace Publishing and has authored seven titles including *Lemuel Haynes: The Black Puritan* and *He Gave Them Judges: Jesus in the Book of Judges.* He and his lovely wife, Angel, have three beautiful children: Aleah Selah, Judah Luke, and Beorn Solomon.

Steve Weaver has been in pastoral ministry for over twenty-five years and has served since 2008 as the senior pastor of Farmdale Baptist Church in Frankfort, Kentucky. Steve has a PhD in church history and historical theology from The Southern Baptist Theological Seminary in Louisville, Kentucky. He is the author of *Orthodox, Puritan, Baptist: Hercules Collins (1647–1702) and Particular Baptist Identity in Early Modern England* (Vandenhoeck & Ruprecht, 2015). Steve has also co-edited, along with Michael A. G. Haykin, a modernized edition of *An Orthodox Catechism* (Reformed Baptist Academic Press, 2013) and *Devoted to the Service of the Temple: Piety, Persecution, and Ministry in the Writings of Hercules Collins* (Reformation Heritage Books, 2007). Steve also contributed to the new edition of Thomas J. Nettles' *Teaching Truth, Training Hearts: The Study of Catechisms in Baptist Life* (Founders, 2017).

Preface

Robert Gonzales Jr.

Over the last few decades, the church has shown a renewed interest in the theology of the Reformation.[1] The reprinting of classic Reformed and Puritan literature as well as the proliferation of conferences focusing on one or more of the Reformation "solas"[2] bear witness to this resurgence. Additionally, an increasing number of Christians and churches have rediscovered the creeds, confessions, and catechisms that were forged during this epochal period of church history. One can find newly published analyses of such Reformed symbols as the Thirty-Nine Articles (1563),[3] the Canons of Dordt (1618–19),[4] the Heidelberg Catechism (1563),[5] or the Westminster Confession (1646).[6]

---

1 For a survey and appraisal of the modern Reformed resurgence, see Collin Hansen's article "Young, Restless, Reformed: Calvinism is Making a Comeback—and Shaking Up the Church," *Christianity Today*, September 22, 2006, https://www.christianitytoday.com/ct/2006/september/42.32.html, and his subsequent full-length book *Young, Restless, Reformed: A Journalist's Journey with the New Calvinists* (Wheaton, IL: Crossway, 2008). More recently, Mark Oppenheimer, "Evangelicals Find Themselves in the Midst of a Calvinist Revival," *The New York Times*, January 3, 2014, https://www.nytimes.com/2014/01/04/us/a-calvinist-revival-for-evangelicals.html.

2 The five "solas" are the following Latin phrases: *sola fide* (by faith alone), *sola gratia* (by grace alone), *sola Scriptura* (by Scripture alone), *solus Christus* (in Christ alone), and *soli Deo gloria* (to the glory of God alone). Each of these phrases highlights a Protestant and Reformed doctrine.

3 Gerald Bray, *The Faith We Confess: An Exposition of the Thirty-Nine Articles* (Latimer Trust, 2009).

4 Cornelis P. Venema, *But for the Grace of God: An Exposition of the Canons of Dordt* (Reformed Fellowship, 2011).

5 Kevin DeYoung, *The Good News We Almost Forgot: Rediscovering the Gospel in a 16th Century Catechism* (Chicago: Moody, 2020).

6 G. I. Williamson, *The Westminster Confession of Faith: For Study Classes*, 2nd ed. (Phillipsburg, PA: Presbyterian & Reformed, 2003); R. C. Sproul, *Truths We Confess: A Layman's Guide to the Westminster Confession of Faith*, 3 vol. (Phillipsburg, PA: Presbyterian & Reformed, 2006, 2007); Chad Van Dixhoorn, *Confessing the Faith: A Reader's Guide to the Westminster Confession of Faith* (Edinburgh: The Banner of Truth, 2014).

Happily, Baptists too find a place at this table. The First London Confession (1644) and the more well-known Second London Confession (1677)[7] evidence a strong continuity with Protestant and Reformed doctrine.[8] Many Baptist churches in colonial America found affinity with the latter of these two and adopted it, with slight modifications, as the Philadelphia Confession (1742) or the Charleston Confession (1767). These confessions, in turn, became the basis for The New Hampshire Confession (1833) and The Abstract of Principles (1858). And a growing number of Baptist churches today are rediscovering this confessional heritage.[9] Indeed, many local churches are beginning to identify themselves as confessional.

The contributors to this book welcome this rediscovery. Indeed, we hope it continues! With that end in view, we have written and compiled these essays to celebrate and commend the use of creeds and confessions in Baptist faith and life. Some of the chapters are written by scholars, others by pastors. The primary audience we have in view are local church leaders and members. Why? Because

---

7 The General Assembly of Baptists churches in London adopted this confession in 1689, from whence the confession derives its more popular name, "The 1689 Baptist Confession." But it was actually published in 1677 by the Petty France Church of London.

8 The Second London Confession is based largely on the text of the Westminster Confession. For a visual comparison of the texts that highlights the high degree of verbal correspondence and the few differences, see James Anderson, "A Tabular Comparison of the 1646 WCF and the 1689 LBCF," *Analogical Thoughts* (blog), accessed January 21, 2021, https://www.proginosko.com/docs/wcf_lbcf.html, or James M. Renihan, *True Confessions: Baptist Documents in the Reformed Family* (Palmdale, CA: Reformed Baptist Academic Press, 2004). For a discussion of the historical context and theology of the Second London Confession, see chapters 4 and 5 of this work.

9 Since the 1970s, a growing number of Baptist churches have adopted the Second London Confession of Faith as their doctrinal standard. Moreover, several local and at least two national associations have formed that are self-consciously confessional: The Association of Reformed Baptist Churches of America (1997) and the Reformed Baptist Network (2016). And organizations like Founders Ministries have labored to help Southern Baptist churches appreciate their theological confessional heritage. Additionally, several seminaries that subscribe to the Second London Confession have formed including The Institute of Reformed Baptist Studies (1997), Covenant Baptist Theological Seminary (2005), Reformed Baptist Seminary (2005), and Grace Bible Theological Seminary (2016). Finally, in 1989 Evangelical Press published Samuel Waldron's *A Modern Exposition of the 1689 Baptist Confession of Faith*, which has gone through five editions (1989, 1995, 2009, 2013, 2016) and has been translated into Spanish, German, Russian, and Romanian.

sound theology is not just the province of the academy but is essential to the health and ministry of the local church.

Part 1 includes two essays that attempt to answer the question, "Why do we need confessions?" The first (chapter 1), by Luke Walker, provides a concise and cogent argument for the importance, necessity, and usefulness of creeds. The second (chapter 2), which I offer, elaborates on the argument of Luke's essay. If you only have time to read one, read Luke's winsome presentation. Hopefully, both chapters will equip pastors to persuade their congregations of the validity and value of confessions of faith.

Part 2 features essays from two well-known and beloved Reformed Baptist historians: Michael Haykin and Tom Nettles. Michael contributes three chapters (3, 4, 5) that explore the historical context and theological content of the First and Second London Confessions of Faith. He demonstrates that these creedal formulas stand firmly within the Reformed and Puritan tradition. Next, Tom tells the story of the New Hampshire Confession (chapter 6) and the Abstract of Principles (chapter 7), and he shows how the theology of these confessions is based on the doctrine contained in the Second London Confession. The analysis these scholars provide is critical for understanding and appreciating the confessional heritage of Baptist churches.

In part 3, the focus shifts from the history and content of the confessions to their practical use in the faith and life of Baptist churches. Steve Weaver reviews the ways in which Southern Baptist churches have historically used confessions (chapter 8). He effectively shows that confessionalism is an inextricable part of the SBC's DNA. Next (chapter 9), I contribute to the topic of confessional "subscription," that is, the nature and degree of commitment an individual or church gives to a creed. Historically, Presbyterians have addressed this issue in more detail than Baptists have. So, I draw much from their discussions. Nevertheless, the issue is also relevant for self-consciously confessional Baptist churches. Finally, I offer a follow-up essay (chapter 10) that raises the questions "What confession?" and "How shall we subscribe?" Then, I suggest several biblical and theological guidelines for answering those questions.

Part 4 includes essays on several of the theological contributions of the Second London Confession of Faith (2LCF) that distinguish it from its parent, the Westminster Confession of Faith (WCF). Jeffrey Johnson (chapter 11) examines how the framers of the 2LCF advance the covenant theology of the WCF in a way that is distinctively Baptist. Here, the reader will behold the beauty of Reformed Baptist "federalism." Then, Tom Ascol (chapter 12) expounds "the Gospel and the Extent of Its Grace," a chapter of the Baptist confession derived from the Savoy Declaration (1658).[10] Tom highlights the abiding relevance this article of the confession holds for healthy missionary endeavors. Sam Waldron follows Tom's presentation with a discussion of the 2LCF's doctrine of civil government (chapter 13). In that chapter, he articulates the view of human authority that underlies the confession's doctrine and touches on the question of civil disobedience within the Reformed tradition. Next, Tom Ascol's second offering (chapter 14) develops a Reformed and Baptist ecclesiology by expounding chapter 26 of the 2LCF, "Of the Church." The reader will see the Second London Confession admirably illustrates the grand Reformation principle, *ecclesia reformata, semper reformanda secundum verbi Dei*.[11] Brian Borgman concludes this part of the book with an examination of the confession's doctrine of baptism and the Lord's Supper (chapter 15). Brian's analysis highlights how the Baptists' doctrine of the sacraments (or ordinances) manifests both continuity and discontinuity within the Reformed tradition. It will be obvious to the reader that the contributors to this volume are quite fond of the Second London Confession, more popularly known as the 1689 Baptist Confession of Faith. For this, we make no apology. We'd like to see more churches embrace this tried-and-true confession as their doctrinal standard and use it as a tool to carry out their mission.

Part 5 features reviews of three important books dealing with the topic of confessionalism. Nick Alford provides a careful assessment of R. Scott Clark's *Recovering the Reformed Confession* (chapter 16). Luke Walker follows with a thoughtful evaluation of Carl Trueman's *The Creedal Imperative* (chapter 17). Finally, Vadim Chepurny takes a close look at J. V. Fesko's recent *The Need for Creeds Today* (chapter 18). These well-written reviews should stimulate the reader's appetite for further research.

---

10 The Savoy Declaration is a Congregationalist modification of the WCF. The Baptists based their confession on both the WCF and the SD.

11 That is, "the church reformed, [is] always [in need of] being reformed according to the Word of God."

The book ends with an appendix on recommended resources for those who wish to go deeper in the study of creeds and confessions.

John Frame has persuasively argued "No Scripture, No Christ." That is, the very nature of our confession of Christ "as Lord" entails the inspired, infallible, and authoritative revelation we find in the Bible.[12] Without that revelation, our professed allegiance to Christ is meaningless. In a more qualified sense, we may insist "No Creed, No Christ." Divine revelation is the basis for our commitment to Christ. Creeds and confessions are a public expression of that commitment. They are one of the important ways in which we confess Christ before men with clarity and precision. Let us, therefore, be *confessing Baptists* in the fullest sense of the word!

Soli Deo gloria.

---

12   See his essay, "No Scripture, No Christ," in John Frame, *The Doctrine of the Word of God* (Phillipsburg, PA: Presbyterian & Reformed, 2010), 563–66.

Part 1

The Legitimacy and
Benefits of Confessions

1

Need for Creed

Luke Walker

C REEDS AND CONFESSIONS OF FAITH have been used by God's people for thousands of years. In fact, they are older than church history itself. It was not the Nicene Creed that gave the early church its creedal moorings but the Scriptures. Creeds and confessions have been utilized by Christians on a mammoth scale, from Nicene trinitarianism and Reformed orthodoxy to contemporary statements on the inerrancy of Scripture.[1] However, the popularity of creeds has waned in modern evangelicalism. "Sadly, we live in a non-creedal, even an anti-creedal, age marked by existential relativism, anti-authoritarianism and historical isolationism."[2] This essay will assert the perpetual legitimacy, importance, and usefulness of creeds and confessions of faith for the modern church.

A Legitimate Form of Biblical Teaching

Before we consider creeds as legitimate forms of biblical teaching, definitions are in order. The word "creed" comes from the Latin *credo*, which means, "I believe." Philip Schaff defines the term: "A Creed, or Rule of Faith, or Symbol, is a confession of faith for public use, or a form of words setting forth with authority certain articles of belief, which are regarded by the framers as necessary for salvation,

---

1 See the Chicago Statement on Biblical Inerrancy, for example.
2 Robert Paul Martin, "Introduction," in Sam Waldron, *A Modern Exposition of the 1689 Baptist Confession of Faith*, 5th ed. (Darlington, Co. Durham, England: Evangelical Press, 2016), 13–14.

or at least for the well-being of the Christian Church."³ A simpler definition is as follows: "Confessions and catechisms, as creeds, are *expressions of faith*. That is, they indicate what a Christian or church understands and believes the Bible to teach regarding faith and life."⁴

Objections to the Legitimacy of Creeds

With definitions like these in mind, one wonders what could possibly produce any opposition to the use of creeds from Christians. To disagree with particular creeds or creedal statements is understandable, but to reject any use of them whatsoever is a shocking position. Why the modern animosity? Besides strong cultural influences which militate against the use of creeds,⁵ the influences of fundamentalism and biblicism have corralled evangelicals into tight hermeneutical quarters. Fundamentalism has tended to be a self-isolating movement, cutting itself off from the creedal productions of the ancient church out of a desire to be faithful to the Bible alone. "Certain strains of anti-intellectual fundamentalism have discouraged an interest in that 'far country' of church history."⁶ Biblicism, on the other hand, has inadvertently taught Christians to rely on rationalism in their handling of Scripture. "Historically, biblicists, although they boast about their devotion to Scripture, are actually devoted to the supremacy of reason."⁷

These forces have established the idea that Christians should only use the Bible for spiritual matters of faith and practice. "If God wanted to give us creeds," one may say, "then he would have given them to us in the Bible." Some even view earlier generations of Christians with suspicion. Do we not understand the language and world of the Bible much more accurately now than older generations of Christians ever did? This kind of "chronological snobbery"⁸ militates against the

3 Philip Schaff, *The History of the Creeds*, in volume 1 of *The Creeds of Christendom* (New York: Harper & Brothers, Publishers, 1878), 3–4.
4 Robert Gonzales Jr., "The Validity and Value of Confessions of Faith," chapter 2 of this book.
5 For example, the growing popularity of anti-authoritarianism.
6 Michael A. G. Haykin, *Rediscovering the Church Fathers: Who They Were and How They Shaped the Church* (Wheaton, IL: Crossway, 2011), 14.
7 R. Scott Clark, "The Difference Between Sola Scriptura and Biblicism," *The Heidelblog*, April 19, 2015, accessed on May 14, 2020, https://heidelblog.net/2015/04/the-difference-between-sola-scriptura-and-biblicism/.
8 See C. S. Lewis, *Surprised by Joy* (New York: HarperCollins, 1955). See also his introduction in Athanasius, *On the Incarnation* (Lexington, KY: Fig, 2012), 1–7.

use of creeds and confessions. Among Calvinistic Protestants, it is contended that creeds oppose the principle of *sola Scriptura*.

These objections are plausible at first glance (which may explain the wide success of clichés such as, "No creed but the Bible"). There are churches who exhibit a chronological snobbery of the opposite sort, revering all things ancient while despising all things present. There are even some churches that place confessional statements above Scripture. Imbalances like these ought to be scrupulously rejected. Nevertheless, these objections, when pressed, do not stand up under scrutiny.

Creeds Are Biblical

Creedal statements are found in the Bible itself. The most basic statements of faith from the Scriptures are creedal, for example, "The Lord our God is one" (Deut. 6:4) and "Jesus is Lord" (Rom. 10:9). The apostle Paul employs creedal expressions that were, apparently, in currency among the earliest churches. Colossians 1:15–20, Philippians 2:6–11, and 1 Timothy 3:16 contain what can only be called creedal assertions. If the apostle found them useful to his own ministry, who are we to disparage them? Creeds bear the sure seal of apostolic usage. "The biblical writers planted the seeds of what would later blossom into the great symbols of the faith. Thus, far from discouraging creeds, the Bible validates their composition and use."[9]

Sola Scriptura and Creeds

The Reformation doctrine of *sola Scriptura* has never asserted that only the Bible is to be used in the life of the believer. The Reformers themselves held to creedal statements and even produced some of their own. The Lutheran *Book of Concord* consists of ancient creeds as well as the creedal work of Martin Luther. John Calvin's *Institutes of the Christian Religion* is patterned after the Apostles' Creed. If these are the bastions of sola Scriptura, then the principle of sola Scriptura is anything but anti-creedal. After all, the phrase *sola Scriptura* is itself a creedal expression.

The position under consideration is something more like *solo Scriptura*, or "the Bible only." Michael Horton says, "The Latin

---

9 Gonzales, "Validity and Value," chapter 2, of this book.

slogan [sola Scriptura] means 'by Scripture alone,' not 'Scripture alone' [solo Scriptura]."[10] Jason Helopoulos says, "Solo Scriptura advocates a radical individualism that rejects the church, creeds, confessions, and tradition as having any authority while embracing private judgment above all else."[11] People are free to align themselves with a position such as this, but they cannot do so while citing the deep magic of sola Scriptura. The doctrine of sola Scriptura actually calls for the use of creeds and confessions. We must, therefore, take our cues from the Scriptures themselves.

Creeds, when used rightly, do not supplant the Scriptures. Rather, they are subject to the Scriptures. A creed is a "*norma normata*, 'a rule that is ruled,' not a *norma normans*, 'a rule that rules.'"[12] Schaff expands upon this: "The Bible is of God; the Confession is man's answer to God's word. The Bible is the *norma normans*; the Confession the *norma normata*. The Bible is the rule of *faith* (*regula fidei*); the Confession the rule of *doctrine* (*regula doctrinæ*)."[13] Faithful creeds are shaped by the Bible and must be reshaped if they do not reflect the teaching of Scripture. The Bible norms the creed and is itself normed by no one.

The Importance of Confessions of Faith

Creeds and confessions are also important. They are not permissible forms of worship which offer no real benefit of their own. Rather, creeds and confessions are a vital aspect of healthy Christians and churches.

Creeds Are Necessary

The need for summaries of faith renders creedal statements not only legitimate but necessary. Saying, "I believe the Bible,"[14] is not enough. "It is naïve to believe that the church wholly discharges its

---

10 Justin Taylor, "Horton: Canon and Covenant/Sola vs. Solo Scriptura," The Gospel Coalition, May 3, 2010, https://www.thegospelcoalition.org/blogs/justin-taylor/horton-canon-and-covenant-sola-vs-solo-scriptura.

11 Jason Helopoulos, "Is Scripture Alone the Same Thing as Scripture Only?" *Tabletalk*, August 7, 2019, https://tabletalkmagazine.com/posts/is-scripture-alone-the-same-thing-as-scripture-only/.

12 Haykin, *Rediscovering the Church Fathers*, 129.

13 Schaff, *The History of the Creeds*, 7.

14 This statement is creedal by definition. The writer has refrained from pressing the treasure trove of ironies in a study of this nature.

duty as the pillar and ground of the truth by proclaiming that it believes the Bible. Most heretics will be willing to say the same thing."[15] False religions claim the Bible.[16] If "no creed but the Bible" means that we only use the words of Scripture to talk about spiritual truth, then preaching is necessarily *unbiblical*. The preacher, after all, must use words that are not found in the Bible itself to communicate the meaning of the words that are found in the Bible. But, whether these summaries of faith appear in the form of elucidating statements from the pulpit or as written statements of faith makes little difference; they are of like kind. Where the former is accepted, the latter may not reasonably be rejected.

Creeds and confessions are the inescapable tools of understanding and teaching the Bible accurately. It matters that we believe the Bible, but it also matters *what* we believe the Bible teaches. Pastors must be able to summarize vital biblical doctrines for their people; Christians must be able to express what they believe to others. To do so, both pastors and Christians must necessarily involve themselves in the use of creedal statements of faith. Whether or not they employ the language of any given historic creed, or that of their own crafting, is irrelevant to the point at hand. The use of creedal statements is simply unavoidable. "Every man who believes anything," C. H. Spurgeon tells us, "must have a creed, whether he write it down and print it or no."[17]

Creeds Are Historical

Creeds are important to the history of the church. They have guided it through countless controversies, trials, and snares. How many saints have been buoyed up by the splendor of the Heidelberg's opening item, for example? "*Ques. 1. What is thy only comfort in life and death?*"[18] This is what makes creedal statements important to church history, namely, they are important to Christians and their faith. Creedal statements have borne much fruit. "The unfolding of your words gives light, it imparts understanding to the simple"

---

15   Martin, in Waldron, *Modern Exposition*, 15.

16   Jehovah's Witnesses and Islam as well as novel groups such as the Black Hebrew Israelites all profess belief in the Bible.

17   Charles Spurgeon, "The Church As She Should Be," *The Spurgeon Center*, January 9, 2018, accessed November 2, 2020, https://www.spurgeon.org/resource-library/sermons/the-church-as-she-should-be/#flipbook.

18   Schaff, *The History of the Creeds*, 539.

(Ps. 119:130). Our spiritual forebears executed this holy unfolding with prayer and care, and their labors are not lightly cast aside. The creeds have settled myriad debates and edified countless believers. The church militant ought not handicap itself in so great a war; the stakes are too high. It needs all the reinforcements church history can afford.

Creeds and confessions form the foundation on which our modern churches exist and minister. We stand on the shoulders of exegetes. When believers read the Bible alongside creeds and confessions, they read the Bible in community with the church of all ages. Clark again says, "If you're not reading the Scriptures with the church and in the communion of the saints you're not following Sola scriptura."[19] It is good for Christians to familiarize themselves with the creeds and confessions of the church to understand the church's historic foundations more fully. Orthodox doctrines, like the Trinity, form so much of the basis of modern Christian thought. This highlights the inconsistency of those who confess, "No creed but the Bible," for many of them also confess Nicene Trinitarianism, Chalcedonian Christology, and Westminster articulations of the attributes of God.

Creeds and confessions have silently shaped a modern evangelicalism that largely rejects them. Just as militant atheism uses the liberties of Christian-formed societies to oppose God's existence, so too modern evangelicalism uses the stable platform of trinitarian orthodoxy to oppose the creeds and confessions which have helped God's people steward the mysteries of faith throughout church history. Whenever modern evangelicals speak of the deity of Christ, or the inerrancy of Scripture, they are participating in creedal behavior. Christians use creeds whether they realize it or not; it is time for a full-on embrace of this mighty gift.

Creeds Are the Future

Historic creeds and confessions of faith have enjoyed lengthened careers among the people of God. Ages have washed over these formulations of truth, and they have stood. Many more centuries would do them no harm. They bear up our churches, as they have borne up the churches of old, and they will bear up tomorrow's church. They will be as relevant in the most distant future of this present evil age as

19 Clark, "Sola Scriptura and Biblicism," *The Heidelblog.*

they ever have been. The creeds are a testament to the timelessness of God's truth.

The Usefulness of Confessions of Faith

As we have seen briefly, creeds and confessions of faith are both legitimate and important forms of theological expression. In addition, they are also useful to the church. They help Christians evangelize, do apologetics, and form into healthy communities of faith led by elders with spiritual integrity.

Creeds Are Useful to Individual Believers

Creedal statements strengthen believers by grounding their faith in the central truths of God's Word. The neatness of thought that creeds promote helps to mature the *believing thinker*, focusing him on God, on Christ, and on the economy of the gospel. Pastors well-armed with creedal truth will prepare sturdier sermons, bringing further clarity and comfort to God's people. Creeds are powerful forces of maturation in Christ. Catechisms in particular are peerless tools in instilling biblical truth in children and young believers. The creeds help Christians to know God, and knowing God makes them to stand, and to grow.

Creeds also furnish believers for their work as ambassadors of Christ. They condense the gospel into bite-sized statements of faith that believers can easily share for the encouragement of other believers, as Paul does in Colossians 1:15–20, or for evangelism purposes, as Paul does in Ephesians 5:14. They also equip believers for personal apologetics. For example, the Nicene Creed and Chalcedonian Definition contain clear treatments of God's triune nature and Christ's dual nature. These two biblical doctrines are especially under constant attack from modern cults and modern culture.

Creeds Are Useful to Churches

Creeds are a strong defense against heresy, doctrinal drift, and downgrade in the pulpit. Preaching pastors who hold themselves and their pulpits to doctrinal standards are well-guarded against the strong sweeps of error and heresy that constantly assault the church in every age. The future of the pulpit is also protected. If future pastors must hold to certain confessional standards, these pulpits will contain men who, though of differing gifts and various convictions both secondary and tertiary, hold to the first principles of the faith. The legacy and effective future mission of the church is protected by providing strong doctrinal safeguards for our pulpits.

They supply common grounds for partnership between likeminded believers and assemblies. Their theological shorthand enables ministries to fly their doctrinal colors clearly. This is a courtesy churches and preachers would do well to afford to potential members. What kind of community are they entering? Will the doctrinal lay of the land drastically change in five or ten years? If new leadership arises, will the fabric of the church be altered? Confessional stakes stabilize churches against these kinds of arbitrary fluctuations.

They are important for drawing and maintaining doctrinal lines. This protects flocks against wild-card elders and men of uncertain conviction. They are also an aid in controversy, not only in defending historic orthodoxy but in resolving disputes between like-minded confessional churches. Confessions in particular tend to give direction for controversy on the church level, such as chapter 26 of the 1689 Second London Baptist Confession.[20]

Confessions of faith have flexible use among churches through different degrees of subscription.[21] This allows a statement of faith to serve God's people at multiple levels. It can keep elder teams in harmony through stricter forms of subscription, and it can give flocks general guidance through looser forms of subscription. Believers in any given church will ideally fall everywhere from brand-new converts to seasoned elders. Confessions of faith embrace all within their pale, introducing novices to the great doctrines of the faith, taking growing believers to a deeper understanding of the great themes of God's Word, and becoming living systems of truth in the minds and hearts of the mature. Requiring loose subscription from church members while requiring stricter subscription among church leaders is a prudent and mature use of confessional statements at the church level.[22]

---

20 Stan Reeves, ed., *Confessing the Faith: The 1689 Baptist Confession for the 21st Century* (Cape Coral, FL: Founders, 2012), 53.

21 "Subscription" refers to the nature and extent of one's affirmation of and commitment to a particular creed or confession. For more about this, see chapter 9 of this book.

22 For a defense of two-level subscription, see Gonzales's essay "Choosing and

Creeds Are Useful for Worship

Finally, creeds and confessions are useful doxological organs. In the end, this is their ultimate purpose, to give shape and vent to the praises of God. They supply God's people with language to address him and to worship him. He is the triune God, the maker of heaven and earth, who speaks by his infallible word and has worked our redemption in his Son, the God-man, who will come again to judge the quick and the dead. Maranatha![23]

Conclusion

Creeds and confessions have been historically important and useful to the church. Yet today, they are unjustly ridiculed and ignored among modern evangelicals. Bad examples of confessional churches do exist. However, when the Bible is consulted, and church history is sounded, and the very act of doing theology is inspected, it will always be found that creeds and confessions of faith are legitimate forms of truth, important foundations of the church, and useful tools in its hand.

Using a Confession," chapter 10 of this book.

23   Trueman expands this point in *The Creedal Imperative* (Wheaton: Crossway, 2012), 135–58.

2

The Validity and Value of Confessions of Faith

Robert Gonzales Jr.

I N JUNE OF 1922, THE Northern Baptist Convention convened under the theme, "Agreed to Differ, but Resolved to Love." One might dispute whether they successfully carried out the resolution. No one will debate that they "agreed to differ." The tensions were high. Perhaps one of the sharpest differences came to a head when William Bell Riley motioned that the Convention adopt the New Hampshire Confession of Faith as its doctrinal standard. Riley was the pastor of First Baptist Church of Minneapolis, and he represented the Fundamentalists who wanted to stem the rising tide of modernism among the churches. Not surprisingly, Riley's motion was challenged with a substitute motion from Cornelius Woelfkin, pastor of Park Avenue Baptist, New York. Woelfkin replied that "the New Testament is the all-sufficient ground of our faith and practice, and we need no other statement."[1]

At first glance, Woelfkin appeared to occupy the higher ground. The Protestant commitment to the supremacy and sufficiency of Scripture (sola Scriptura) would seem to entail something close to a "no-creed-but-Scripture" stance on matters of Christian faith and life. However, this essay aims to show that Riley's call for a confession

---

1 David O. Beale, *In Pursuit of Purity: American Fundamentalism Since 1850* (Greenville: Unusual Publications, 1986), 206.

of faith is the higher and more solid ground on which we may erect the edifice of Christian faith and life. Indeed, a careful consideration of the biblical data not only supports the use of creeds and confessions, but it also exposes Woelfkin's "biblicist" approach as sinking sand. The argument that follows consists in two parts. First, we will examine the biblical basis for using confessions of faith and address some common objections to their use. Second, we shall highlight several ways in which a solid confession of faith can promote the church's health and facilitate its mission. To ensure clarity, we begin by defining what we are defending.

A Definition of a Confession of Faith

One of the most thorough and helpful studies on this subject is Philip Schaff's three-volume work, *The Creeds of Christendom*.[2] According to Schaff, confessions of faith and catechisms are types of creeds.[3] The term "creed" comes from the Latin word *credo*, which means, "I believe." Thus begins the so-called Apostles' Creed: "*I believe* [credo] in God the Father Almighty." Creeds, then, are *expressions of faith*.[4] That is, they indicate what a Christian or church understands and believes the Bible to teach regarding faith and life. But Schaff offers us a more formal definition as well. In his words, "A Creed, or Rule of Faith, or Symbol, is a confession of faith for public use, or a form of words setting forth with authority certain articles of belief, which are regarded by the framers as necessary for salvation, or at least for the well-being of the Christian Church."[5]

We should highlight three elements in that definition. First, Schaff refers to a creed as a "confession of faith *for public use*" (emphasis added). Since creeds are intended for public use, they are usually

---

2 Philip Schaff, *The Creeds of Christendom*, 3 vol. (1877; repr., Grand Rapids: Baker Book House, 1990).

3 The primary difference between a confession and catechism is that the latter, derived from the Greek κατακειν, "to teach with the mouth," is written in question-and-answer form.

4 The Apostles' Creed was once thought to be of apostolic origin. More correctly, it should be viewed as a summary of apostolic teaching, which eventually reached its final form by the end of the fifth century. See Schaff, 1:16–20.

5 Schaff, 1:3, 4. Millard Erickson offers a more concise definition. He defines a creed as "a summary of the beliefs of a person or group, often a denomination." *The Concise Dictionary of Christian Theology* (Grand Rapids: Baker Book House, 1986), 39. This definition is too general for our purposes.

written to ensure transmission and dissemination. That is what this essay will defend: a *written* creed or confession.

Second, Schaff acknowledges that creeds set forth articles of faith "with authority." That is, creeds call upon Christians to believe and affirm specific articles of faith or dogma. Yet, their authority is subordinate to Scripture. Schaff writes, "The Bible is the rule of *faith* (*regula fidei*); the Confession [is] the rule of *doctrine* (*regula doctrinae*). The Bible has, therefore, a divine and absolute [authority], the Confession only an ecclesiastical and relative authority."[6] Unlike the Catholic and Orthodox churches, Protestants do not accord creeds authority equal with Scripture.[7]

Third, with respect to Schaff's definition, creeds and confessions may contain articles of faith that *vary in level of importance.* Some of the articles are vitally important, being "necessary for salvation." Other articles are of relative importance for "the well-being [i.e., spiritual health] of the church." For example, the Westminster Confession of Faith (WCF) and the Second London Confession of Faith (2LCF) contain, as do all good creeds, some doctrines that we view as *essential for salvation.* Some of those doctrines would include the divine authority of Scripture, the deity of Christ, man's sinfulness and need for salvation, the vicarious atonement of Christ on the cross, justification by faith alone, the bodily resurrection, and so on. To reject any one of those doctrines would call into question one's Christian profession. On the other hand, we do not believe or claim that one must agree with all the doctrines in a confession like the WCF or 2LCF in order to be saved. In fact, it is possible to be a genuine Christian and yet disagree at some points with these

---

6 Schaff, 1:7.

7 Two ramifications follow: (1) The confession's authority is always *subordinate* to the authority of Scripture. The Bible is our *supreme* authority in matters of faith and practice because it is the inspired Word of God. A creed or confession, on the other hand, represents the church's interpretation of God's word and is, therefore, an expression of human authority. The creed or confession is the *norma normata* ("a rule that is ruled"), and the Bible is the *norma normans* ("the rule that rules"). Moreover, (2) confessions, unlike Scripture, are fallible. Therefore, confessions are subject to correction, modification, and improvement. A case in point is the Westminster Confession of Faith (WCF). The Westminster Confession is perhaps the greatest creed ever written. Nevertheless, the Congregationalists as well as our Baptist forefathers recognized that certain doctrines in that Confession needed to be corrected or revised. As a result, they produced the Savoy Declaration (SD) and the Second London Confession of Faith (2LCF), respectively. These two confessions may be viewed as modified versions of the Westminster.

confessions. Of course, to reject the non-essential teachings of these confessions may affect one's spiritual health or the spiritual health of the church.[8] Nevertheless, we want to make it clear that we are neither asserting nor defending full agreement with a confession like 2LCF or the WCF as a requisite for salvation.

The Validity of a Confession of Faith

First, we will present arguments for the validity of adopting and using creeds and confessions in the church. Second, we will address three of the primary objections raised against the use of creeds and confessions. Others have provided a more comprehensive defense of creeds.[9]

Three Biblical Arguments for Confessions

We will confine ourselves to three main arguments.

1. The Bible commands us to confess our faith publicly.

The Lord Jesus Christ expresses this duty pointedly in Matthew 10:32–33. In the context, the Lord has warned his twelve disciples that they will be persecuted because of their commitment to him. He exhorts them not to fear those who only have power to kill their body but have no power over their soul. Rather, they should fear God, who has the power to destroy both the body and the soul. To enforce that exhortation, Jesus adds, "Everyone who *acknowledges* [ὁμολογήσει] me before men, I also will *acknowledge* [ὁμολογήσω] before my Father who is in heaven, but whoever denies me before men, I also will deny before my Father who is in heaven." The Greek verb ὁμολογέω translated "acknowledge" means "to express openly one's allegiance to a proposition or person.[10] In this case, Jesus expects his disciples to confess publicly their allegiance to him. Obviously, he wants them to do more than "mouth" the right words. Merely reciting the Apostles'

---

8 If a doctrine or teaching has no bearing whatsoever on the spiritual health of a Christian or a church, then, in my opinion, it has no business whatsoever in a creed.

9 We do not intend to be exhaustive. For a more developed argument for the legitimacy of creeds, see Carl Trueman, *The Creedal Imperative* (Wheaton: Crossway, 2012), 21–80.

10 Johannes P. Louw and Eugene Albert Nida, *Greek-English Lexicon of the New Testament: Based on Semantic Domains* (New York: United Bible Societies, 1996), 417.

Creed or the Lord's Prayer, for example, will not guarantee anyone a place in heaven. The Lord is calling for a heart-deep commitment. And such a genuine heart commitment to Jesus should result in a verbal confession of that commitment. The two go hand-in-hand. We should question the one where we do not find the other.

Similarly, the apostle Paul connects a public confession of faith with a heart commitment of faith: "If you confess with your mouth that Jesus is Lord and believe in your heart that God raised him from the dead, you will be saved. For with the heart one believes and is justified, and with the mouth one confesses and is saved" (Rom. 10:9–10). One should note that the confession of Christ as Lord entails some degree of understanding of and agreement with what his lordship means. Both the immediate and larger context of Scripture indicates that Christ's lordship includes both his Messianic kingship[11] and also his deity.[12] Thus, when a first century Jew or Gentile confessed Christ as "Lord," he was publicly affirming that Christ was his king and his God.[13] Moreover, a public confession of Christ's lordship apart from a heart commitment to that lordship is insufficient for salvation. Many who say, "Lord, Lord," will be rejected in the last day because their lives did not match up to their public profession (Matt. 7:21–23). Conversely, a public confession of faith is, like good works, a necessary evidence of saving faith. Charles Hodge's comment is to the point: "The public profession of religion or confession of Christ is an indispensable duty. That is, in order to salvation, we must not only secretly believe, but also openly acknowledge that Jesus is our prophet, priest, and king."[14]

How does this square with the claim that faith and religion are personal and private matters? Many people today, especially

---

11 Accordingly, the verse parallels Christ's lordship with his resurrection, which marked Christ's installment as the Messianic king and Son of Yahweh (see Ps. 2:6–7; Acts 13:33; Rom. 1:4; Eph. 1:20–23; Heb. 1:5, 8). See further John Murray, *The Epistle to the Romans*, vol. II (Grand Rapids: Eerdmans, 1968), 55.

12 The Greek term employed for "Lord" (i.e., κύριος) is commonly used in the Septuagint for Yahweh. Paul brings out this connection in this very passage when he quotes an Old Testament passage referring to Yahweh (Joel 2:32) and applies it to Jesus (Rom. 10:13). Thus, to confess Jesus as Lord is to worship him as Yahweh (see John 5:23).

13 Such was the confession of Thomas, "My Lord and my God!" (John 20:28).

14 Charles Hodge, *A Commentary on Romans* (1835; repr., Edinburgh: Banner of Truth, 1983), 343. Along the same lines, Murray writes, "Confession without faith would be vain (cf. Matt. 7:22, 23; Tit. 1:16). But likewise, faith without confession would be shown to be spurious." *The Epistle to the Romans*, 2:56.

politicians, claim to have faith and religion. Yet they studiously avoid any public affirmation of what that means. Contrary to that practice, the Bible calls God's people to confess their faith unashamedly and publicly. This is precisely what we do by publishing and affirming a written confession of faith. We proclaim to the world and to one another both the reality and also the substance of our faith.

2. The Bible commends the interpretation and application of Scripture.

We could appeal to a number of passages to establish this point,[15] but we will confine ourselves to Luke's account of Paul's initial ministry in Thessalonica:

> Now when they had passed through Amphipolis and Apollonia, they came to Thessalonica, where there was a synagogue of the Jews. And Paul went in, as was his custom, and on three Sabbath days he reasoned with them from the Scriptures, explaining and proving that it was necessary for the Christ to suffer and to rise from the dead, and saying, "This Jesus, whom I proclaim to you, is the Christ." And some of them were persuaded and joined Paul and Silas, as did a great many of the devout Greeks and not a few of the leading women (Acts 17:1–4).

When Paul preached in the synagogues, he did not merely read the Old Testament and sit down. Rather, he "reasoned ... from the Scriptures." According to verse 3, his reasoning included *interpretation* and *argumentation*. The first Greek participle, διανοίγων, simply means, "to open." Applied to Scripture, figuratively, it refers to opening up the meaning of a passage; hence, interpretation. The second participle, παρατιθέμενος, means, "to put forth." Here, it refers to the setting forth of arguments. Furthermore, verse 4 indicates that Paul *applied* his conclusions to his audience, calling on them to receive Jesus as the Messiah. Obviously, Paul did not hesitate to go beyond the mere text of Scripture and offer his own explanation of what Scripture meant.

Someone may object that Paul was an inspired apostle. Certainly, he may tread where others may not. However, Ephesians 4:11–14

---

15   A few examples included Neh. 8:5–8; Acts 8:26–35; 28:23; Eph. 4:11–14; 2 Tim. 2:15; 3:16–17; 4:2.

indicates that non-inspired pastor-teachers, as well as apostles, have been given to the church in order to equip the saints with sound doctrine until the unity of the faith is attained. And no one in the history of the church has ever argued that pastors fulfill that duty by merely quoting or reading passages of Scripture. To the contrary, they do exactly what Paul did. They interpret and apply God's word. Now if a pastor-teacher may interpret and apply God's word in the form of a sermon, why not in the form of a creed? Both are interpretations and applications of Scripture. Thus, a creed or a confession of faith is no different *in principle* than a sermon except that the former is often the product of several minds and, as a result, more precise.[16] And if creeds, like sermons, are essentially expositions of Scripture, then their validity is a given. As Alexander Hodge points out in his defense of creeds:

> While, however, the Scriptures are from God, the understanding of them belongs to the part of men. Men must interpret to the best of their ability each particular part of Scripture separately, and then combine all that the Scriptures teach upon every subject into a consistent whole.[17]

3. The Bible contains rudimentary creeds and confessions of faith.

When Jesus asked His disciples, "Who do you say that I am?" Peter answered on behalf of the others with a confession of faith: "You are the Christ, the Son of the living God." This miniature confession of faith was an essential part of the "rock" upon which Jesus built His church (Matt. 16:15–18).[18] Furthermore, there is some evidence that this brief confession of faith later became a standardized formula and prerequisite for baptism. For example, when the Ethiopian

---

16   The Westminster Confession of Faith was the product of over one hundred ministers.

17   Archibald Alexander Hodge, *A Commentary on the Confession of Faith* (Philadelphia: Presbyterian Board of Publication and Sabbath-School Work, 1901), 19.

18   Since the Reformation, most Protestant commentators have avoided identifying the "rock" as Peter (a Roman Catholic interpretation), and instead they have identified it as Peter's confession. However, the play on words—"You are *Peter* [Πέτρος], and upon this *rock* [πέτρα] I will build My church" (v. 18)—makes it likely that Peter himself is the rock. Yet, it is not upon Peter merely as an individual, but upon Peter as the spokesman for the apostles, bearing witness to Jesus' identity as the Christ, the Son of the Living God, that Jesus builds His church. Thus, Peter's confession of faith is an inseparable part of the church's foundation. This interpretation does not demand that we view Peter as the first pope.

eunuch says to Philip, "Look! Water! What prevents me from being baptized?" Philip replies, "If you believe with all your heart, you may." To which the eunuch responded, "I believe that Jesus Christ is the Son of God" (Acts 8:36–37, NASB95).[19]

Not surprisingly, some scholars believe that the confession of Jesus "as Lord" was also a rudimentary Christian creed (Acts 10:36; Rom. 10:9; 1 Cor. 12:3; 2 Cor. 4:5; Phil. 2:11).[20] This creed may have expanded over time to include various elements of Christ's person and work stated in concise form. Perhaps, we have such an example in 1 Timothy 3:16:

> By common confession, great is the mystery of godliness:
>
> > He who was revealed in the flesh,
> > Was vindicated in the Spirit,
> > Seen by angels,
> > Proclaimed among the nations,
> > Believed on in the world,
> > Taken up in glory. (NASB95)

Paul did not compose these words on the spur of the moment. Nor do they reflect his private opinion. Rather, this "mystery of godliness" formula is commonly confessed—that is, widely known and affirmed.[21] Because of the symmetrical structure of the phrases, some commentators believe that this was part of an early creed or perhaps even a hymn.[22]

---

19 Even if this confession is a later interpolation, it still reflects an early practice. See F. F. Bruce, *The Book of the Acts* (Grand Rapids: Eerdmans, 1989), 178.

20 Commenting on Romans 10:9, C. E. B. Cranfield writes, "In view of the evidence of this verse, in which the presence of 'confess' is suggestive, and of 1 Cor. 12:3; 2 Cor. 4:5; Phil. 2:11, it seems clear that 'Jesus is Lord' was already an established confessional formula. It is probable that it was used in connexion [*sic*] with baptism, but also in Christian worship generally." *Romans: A Shorter Commentary* (Grand Rapids: Eerdmans, 1985), 257.

21 For this reading of the Greek adverb ὁμολογουμένως (translated above as "by common confession," NASB95), see Louw and Nida, *Greek-English Lexicon of the New Testament: Based on Semantic Domains*, 2nd ed. (New York: United Bible Societies, 1988, 89), §33.276.

22 Newport White writes, "It is difficult to avoid the conclusion that what follows is a quotation by St. Paul from a primitive creed or summary of the chief facts to be believed about Jesus Christ." *The First and Second Epistles of Timothy* in *The Expositor's Greek New Testament*, ed. W. Robertson Nicoll (reprint, Grand Rapids: Eerdmans, 1988), 118; see also J. J. van Oosterzee, *The Two Epistles of Paul to Timothy*, trans. E. A. Washburn and E. Harwood, in *A Commentary on the Holy Scriptures*, ed. Johann Peter Lange, trans. Philip Schaff (New York: Charles Scribner & Co., 1869), 45–46; William Hendriksen, *Thessalonians, Timothy, and Titus* in *New*

Other rudimentary or seminal creeds in the Bible include the ancient *Shema* (Deut. 6:4), the "Exodus Confession" (Deut. 26:1–11), and the great "Church Unity Creed" (Eph. 4:4–6). These and the ones described above became the models for later, more fully developed creeds, such as the Apostles' Creed.[23] The biblical writers planted the seeds of what would later blossom into the great symbols of the faith. Thus, far from discouraging creeds, the Bible validates their composition and use.

Three Common Objections against Confessions

Despite the biblical evidence supporting the use of creeds and confessions, some Christians have raised objections to their use. Below are the three most common.

1. Confessions undermine the authority of Scripture.

This can and does happen. For instance, the Roman Catholic and the Orthodox churches extend the claim of infallibility to several of their creeds, elevating their authority to a place equal with Scripture. Some Protestant churches have also been guilty of a kind of "hyper-confessionalism" that gives the creed a kind of practical authority equal to Scripture.[24] This approach to confessions borders on "symbolatry," which Schaff defines as "a species of idolatry [that] substitutes the tyranny of a printed book for that of a living pope."[25] However, the problem is not with creeds per se, but with *the church's attitude toward creeds*. We have already stated that a creed is merely an extension of ecclesiastical, and therefore human, authority. The Protestant doctrine of *sola Scriptura* does not deny the place of legitimate human authorities but subordinates them to Scripture. As a result, all creeds—except those found in Scripture—must be viewed as authorities subordinate to Scripture. The WCF and 2LCF articulate this point with clarity and conviction:

> The supreme judge, by which all controversies of religion are to be determined, and all decrees of councils, opinions of ancient writers, doctrines of men, and private spirits are to be examined, and in whose sentence we are to rest, can

Testament Commentary (Grand Rapids: Baker Book House, 1990), 137–141.
23   Schaff, 1:4–7; 16–20.
24   Schaff, 1:7–8.
25   Schaff, 1:7.

be no other but the Holy Scripture delivered by the Spirit, into which Scripture so delivered, our faith is finally resolved (WCF/2LCF 1.10).

Additionally, the WCF adds,

All synods or councils, since the Apostles' times, whether general or particular, may err; and many have erred. Therefore, they are not to be made the rule of faith, or practice; but to be used as a help in both (WCF 31.3).

Therefore, as long as we maintain a strong commitment to the supremacy of Scripture, we need not fear the unlawful intrusion of human creeds.

2. Confessions contradict the sufficiency of Scripture.

Does not Paul assure Timothy that Scripture is sufficient to equip him for "every good work" (2 Tim. 3:16–17)? If the Bible is sufficient, why do we need confessions?

This objection misunderstands *the nature* of Scripture's sufficiency. For example, when we say that the Bible is sufficient as a rule of faith, we do not mean to exclude sermons. We would not conclude a pastor faithfully carries out his role to "preach the word" (2 Tim. 4:2) if he stands behind the pulpit every Sunday and simply reads from the Bible without comment. We expect more—some doctrine, reproof, correction, and training in righteousness! In other words, we expect the pastor-teacher to exegete, illustrate, and apply the words of the Bible. The Bible alone is sufficient for its God-ordained role, but the Bible alone is not "omni-sufficient" for every task. As Sam Waldron explains, "The Scripture was not given to be a complete catalog of all the sermons the church would ever need. It is not sufficient for that, and in the same way it is not sufficient to serve the church as a confession of faith."[26]

Perhaps the best way to illustrate the nature of Scripture's sufficiency is to view the Bible as the foundation upon which the super-structure of Christian doctrine and practice is built. As a foundation for our faith the Bible alone is sufficient. And yet, like a foundation, the Bible was never intended to stand by itself. God's

26 From an unpublished lecture, "Why Should the Church Hold to a Confession of Faith?"

written word is meant to be interpreted and applied. That is precisely what a confession does.

3. Confessions intrude upon liberty of conscience.

When creeds exceed the bounds of Scripture, they may infringe on liberty of conscience. Certainly, then, we must take care that our creed does not "add" to Scripture (Deut. 4:2; Rev. 22:18). What is more, we must beware of requiring an affirmation that precedes understanding. We should give each conscience a sufficient amount of time to be instructed and an appropriate degree of latitude with respect to the actual wording or even some non-essential teachings of the confession.[27] Moreover, when one has a confession as detailed and comprehensive as the Westminster or the Second London, the church may allow its officers to take exception to wording or propositions that are not deemed essential to the confession's overall system and Reformed distinctives. For example, adherents of the WCF or 2LCF usually do not view an affirmation of the Pope of Rome as "that Antichrist" essential to one's commitment to these confessions.[28]

However, if the creed or confession of faith is an accurate guide to what the Bible teaches, it cannot be viewed as an intrusion upon our liberty of conscience. Our minds have been freed from the shackles of sin, so that they might freely embrace God's truth, not reject it. Indeed, the rejection of biblical truth may be an indication of a bad conscience (1 Tim. 1:19–20; 2 Tim. 2:17–18). As Samuel Miller has wisely observed, "Men are seldom opposed to creeds, until creeds have become opposed to them."[29] Consequently, the rejection of a creed may not reveal a problem with the creed, but rather a problem with the heart.

---

27 The term "subscription" when applied to creeds or confessions denotes the nature and level of one's adherence to the wording of the symbol. I discuss this in more detail in chapter 10.

28 Though a good case can be made that the Roman pontiff is *an* antichrist. As Charles Spurgeon is alleged to have said, "He should at least be arrested on suspicion."

29 Samuel Miller, *The Utility and Importance of Creeds and Confessions* (reprinted, A Press, 1987), 40, quoted in Robert P. Martin, "The Legitimacy and Use of Confessions," in Samuel E. Waldron, *A Modern Exposition of the 1689 Baptist Confession of Faith* (Durham: Evangelical Press, 1995), 14.

In conclusion, a public confession of biblical truth in the form of a creed need not be inconsistent with the liberty of conscience. Nor is a confession, when viewed and used rightly, inconsistent with the sufficiency and ultimate authority of Scripture.

The Value of Confessions of Faith

In pointing out the value of a confession of faith, we are in a sense presenting another argument for the validity of a confession. According to 1 Timothy 3:15, God has ordained that the church function as "the pillar and support of the truth." This does not mean that Scripture's authenticity or authority depends upon the church, as Rome claims. In that sense, God's truth does not need a pillar or support. What the text does mean, in the words of Albert Barnes, is that the church "is entrusted with the business of maintaining the truth, of defending it from the assaults of error, and of transmitting it to future times."[30] A confession of faith is of great value in assisting the church to carry out this task.

Qualifying a Confession's Value

Before we underscore the value of a good confession of faith, we must qualify its value. Adopting and using a good confession of faith does not guarantee a vibrant and healthy church. Orthodoxy is an essential element of vital Christianity. That is one of the main reasons we need good confessions of faith, just as we need good sermons and solid Christian literature. However, *orthodoxy* (right doctrine) is not the only element of vital Christianity. Jesus commends the church of Ephesus for its orthodoxy but rebukes it for having lost its "first love" (see Rev. 2:1–7). The reference to "first love" may be a reference to a loss of affection for the person of Christ. It may be a reference to a loss of affection among the brothers. Or it may be referring to a loss of concern for the lost. In any case, Jesus underscores the need for something more than mere orthodoxy. We also need *orthopraxy* (right practice) and *orthopathos* (right affections). Thus, we cannot assume that simply having the right confession or adopting the right confession will result *automatically* in a vibrant

---

30   *Barnes' Notes on the New Testament* (Grand Rapids: Kregel Publications, 1962), 1142.

and healthy church. We cannot assume that theological proficiency and correctness *necessarily* result in a closer walk with God. As Roy Taylor cautions, "Any Christian who takes theology seriously should realize that there is a danger of concentrating on theological precision so earnestly that we fall into the trap of loving theology as a formal academic discipline more than loving the Lord God himself. We can become so enamored of the system of theology we espouse that we do not grow in our love for the triune God."[31]

Taylor is not suggesting we can have a genuine relationship with and love for God apart from propositional truth. Propositional truth is the vehicle through which God reveals himself to us, communicates to us, and communes with us. In that sense, we can say, "No creed, no Christ."[32] But Taylor's concern is that mere head knowledge and theological precision are not an end in themselves.

We would say it this way: when the confession of faith engenders within us stronger love for and devotion to the Person, Word, and Works of Jesus, we are using the confession rightly. In that sense, we may liken the confession to John the Baptist—the confession is not itself "the Christ" but only a pointer to the Christ. However, when our devotion to the confession of faith exceeds our devotion to the Person, Word, and Works of Christ, we have begun to misuse the confession. The confession no longer functions in the role of John the Baptist since *it* has "increased," whereas Christ has "decreased." This sort of "hyper-Confessionalism" becomes an enemy to vital Christianity and subtly undermines the very solas of the Reformation it was written to affirm and promote.

In summary, adopting and using a good confession of faith does not guarantee we will have a vibrant and healthy church. By itself a good confession is not the "silver bullet" or the "panacea" for all the church's needs.

---

31 L. Roy Taylor, "Practical Benefits and Dangers of Subscription," in *The Practice of Confessional Subscription*, ed. David W. Hall (Oak Ridge, TN: Covenant Foundation, 1997), 317 (hereafter, *PCS*).

32 Carl Trueman develops this point in some detail in *The Creedal Imperative*, 52–66. See also John Frame, who argues that we can have no personal and saving relationship with Christ apart from propositional revelation. "No Scripture, No Christ," in *The Doctrine of the Word of God*, 563–66.

Affirming a Confession's Value

With that important qualification aside, there are a number of ways
in which a good confession of faith can assist the church in its task of
fulfilling the Great Commission.

1. Confessions help churches carry out the Great Commission.

Prior to his ascension, the Lord Jesus Christ commissioned the elev-
en apostles with the awesome task of making disciples and teaching
them *everything* that he had commanded (Matt. 28:19–20). The
apostle Paul also received this commission, and he faithfully en-
deavored to teach God's people "the whole purpose of God" (Acts
20:18–27). This same commission has been passed on to the church
to carry out until the end of the age.[33]

Now the overwhelming volume of biblical truth makes this a
formidable task. The Bible consists of 66 books divided into 1,189
chapters containing over 773,000 words. The church cannot convey
that huge mass of truth all at once. Accordingly, the church must
isolate the most basic and fundamental truths. Then it must system-
atize them in summary form so that they can be easily taught and
easily learned.[34] Historically, this has been one of the functions of a
creed.[35] Creeds or confessions of faith are comprehensive yet concise
summaries of biblical doctrine. Like good sermons or Christian literature, they distill gospel truth in expository form. As noted above,
their accuracy is enhanced since they are in many cases the product
of many minds. This makes creeds and confessions valuable aids to
assist the church in carrying out its commission.

Not surprisingly, this is the reason Charles Spurgeon gave for
reprinting the Second London Confession. In 1855, the second year
of his ministry at New Park Street Chapel, he wrote,

> I have thought it right to reprint in cheap form this excellent
> list of doctrines, which were subscribed to by the Baptist
> Ministers in the year 1689. We need a banner because of the
> truth; it may be that this small volume may aid the cause of
> the glorious gospel by testifying plainly what are its leading

---

33 The fact that Christ promises his special presence "until the end of the age"
proves that the commission was intended to extend beyond the life span of the elev-
en apostles.

34 Kenneth Gentry, "In Defense of Creedalism," *Penpoint*, (December 1998), 2.

35 Schaff, 1:8.

doctrines.... This little volume is not issued as an authoritative rule, or code of faith, whereby you are to be fettered, but as an assistance to you in controversy, a confirmation in faith, and a means of edification in righteousness. Here the younger members of our church will have a body of divinity in small compass, and by means of the Scriptural proofs, will be ready to give a reason for the hope that is in them.... Cleave fast to the Word of God, which is here mapped out for you.[36]

We concur with Spurgeon. A good confession of faith provides a valuable summary of that glorious truth, which is contained in God's word. As such, a confession serves as a doctrinal standard for the church's shepherds tasked with feeding the flock (Matt. 28:19–20; 1 Tim. 3:2; 6:2a–3; 2 Tim. 1:13; 2:2; 4:1–5; Titus 1:9; 2:1).[37] Moreover, the confession equips the pastor-teacher with a tool for grounding God's people in the truth. By working through a confession like the 2LCF, exegeting the proof texts and expounding the doctrines, he can provide a local church with a course on systematic theology in a fairly comprehensive yet concise form. In addition, some creeds have even been put to song and can be used for worship. The most common creedal song is probably the Apostles' Creed, which one can find in several different renditions and tunes. "Catechism Songs" is a project to put the Shorter Catechism into song that can be used in public or private worship.[38] One might even classify many of the great hymns we sing, such as "Holy, Holy, Holy," "Immortal, Invisible, God Only Wise," or "Come Thou Almighty King," as creeds put to song.[39]

2. Confessions help churches defend the truth from error.

The church is called not only to maintain the truth, but also to defend it from error. Thus, Jude, the "bondservant [and half-brother] of Jesus Christ, and brother of James," makes the plea: "Beloved,

---

36 Quoted in the foreword to *The Baptist Confession of Faith of 1689* (Carlisle, PA: Grace Baptist Church), 7–8.

37 Of special note is the participle of the verb ὑγιαίνω, which is translated "sound" and modifies "words" and "doctrine" in the Pastoral Epistles. The verb means "to be healthy." The participle functions as an adjective and when modifying words or doctrine signifies that which is correct, accurate, and orthodox.

38 See http://catechismsongs.com (accessed January 30, 2021).

39 For more on this point, see Carl Trueman's discussion on the use of creeds for worship in *The Creedal Imperative*, 156–57.

although I was very eager to write to you about our common salvation, I found it necessary to write appealing to you to contend for the faith that was once for all delivered to the saints" (Jude 3).

The Greek word translated "contend" denotes an intense struggle or fight.[40] It is a battle waged for "the faith once for all handed down to the saints," that is, for the body of divinely revealed truth, which we now possess in the Scriptures of the Old and New Testaments. In this case, our enemy consists of those who pervert the truth, reject authority, cause divisions, and live ungodly lives (see Jude 4–19). Such, according to Jude, "have crept in [and may creep in today] unnoticed" (Jude 4). And as a consequence, God's people must contend for the faith. The present tense of "contend" suggests the need for an ongoing struggle until the end of the age.[41]

Historically, creeds have been the weapons that the church has forged from the Scriptures to wage this ongoing war. As the passage from Jude and others demonstrate, the battle began in the apostolic church. As heresy attacked the church from within and without, the church responded with doctrinal formulations. For example, the Jerusalem Council formulated and published certain dogmas designed to protect the churches against the heresy of the Judaizers (Acts 15:1–30). The apostle Paul confronted a denial of the resurrection with an elaborate defense and exposition of the doctrine (1 Cor. 15:1–58; see also 1 Tim. 1:19–20; 2 Tim. 2:17–18).

And the apostle John fortified the church against the attacks of incipient Gnosticism with an apologetic for Christ's full humanity (1 John 1:1–3; 4:1–6; 5:1–6).[42] The early church continued the polemic and responded to the Arian, Apollinarian, Nestorian, and Eutychian heresies with such confessional formulas as the Nicene Creed, the Chalcedonian Creed, and the so-called Athanasian Creed.[43] In time,

---

40 The word is ἐπαγωνίζομαι, which is the intensified form of the Greek verb from which we derive the English verb, "to agonize." The more common form of the word, ἀγωνίζομαι, "was much used in connection with athletic contests to describe a strenuous struggle to overcome an opponent, as in a wrestling match." D. Edmond Hiebert, *Second Peter and Jude* (Greenville: Unusual, 1989), 218.

41 Heibert, 218–19.

42 Because Gnostics viewed matter as inherently evil, they denied that Christ had a material body, thus denying his full humanity. This view has also been called "Docetism," from the Greek word δοκέω, "to appear." They argued that Jesus only appeared to have a body.

43 Schaff, 1:24–42; Archibald A. Hodge, *Outlines of Theology* (reprint, Edinburgh: Banner of Truth Trust, 1983), 115–19.

the doctrinal decay and corruption of the Roman church provoked the Reformers to defend the faith. The many creeds, confessions, and catechisms that grew out of the Reformation bear witness to that defense.[44]

Unfortunately, the ecumenism of our day has blinded many churches and denominations to the duty of defending the faith. Many modern creeds require a minimal amount of doctrinal homogeneity and allow for a great amount of doctrinal diversity. Such an approach not only rejects the church's duty to expose and refute error, but it misses one of the primary functions of a creed. Concerning this modern approach to creeds, J. Gresham Machen remarked in the early part of the twentieth century,

> The historic creeds were exclusive of error; they were intended to set forth the biblical teaching in sharp contrast with what was opposed to the biblical teaching, in order that the purity of the church might be preserved. These modern statements, on the contrary, are inclusive of error. They are designed to make room in the church for just as many people and for just as many types of thought as possible.[45]

The church must resist the modern overemphasis on doctrinal latitude. God's people should not embrace but reject deviant forms of doctrine. We are explicitly warned "Do not be led away by diverse and strange teachings" (Heb. 13:9). Again, "Beloved, do not believe every spirit, but test the spirits to see whether they are from God, for many false prophets have gone out into the world" (1 John 4:1). One of the ways that we can test the spirits is to compare their views of Scripture with the tried and proven creeds of historic Christianity. A good creed or confession of faith will serve as a check to prevent the church from too hastily adopting doctrines that are novel and that deviate from mainstream Christian thought. As Kenneth Gentry observes, "Creeds help to preserve the essential core of true Christian faith from generation to generation."[46]

---

44 Schaff, 1:203–813.

45 "Creeds and Doctrinal Advance," *Banner of Truth* (November 1970), quoted in *A Modern Exposition of the 1689*, 21.

46 Kenneth Gentry, "In Defense of Creedalism," *Penpoint*, vol. 9, no. 4 (1998), 2. As the Scottish theologian James Bannerman perceptively notes, "Had the adoption of confessions and creeds not been a duty laid upon the Church by a regard to her own members, it would have been a necessity laid upon the Church by a regard to those not her members, but her enemies." James Bannerman, *The Church*

At this point, an important clarification is in order. Excluding heretical doctrine is not the same as disallowing legitimate differences. Thus, the mark of a good confession is not that it answers every conceivable question but that it preserves the integrity and health of the church. As J. V. Fesko observes, "The best confessions have doctrinal flexibility built in, to make room for differing opinions on challenging topics."[47] Fesko offers several examples where the framers of the WCF purposely employed language for certain points of doctrine that was flexible enough to accommodate more than one particular understanding of the doctrine.[48] The same is true with respect to the 2LCF. For example, the First London Confession (1644) in its second and subsequent editions (1646, 1651, 1652, 1653) supported closed communion.[49] This was the majority view among Particular Baptists in the seventeenth century. Nevertheless, William Collins and Nehemiah Coxe, who drafted the Second London Confession in 1677, purposely avoided language that required an affirmation of closed Communion in order to accommodate the minority position of open communion.[50] In this case, the framers of the 2LCF wisely allowed for some diversity within the boundaries of orthodoxy.

---

of Christ, (1868; repr., Still Waters Revival Books, 1991), 1:301.

47   *The Need for Creeds Today: Confessional Faith in a Faithless Age* (Grand Rapids: Baker Academic, 2020), 87.

48   These examples include language concerning the divine degrees, the covenants, and assurance. *The Need for Creeds Today*, 83–89.

49   This is seen in the addition to Article 39, which is italicized: "That Baptisme is an Ordinance of the new Testament, given by Christ, to be dispensed onely upon persons professing faith, or that are Disciples, or taught, who upon profession of faith, out to be baptized *and after to partake of the Lord's Supper.*" See William L. Lumpkin, *Baptist Confessions of Faith*, rev. ed. (Valley Forge: Judson, 1969), 167b.

50   In an appendix to the confession, the authors write, "We are not insensible that as to the order of God's house, and entire communion therein there are some things wherein we (as well as others) are not at a full accord among our selves, as for instance; the known principle, and state of the consciences of diverse of us, that have agreed in this Confession is such; that we cannot hold Church-communion, with any other than Baptized-believers, and Churches constituted of such; yet some others of us have a greater liberty and freedom in our spirits that way; and therefore we have purposely omitted the mention of things of that nature, that we might concurre, in giving this evidence of our agreement, both among our selves, and with other good Christians, in those important articles of the Christian Religion, mainly insisted on by us: and this notwithstanding we all esteem it our chief concern, both among our selves, and all others that in every place call upon the name of the Lord Jesus Christ our Lord, both theirs and ours, and love him in sincerity, to endeavour to keep the unity of the Spirit, in the bond of peace; and in order thereunto, to exercise all lowliness and meekness, with long-suffering, forbearing one another in love." *A Confession of Faith. Put forth by the Elders and Brethren of many Congregations of Christians (baptized upon Profession of their Faith) in London and the Country. Printed*

3. Confessions help churches cooperate with one another.

Christ never intended local churches to work alone. One local church cannot carry out the Great Commission by itself. Instead, it should unite with other like-minded churches to carry out such cooperative efforts as benevolence, evangelism, missions, ministerial training, and the publication of Christian literature (Acts 15; 2 Cor. 8:18–24; Gal. 1:1–2, 18–22; Col. 4:13–18). In a day when denominations and cults abound, *substantial doctrinal agreement* is important if such co-operative efforts are to be healthy and productive. If two are to walk together, they must be agreed (Amos 3:3). True fellowship and harmony exist when God's people are of "one mind" (1 Cor. 1:10; Phil. 2:1–4). The "unity of the Spirit" (Eph. 4:3) will not be achieved apart from the "unity of the faith" (Eph. 4:13), which, in the context of Ephesians 4, includes *doctrinal agreement*. Since good confessions identify and expound doctrines essential to the faith as well as doctrines vital for the health of the church, they may serve as a helpful reference point for ascertaining whether there is sufficient doctrinal agreement to attain such unity.

Again, we need to qualify this point. Christ prayed for unity among all his true disciples (John 17). Not surprisingly, the WCF and 2LCF teach that believers are to have some level of "communion" with "all those who in every place call upon the name of the Lord" (WCF 26.2; 2LCF 27.2). Thus, we are not advocating a kind of "sectarian" spirit in which we only have inter-church fellowship with other Christians and churches that dot their i's and cross their t's precisely in the same manner we do.[51] We should pray for and exercise brotherly love to all true Christians and true churches of Christ. We may engage in larger or broader kingdom endeavors with churches that may not adhere to the same confession we affirm.

---

in the Year 1677. Facsimile Ed. (Auburn, MA: B&R Press, 2000), 137–38.

51 For example, many of the eighteenth-century Calvinistic Baptist churches did not experience the fruits of the English "evangelical revival" because they became too ingrown and doctrinally exclusive, refusing to acknowledge God's blessing on the labors of men like George Whitefield because he was an Anglican. See Michael Haykin's *One Heart and One Soul: John Sutcliff of Olney, his friends and his times* (Durham, UK: Evangelical Press, 1994), 26–28. Certainly, they were right to be wary of the Arminian elements of the revival promoted by men like John Wesley. But as Iain Murray argues, a Reformed Christian may even learn some helpful lessons from an Arminian like Wesley. See his *The Old Evangelicalism: Old Truths for a New Awakening* (Carlisle, PA: Banner of Truth, 2005). Chapter 5 is entitled, "What Can We Learn from John Wesley?"

Nevertheless, when we contemplate kingdom endeavors with a narrower focus, such as church planting, missions, theological education, and the publication of solid Christian literature, a solid confession of faith provides a helpful "compass" to ensure we are traveling in the same direction and pursuing the same goals.

Conclusion

"No creed but the Bible" has never been the historical position of orthodoxy. Rather it has always been the pious cloak of heretics, cultists, and modernists. It should be no surprise, then, that the Northern Baptist Convention opened the door wide for modernism when it voted to reject Riley's motion to adopt the New Hampshire Confession and to approve Woelfkin's proposal that "the New Testament is the all-sufficient ground of our faith and practice." That denomination has since become apostate.[52] Unfortunately, some Christians today have failed to see this danger and have rallied against creeds. Our goal in this study has been to ensure that we do not make that mistake. Our aim has been to persuade you of the validity and value of a confession of faith. We hope we have succeeded!

---

52 The Northern Baptist Convention has since become the American Baptist Churches USA (ABCUSA). For more about its history and decline, see Beale, *In Pursuit of Purity*, 171–229.

Part 2

A Survey of Some Reformed Baptist Confessions

3

"The Lifting up of the Name of the Lord Jesus in sinceritie"

An Introduction to The First London Confession of Faith

Michael A. G. Haykin[1]

O N OCTOBER 16, 1644, A BOOKSELLER by the name of
George Thomason, whose shop was located next to St.
Paul's Churchyard in London, purchased a small twenty-
four-page booklet entitled *The Confession of Faith, Of those Churches
which are commonly (though falsly) called Anabaptists*.[2] It was clearly
designed for easy conveyance, as it measured roughly seven inches
by six inches. The authors of the booklet were not named on the title
page, though at the foot of the introductory preface there did appear
fifteen names—the pastoral leadership of the seven Particular Baptist
churches then in existence, all of them located in the capital.[3] As to

---

1   Much of this chapter first appeared as a chapter in my *Kiffen, Knollys, and
Keach: Rediscovering our English Baptist Heritage*, 2nd ed. (Peterborough, ON:
H&E, 2019) and as the "Historical Introduction" to *The First London Confession of
Faith 1646 edition* (Springfield, MO: The Particular Baptist Press, 2017). Used by
permission of both publishers. The material has been rewritten in places, expanded
in others, and the footnotes updated throughout.
2   Murray Tolmie, *The Triumph of the Saints: The Separate Churches of London
1616–1649* (Cambridge: Cambridge University Press, 1977), 56.
3   The second edition of 1646 lists a slightly different set of names. It has fourteen
names from seven Baptist churches, including Hanserd Knollys (1599–1691) and
Benjamin Coxe (1595–*c.*1676), as well as two elders of a French Huguenot congregation: Denis le Barbier and Christopher Duret. See "To the judicious and im-

which of these leaders were the actual authors of this confession, later known simply as The First London Confession of Faith, it appears that William Kiffen (1616–1701), John Spilsbury (1593–*c.*1668), and Samuel Richardson (fl.1637–1658) played the most prominent role in drawing it up.[4]

partial Reader" in *A Confession of Faith Of seven Congregations or Churches of Christ in London, which are commonly (but uniustly) called Anabaptists*, 2nd ed. (London: Matthew Simmons, 1646), [A4 verso]. Coxe also drew up an appendix for the second edition of the *Confession*: *An Appendix to A Confession of Faith, or A more full Declaration of the Faith and Judgement of Baptized Believers* (London, 1646). This appendix had twenty-two articles that dealt with such matters as the fall of Adam, human responsibility, particular redemption, the free offer of the Gospel, the nature of irresistible grace, the necessity of good works and sanctification, the means of grace and perseverance, and closed communion.

For a side-by-side listing of the names on the first two editions of the confession, see Tolmie, *Triumph of the Saints*, 58. And for details regarding the men who signed the confession, see Tolmie, *Triumph of the Saints*, 57–61. References to the First London Confession of Faith will identify it as *Confession of Faith* with the specific year of the edition noted in parentheses.

By describing these churches as "Particular Baptists," I am aware that I am employing a term that only comes into vogue somewhat later as an identity-marker for these congregations. See the discussion by Matthew C. Bingham, *Orthodox Radicals: Baptist Identity in the English Revolution* (Oxford: Oxford University Press, 2019).

4 Joseph Ivimey, *The Life of Mr. William Kiffin* (London, 1833), 99; B. R. White, "The Doctrine of the Church in the Particular Baptist Confession of 1644," *The Journal of Theological Studies* n.s., 19 (1968): 570; William L. Lumpkin, *Baptist Confessions of Faith*, 2nd ed. (Valley Forge, PA: Judson Press, 1969), 145–146. Tolmie (*Triumph of the Saints*, 57), regards Kiffen as "perhaps the principal author of the Confession."

On Kiffen, see especially William Orme, *Remarkable Passages in the Life of William Kiffin* (London: Burton and Smith, 1823); Ivimey, *The Life of Mr. William Kiffin*; Barrie R. White, "William Kiffin—Baptist Pioneer and Citizen of London," *Baptist History and Heritage*, 2, no.2 (July, 1967): 91–103, 126; and now, Larry J. Kreitzer, *William Kiffen and His World*, 7 vols (Oxford: Regent's Park College, 2010–2020). For the spelling of Kiffen's name, I am following Kreitzer, who is the leading authority on the life and ministry of Kiffen.

On Spilsbury, who was probably a cobbler by trade, see R. L. Greaves, "Spilsbury (or Spilsbery), John" in his and Robert Zaller, ed., *Biographical Dictionary of British Radicals in the Seventeenth Century* (Brighton, Sussex: The Harvester Press, 1984), 193–194; Robert W. Oliver, *From John Spilsbury to Ernest Kevan: The Literary Contribution of London's Oldest Baptist Church* (London: Grace Publications Trust on behalf of the Evangelical Library, 1985), 8–9; B. R. White, "The London Calvinistic Baptist Leadership 1644–1660" in J.H.Y. Briggs, ed., *Faith, Heritage and Witness* (London: The Baptist Historical Society, 1987), 37–38.

On Richardson, see Paul Linton Gritz, "Samuel Richardson and the Religious and Political Controversies Confronting the London Particular Baptists, 1643 to 1658" (PhD thesis, Southwestern Baptist Theological Seminary, 1987).

The Reasons for the Confession

These churches issued the confession mainly to defend themselves against various false charges that were being circulated in the capital. The title page said it all: the confession was being issued "for the taking off those aspersions which are frequently both in Pulpit and Print" levelled against them.[5] As they explained further in the preface, they had been depicted as men and women "lying under that calumny and black brand of Heretickes, and sowers of division." From the pulpits and in the writings of fellow Puritans, they had been accused of "holding Free-will, Falling away from grace, denying Originall sinne, disclaiming of Magistracy, denying to assist them either in persons or purse in any of their lawfull Commands, doing acts unseemly in the dispensing the Ordinance of Baptism, not to be named amongst Christians."[6] From the first three of these charges it would appear that the Particular Baptists were being confused with the General Baptists, who had emerged in the 1610s under the leadership of John Smyth (*c.* 1570–1612) and Thomas Helwys (died *c.* 1615) and who were explicitly Arminian in their theology.[7] The next two charges are ones relating to political subversion and rebellion. Such accusations were probably levelled on the misunderstanding that the Particular Baptists were akin to the revolutionary, continental Anabaptists of the previous century. It is noteworthy that in the title of their confession, the Particular Baptists emphasized that they were "commonly (though falsly) called Anabaptists." The final charge—that of sexual immorality in the administration of baptism—was pure slander, but one that was frequently made against the early Baptists. For example, Daniel Featley (1582–1645), an influential, outspoken minister devoted to the Church of England and critical of Puritanism, penned a scurrilous attack on the Baptists entitled *The Dippers dipt. Or, The Anabaptists duck'd and plunged Over Head and Eares* (1645). In it he maintained that the Baptists were in the habit of stripping "stark naked, not onely when they flocke in

---

5 *The Confession of Faith, Of those Churches which are commonly (though falsly) called Anabaptists* (London: Matthew Simmons, 1644), title page.

6 "To All That Desire The Lifting up of the Name of the Lord Jesus in sinceritie, the poor despised Churches of God in London send greeting, with prayers for their farther increase in the knowledge of Christ Jesus" in *Confession of Faith* (1644), A2 recto and verso.

7 On Smyth and Helwys and the General Baptists, see Haykin, *Kiffen, Knollys, and Keach*, 11–17.

great multitudes, men and women together, to their Jordans to be
dipt; but also upon other occasions, when the season permits"![8]

The upshot of such charges—charges that the authors of this
preface vehemently asserted were "notoriously untrue"—was that
many godly believers wanted nothing at all to do with the Particular
Baptists. Many unbelievers were encouraged, "if they can finde the
place of our meeting, to get together in Clusters to stone us, as looking upon us as a people... not worthy to live."[9] John Spilsbury, for
example, mentioned in 1643 that his convictions regarding believer's
baptism had made his opponents "so incensed against me, as to seeke
my life."[10]

Consequently, in 1644 the London Particular Baptist leadership
decided to issue a confession of faith which would demonstrate
once and for all their fundamental solidarity with the international
Calvinist community. Study of the theological sources behind the
confession has shown that Kiffen, Spilsbury, and Richardson did
not create the confession *ex nihilo*. There is clear evidence that they
used a variety of resources, but it is noteworthy that in some of the
key articles dealing with soteriology and ecclesiology, the authors
did indeed make "original compositions."[11]

Criticism of the First London Confession of Faith from their fellow
Puritans compelled these Particular Baptists to issue an expanded
second edition in January of 1646.[12] Richardson and one of the new
signatories of the second edition, Benjamin Coxe, boldly handed out
copies of the confession to the members of Parliament at the doorway

---

8 Cited Gordon Kingsley, "Opposition to Early Baptists (1638–1645)," *Baptist
History and Heritage* 4, no.1 (January 1969): 29. On Daniel Featley, see further W.
J. McGlothlin, "Dr. Daniel Featley and the First Calvinistic Baptist Confession,"
The Review and Expositor 6 (1909): 579–589. For the charge of sexual immorality,
see also J. F. McGregor, "The Baptists: Fount of All Heresy" in his and B. Reay,
ed., *Radical Religion in the English Revolution* (Oxford: Oxford University Press,
1984), 41–42; James Barry Vaughn, "Public Worship and Practical Theology in the
Work of Benjamin Keach (1640–1704)" (PhD Thesis, University of St. Andrews,
1989), 60.
9 "To All That Desire The Lifting up of the Name of the Lord Jesus," A2 verso.
10 White, "Doctrine of the Church," 571n1.
11 Jay Travis Collier, "The Sources Behind the First London Confession,"
American Baptist Quarterly 21, no.2 (June 2002): 196–214. For what Collier calls
"original compositions," see Articles 21–32, XLI, and 49 in the 1644 edition (Collier, "The Sources Behind the First London Confession," 212).
12 For some of this critique, see Tolmie, *Triumph of the Saints*, 61–65.

of the House of Commons, for which they were arrested, though soon released![13] *Confession* soon became the doctrinal standard for the first period of Particular Baptist advance, which ended in 1660 with the restoration of Charles II (r.1660–1685).[14]

The Contents of the Confession

The 1646 edition of the confession consists of fifty-two articles. The first twenty articles dealt with the nature and attributes of God, the doctrine of the Trinity,[15] divine election, the fall and sinfulness of all humanity, and the person and work of Christ in his offices of prophet, priest, and king. Articles 21 to 32 dealt with the work of salvation and unequivocally reveal the confession's Calvinism.[16] For instance, Article 22, discussing saving faith, stated that "Faith is the gift of God wrought in the hearts of the Elect by the Spirit of God."[17] And as the gift of God, this faith cannot be lost: "Those that have this precious faith wrought in them by the Spirit, can never finally nor totally fall away."[18] Moreover, such saving faith was possessed only by the elect of God: "Christ Jesus by his death did purchase salvation for the Elect that God gave unto him."[19] Yet, as Robert W. Oliver has noted, this "belief in Particular Redemption did not inhibit evangelism."[20]

Articles 48–51 of the confession effectively rebutted the charge that the London Particular Baptists were Anabaptist revolutionaries by emphasizing that the civil power was ordained by God and that this power was not only to be obeyed, but also defended in all civil

---

13 See Samuel Renihan, "Benjamin Coxe 1595–ca.1676" in Michael A. G. Haykin and Terry Wolever, ed., *The British Particular Baptists. Volume I: A Series of Biographical Essays on Notable Figures*. Rev. ed. (Springfield, MO: Particular Baptist Press, 2019), 49–50 and n.54.

14 White, "Doctrine of the Church", 570; *idem*, "The Origins and Convictions of the First Calvinistic Baptists," *Baptist History and Heritage*, 25, no.4 (October 1990): 45.

15 The article on the Trinity, Article 2, is one of the articles identified by Collier as being original to the framers of this *Confession* ("The Sources Behind the First London Confession," 212).

16 Robert W. Oliver, "Baptist Confession Making 1644 and 1689" (Unpublished paper presented to the Strict Baptist Historical Society, March 17, 1989), 4.

17 *Confession of Faith* (1646), Article 22.

18 *Confession of Faith* (1646), Article 23.

19 *Confession of Faith* (1646), Article 21.

20 Oliver, "Baptist Confession Making," 4.

matters. Article 50, an addition to the second edition of the confession, stated that it was perfectly legitimate for "a Christian to be a Magistrate or Civill Officer" and "to take an Oath," both of which the continental Anabaptists of the sixteenth century had disputed.[21] The final article affirmed the resurrection.

The Ecclesiology of the Confession

The fifteen articles that lay between those discussing God's work in the salvation of sinners and those detailing the relationship of local churches to the state contained a thorough discussion of the nature of the church and its life. The local church, Article 33 affirmed, "is a company of visible Saints, called and separated from the world by the Word and Spirit of God, to the visible profession of the faith of the Gospel, being baptized into that faith, and joyned to the Lord, and each to other, by mutuall agreement."[22] In other words, the local church should consist only of those who have professed faith in Christ and have borne visible witness to that faith by being baptized. What is meant by placing baptism after the profession of faith in this article was later made explicit in Articles 39 and 40.[23] In the first of these articles, it was clearly stated that only those who have professed faith or who are "Disciples, who upon profession of faith, ought to be baptized, and after to partake of the Lord's supper."[24]

Article 40 then went on to describe the proper mode and meaning of baptism. It should be by immersion, or by "dipping or plunging the body under water." As to its meaning, the authors of the confession noted two significations of baptism.[25] First, it signified the believer's "death, burial, and resurrection" with Christ. Second, it helps to give the believer assurance that, just as he or she is raised up from the waters of baptism, "so certainly shall the bodies of the Saints be

---

21 See the discussion of this Article L by Paul Lusk, "Reappraising the English Anabaptists in the time of the Revolution: Article 50 of the 1646 confession," *Anabaptism Today*, 1, no.2 (October 2019): 15–25.

22 *Confession of Faith* (1646), Article 33.

23 White, "Doctrine of the Church," 580.

24 *Confession of Faith* (1646), Article 39. The final clause that limited participation in the Lord's Supper to baptized believers is not present in the first edition of 1644.

25 In the *Confession of Faith* (1644) these two meanings of baptism were given along with a third: it bore witness to the inner washing of the believer by the blood of Christ. Beginning with the second edition of the *Confession*, this meaning was omitted.

raised by the power of Christ, in the day of the resurrection." In the margin alongside this article, there was also a pointed refutation of the charge that the Baptists, in their administration of the ordinance of baptism, engaged in acts of immorality. The baptism of believers was carried out, it said, with "convenient garments be both upon the Administrator and subject, with all modesty."[26]

In entering the local church through the doorway of baptism, believers are declaring their acknowledgment of Christ as "their Prophet, Priest, and King" and placing themselves under "his heavenly conduct and government, to lead their lives in this walled Sheepfold, and watered Garden."[27] The final image used here to describe the church, "watered garden," would have a noteworthy history among the Particular Baptists. The phrase is drawn from Song of Solomon 4:12: "A garden inclosed is my sister, my spouse; a spring shut up, a fountain sealed" (KJV) and over the next century it would recur again and again in Particular Baptist documents that talked about the nature of the church.[28]

A significant number of homes in seventeenth-century England had enclosed gardens attached to them. While some of these gardens were developed for aesthetic reasons and consisted primarily of flowers and shrubs, many of them were kitchen gardens, designed

---

26 *Confession of Faith* (1646), Article 40. For the meaning of baptism in the writings of one of the signatories of this confession, see B. R. White, "Thomas Patient in England and Ireland," *Irish Baptist Historical Society Journal* 2 (1969–1970): 43–45.

27 *Confession of Faith* (1646), Article 35.

28 See, for example, Benjamin Keach, *Gospel Mysteries Unveiled* (London: L.I. Higham, 1815), 2:332: "Some part of a wilderness hath been turned into a garden or fruitful vineyard: so God hath out of the people of this world, taken his churches and walled them about, that none of the wild beasts can hurt them"; and Keach, *Gospel Mysteries Unveiled*, 2:339: "the church of Christ, is a garden inclosed, or a community of christians distinct from the world: 'A garden inclosed is my sister, my spouse.' Cant. iv.12." The covenant of Bourton-on-the-Water Baptist Church, Gloucestershire, drawn up around 1720, stated that members of the church must "promise to keep the Secrets of our Church entire without divulging them to any that are not Members of this particular Body, tho' they may be otherwise dear & near to us; for we believe the Church ought to be as a Garden enclosed & a fountain sealed" (cited in Charles W. Deweese, *Baptist Church Covenants* [Nashville: Broadman, 1990], 124).

It is noteworthy that Keith W. F. Stavely describes this image of an enclosed garden as "the image most frequently employed to describe the church" in "seventeenth-century ecclesiastical discourse" ("Roger Williams and the Enclosed Gardens of New England" in Francis J. Bremer, ed., *Puritanism: Transatlantic Perspectives on a Seventeenth-Century Anglo-American Faith* [Boston: Massachusetts Historical Society, 1993], 261).

to produce small fruits, herbs, salad greens and other vegetables. Generally rectangular in shape, they were enclosed by walls, fences, or hedges that might reach as high as sixteen feet. These walls provided both protection from the cooling effects of the wind and privacy for the owner.[29] In fact, during the turbulent era of the 1640s, when the British Isles experienced the horrors and ravages of civil war, such gardens came to be increasingly seen as "places of secure retreat from the dangers of political and religious strife."[30]

Given the insularity of such enclosed gardens, the regular use of this term by Particular Baptists in the late seventeenth and the early eighteenth centuries as a favored description of their churches can hardly be considered fortuitous. As the Particular Baptists moved into the eighteenth century, their community was increasingly insular. The use of this phrase, with all its introspective overtones, would only encourage the Particular Baptists to closet themselves within their meetinghouses and limit their horizons to the maintenance of church life. But all this was far in the future when this confession was drafted, and the men who drew it up were far from being inward-looking. They were firmly convinced that "the Gospel ... is to be preached to all men."[31]

Articles 36 and 42 to 45 were a classic description of congregational church government. On the basis of Matthew 18:17 and 1 Corinthians 5:4–5, it was affirmed that "Christ hath ... given power to his Church to receive in, and cast out, any member that deserves it; and this power is given to every Congregation, and not to one particular person, either member or officer, but in relation to the whole body."[32] The members of the local church acting together have the authority and power to receive new members into their midst as well as to excommunicate those who refuse to walk under Christ's lordship. Furthermore, "every Church hath power given them from Christ, for their well-being to chuse among themselves meet persons for Elders and Deacons."[33] It was also stressed that "none other have

29 David C. Stuart, *Georgian Gardens* (London: Robert Hale Ltd., 1979), 142–143.
30 Tom Turner, *English Garden Design: History and styles since 1650* (Woodbridge, Suffolk: Antique Collectors' Club Ltd., 1986), 9.
31 *Confession of Faith* (1644), Article 21. The 1646 edition did not have this clause, though the men who issued it clearly still held it.
32 *Confession of Faith* (1646), Article 52.
33 *Confession of Faith* (1646), Article 36.

power to impose" leaders on the congregation from the outside. This statement was a powerful declaration that "the ministry was ... firmly subordinated to the immediate authority of the covenanted community."[34] As B. R. White has pointed out, this jealous concern for congregational autonomy was motivated by a deep desire to be free to obey Christ, and not to be bound by the dictates of men and human traditions.[35] In sum, Christ has entrusted to individual congregations the authority and right to order their lives together as believers. The understanding of the local church displayed in these articles placed upon church members a great responsibility. In the words of Stanley Grenz, late professor of theology at Carey Hall in Vancouver, "Believers are initiated into a corporate life in which they are to become personally involved and over which they are to take personal ownership. Because the people are the church, ongoing Baptist congregational life demands the involvement of each member in a way unparalleled by the leader-centered polity of both the traditional churches and the newer charismatic groups."[36]

Baptist Associations

This strong affirmation of congregational autonomy in the texts cited above, which could easily lead to isolationism, was balanced by Article 47, in which it was stated that "although the particular congregations be distinct and severall bodies, every one as a compact and knit Citie within it selfe; yet are they all to walke by one rule of truth; So also they (by all meanes convenient) are to have the counsell and helpe one of another, if necessitie require it, as members of one body, in the common faith, under Christ their head."[37] The autonomy of each local congregation was recognized as a biblical given, but so was the fact that each congregation ultimately belonged to only one Body and each shared the same head, the Lord Christ. Therefore, local congregations should endeavor to help one another.

---

34 White, "Doctrine of the Church," 581; *idem*, "Origins and Convictions of the First Calvinistic Baptists," 46. The first of these articles by White has been very helpful in thinking through the ecclesiology of this confession. On the fact that there should be only two church offices, those of elder and deacon, see the remarks of Benjamin Keach, *The Glory of a True Church, and Its Discipline Display'd* (London, 1697), 15–16.

35 White, "Doctrine of the Church," 584.

36 Stanley Grenz, "A Baptist Ecclesiology for the Contemporary World," *Search* 22, no.4 (Summer 1993): 8–9.

37 *Confession of Faith* (1646), Article 47.

The sort of help envisioned by the authors of this confession can
be discerned in the proof texts that were placed alongside this article
in both its 1644 and 1646 editions. The first edition cited, among
other verses, 1 Corinthians 16:1, which refers to the collection of
money that Paul gathered from congregations in Greece and Asia
Minor for the poor in the church at Jerusalem, and Colossians 4:16,
in which the church at Colossae is urged to share Paul's letter to them
with the church at Laodicea and vice versa. In the 1646 edition,
some proof texts were dropped and among those added were Acts
15:2–3, which deals with the Jerusalem Council, and 2 Corinthians
8:1–4, which also has to do with the collection of money for the
church at Jerusalem. In other words, the authors of this confession
envisioned the churches helping one another in areas of financial
need as well as in giving advice with regard to doctrinal and ethical
matters. Ultimately what bound the churches together was a common determination to walk according to the "one rule of truth," that
is, the Scriptures. Only where there is such genuine agreement as to
the source of final authority for life and doctrine can local churches
walk and work together.[38]

Here, in Article 47, is the genesis of what would later become a
characteristic feature of the early Particular Baptists, namely, their
regional associations which linked together local congregations in
specific geographical areas of Great Britain. These associations were
to be a key factor in the great growth that the Particular Baptist cause
witnessed during the late 1640s and the 1650s. These were tumul-
tuous years in English history, as the land was convulsed in civil war
and experienced massive social, political, and economic upheaval.
The Particular Baptists flourished, however, and their commitment
to associations played a vital part in their growth. Associations provided mutual strength and fellowship, an instrument for preserving
congregational integrity and orthodoxy, a means of providing for
the financial needs of poorer congregations, and a way of supporting
church-planting and evangelistic endeavors. The important place
that these first-generation Baptists accorded to their associations is
well expressed by B. R. White when he states that "they no more
believed that an individual congregation should be free to go its own
way than that an individual believer could be a serious Christian
without commitment to a local, visible congregation."[39]

---

38 White, "Doctrine of the Church," 583–584.
39 White, "Origins and Convictions of the First Calvinistic Baptists," 47.

Coda

The Particular Baptist cause expanded from the seven churches in London in the mid-1640s to around 130 throughout England, Wales, and Ireland by the late 1650s. Helping to win converts to the Baptist position and bind them together was the *First London Confession of Faith*, which appeared in three further editions: two published in London in 1651 and 1652, and a Scottish edition in 1653.[40] The printing of these three further editions bespeaks the flourishing state of these Baptists. In many ways, it was a halcyonic era in Baptist history.

---

40 *A Confession of Faith Of the several Congregations or Churches of Christ in London, which are commonly (though unjustly) called Anabaptists*, 3rd ed. (London: M[atthew] S[immons], 1651). This third edition was signed by fourteen London Baptists, of whom only Kiffen and Spilsbury had signed the earlier editions ("The Epistle to the Reader," [A3 verso]). It also had an appendix entitled "Heart Bleedings for Professors Abhominations" (*Confession of Faith* [1651], 13–26), which is aimed at refuting such rival sects as the Quakers and the Ranters. This appendix had previously appeared as a separate publication: *Heart-Bleedings for Professors Abominations* (London: Francis Tyton, 1650). This 1650 version was signed by sixteen London Particular Baptists, half of whom would sign the 1651 edition of the Confession; *A Confession of Faith Of the several Congregations or Churches of Christ in London, which are commonly (though unjustly) called Anabaptists*, 4th ed. (London: M[atthew] S[immons], 1652). This fourth edition also has the appendix of that of 1651; *A Confession of Faith Of the several Congregations or Churches of Christ in London, which are commonly (though unjustly) called Anabaptists*, 4th ed. corrected (Leith, 1653). This edition of the confession has the appendix of the third and fourth editions as well as an additional preface signed by, presumably, the leaders of a Particular Baptist congregation that met in "Leith and Edinburgh": "Thomas Spenser, Abraham Holmes, Thomas Powell, and John Brady" ("To the impartiall Reader" in *Confession of Faith* [1653], [A1 verso]).

4

"Declaring before God, Angels, and Men . . . that wholesome Protestant Doctrine"

The Historical Context of the Second London Confession

Michael A. G. Haykin

T HE FIRST LONDON CONFESSION OF FAITH had gone through
five editions between 1644 and 1653, but by the mid-1670s,
a copy of it appears to have been a rarity in the British Isles.[1]
The Particular Baptists were still continuing to flourish despite the
fact that they, and other Dissenting bodies (like the Presbyterians,
Congregationalists, and Quakers), had been subject to vicious state
persecution since the restoration of the monarchy in 1660. These
"many others" who had "embraced the same truth" set forth in the
First London Confession needed a statement of their faith.[2] So it
was that in 1677, two London Particular Baptists, William Collins
(d. 1702) and Nehemiah Coxe (d. 1689), co-pastors of the Petty

---

1   Much of this chapter first appeared as a chapter in my *Kiffen, Knollys, and
Keach: Rediscovering our English Baptist Heritage*, 2nd ed. (Peterborough, ON:
H&E, 2019). Used by permission of the publisher. The material has been largely
rewritten and expanded and the footnotes updated throughout.

2   "To the Judicious and Impartial Reader" in *A Confession of Faith Put Forth by the
Elders and Brethren Of many Congregations of Christians (baptized upon Profession of
their Faith) in London and the Country* ([London,] 1677), A3 verso. This, and later
editions of the confession, will be cited as "Confession of Faith" with the respective
year in parentheses in which it was published.

France Baptist Church in London, published a confession, what is now called the Second London Confession, for these "many others." Yet, it may be asked, why did they not simply reprint the First London Confession of Faith? The answer to this vital question is to be found in certain key events that had taken place between the publication of the First London Confession and that of the Second London Confession.

"No itch to clogg Religion with new words"

The First London Confession of Faith served the Particular Baptists well during the 1640s and 1650s when the rule of Parliament and then that of Oliver Cromwell (1599–1658) afforded them an unprecedented degree of freedom to evangelize and plant new churches. This situation was completely altered, though, after Cromwell's death, and a number of his generals supported the restoration of the monarchy in the person of Charles II. Persecution now became the order of the day, for those who came to power with Charles were determined to destroy the Puritans as a political force and religious power. Interestingly enough, Charles II, who was a crypto-Roman Catholic and was received into the Roman Church on his deathbed, seems to have had a sincere desire for religious toleration. This desire probably stemmed from the fact that toleration would have given security to fellow Roman Catholics. But, as British historian Michael R. Watts has noted, "though Charles wanted religious toleration, he wanted the crown more."[3] To keep his crown, Charles needed Parliament, and the Parliament that came to power with Charles in 1660 had little sympathy for Puritanism either within or outside of the Church of England. Consequently, for the next twenty-eight years, those who would not conform to the Church of England were subjected to "calculated and often malicious persecution."[4] For instance, in June of 1662, the Petty France Particular Baptist Church in London was attacked by a group of soldiers, who, one record states, "came to Petty France full of Rage and Violence, with their Swords drawn; they wounded some, and struck others, broke down the Gallery, and made much spoile."[5]

---

3 Michael R. Watts, *The Dissenters: From the Reformation to the French Revolution* (Oxford; Clarendon Press, 1978), 222. For a recent study of Charles II, see Clare Jackson, *Charles II: The Star King* ([London]: Allen Lane, 2016).

4 Watts, *Dissenters*, 222.

5 Cited in T. E. Dowley, "A London Congregation during the Great Persecu-

Of course, the Particular Baptists were not the only ones to suffer during this time of great persecution; all who dissented from the rites and practices of the Church of England suffered to one degree or another. This furnace of common affliction only served to reinforce in the minds of many Particular Baptists just how much they shared with fellow Calvinists who were either Presbyterians or Congregationalists, the latter being then known as Independents. Moreover, there was at hand a document which could concretely demonstrate the essential doctrinal unity between these three groups, namely, the Westminster Confession of Faith. This confession, the authoritative statement of faith of both the Church of Scotland and the English Presbyterians, had been issued by the Westminster Assembly in 1646. The Independents had subsequently used it as the basis of their statement of faith, known as the Savoy Declaration, which was drawn up in 1658 by such leading Puritan authors as John Owen (1616–1683) and Thomas Goodwin (1600–1680).[6] The desire to present a united Calvinist front in the face of persecution and to demonstrate their unity in the "wholesome Protestant Doctrine" of their fellow Puritans consequently led the Particular Baptists to employ the Westminster Confession, as modified by the Savoy Declaration, as the basis of a new confession.[7] In their words, they had "no itch to clogg Religion with new words."[8]

---

tion: Petty France Particular Baptist Church, 1641–1688," *The Baptist Quarterly* 27 (1977–1978): 233. For two excellent monographs on this persecution, see G. R. Cragg, *Puritanism in the Period of the Great Persecution 1660–1688* (Cambridge: Cambridge University Press, 1957) and Raymond Brown, *Spirituality in Adversity: English Nonconformity in a Period of Repression, 1660–1689*, Studies in Evangelical History and Thought (Milton Keynes, Buckinghamshire: Paternoster, 2012).

6   While most of the articles in the Savoy Declaration are taken word for word from the Westminster Confession, there are a number where the authors of the Savoy Declaration have either altered the wording or added brand new articles. For some of these changes, see Peter Toon, *Puritans and Calvinism* (Swengel, PA: Reiner, 1973), 77–84; Robert W. Oliver, "Baptist Confession Making 1644 and 1689" (Unpublished paper presented to the Strict Baptist Historical Society, March 17, 1989), 11–12.

7   "To the Judicious and Impartial Reader" in *A Confession of Faith Put Forth by the Elders and Brethren Of many Congregations of Christians (Baptized upon Profession of their Faith) in London and the Country* (London: John Harris, 1688), A5 recto–[A6 recto].

8   "To the Judicious and Impartial Reader" in *Confession of Faith* (1688), A6 recto.

"All religion would be cashiered"

A second reason for a new confession was the appearance of hyper-Calvinism in the West Country. Andrew Gifford Sr. (1642–1721), pastor of the Pithay Particular Baptist Church in Bristol, knew "some ministers who were of the opinion that as none could pray acceptably without the influences of the Holy Spirit, and unconverted men being destitute of those influences, that therefore it was not their duty to pray, nor the duty of ministers to exhort them to seek for spiritual blessings."[9] Gifford wrote to the Particular Baptist pastors in London seeking their opinion on the matter.

A letter was drawn up in January of 1675 by William Kiffen and a number of other London Baptists in which it was unequivocally stated that "prayer is a part of that homage which every man is obliged to give to God" and that it is "a duty belonging to natural, and not only to instituted religion." Support for this position was found in Acts 17:26–27, where the apostle Paul declared to the Athenian philosophers on the Areopagus that God has so ordered the history of the world that men and women "should seek the Lord." As Kiffen and his fellow Baptists went on to note: "Whatever in that text is meant by seeking, prayer cannot (by any just reason) be excluded; and if prayer be intended, 'tis comprehensive of all mankind. It cannot be supposed that man, being such a creature as he is, should not be obliged to love, fear, and obey God." In response to the objection that "such persons have not the Spirit, [and] therefore ought not to pray," the London Baptists were unequivocal in their reply:

> This objection is not cogent, forasmuch as neither the want of the Spirit's immediate motions to, or its assistance in the duty, doth not take off the obligation to the duty. If it would, then also, from every other duty; and consequently all religion would be cashiered. If the obligation to this and other duties were suspended merely for want of such motions or assistance, then unconverted persons are so far from sinning in the omission of such duties, that it is their duty to omit them. 'Tis certain no man can, without the assistance of the Holy Spirit, either repent or believe; yet it will not therefore follow, that impenitency and unbelief are no sins; if these be sins, then the contrary must be their duty.[10]

9 Cited in Joseph Ivimey, *A History of the English Baptists* (London, 1811), 1:416.
10 Cited in Ivimey, *History*, 1:417–418.

Coming only a couple of years before the publication of the Second London Confession, this issue was certain to be on the minds of those who compiled this confession.

"A great dispute . . . concerning the rule"

Yet another reason which prompted the desire to issue a new confession was the threat posed by the Quakers.[11] The Quaker movement had started in the late 1640s when George Fox (1624–1691), a shoemaker and part-time shepherd, began to win converts to a perspective on the Christian faith which rejected much of orthodox Puritan theology. Fox and the early Quakers proclaimed the possibility of salvation for all humanity and urged men and women to turn to the light within them to find salvation. We "call All men to look to the Light within their own consciences," wrote Samuel Fisher (1605–1665), a General Baptist turned Quaker, "by the leadings of that Light . . . they may come to God, and work out their Salvation."[12] This emphasis on the light within, which the Quakers variously called the indwelling Christ or Spirit, often led them to elevate it above the Scriptures.

For the Puritans, including the Particular Baptists, the nature of the Spirit's work in the authors of Scripture was unique and definitely a thing of the past. The Spirit was now illuminating that which he had inspired, and their experiences of the Spirit were to be tried by the Scriptures.[13] Thus, when some Baptists in Huntingdonshire and Cambridgeshire became Quakers and declared that the "light in their consciences was the rule they desire to walk by," not the Scriptures, they were simply expressing what was implicit in the entire Quaker movement.[14]

This desire to live by what they regarded as the dictates of the indwelling Spirit rather than by the written Word sometimes led the early Quakers into quite bizarre patterns of behavior. Probably the

---

11 Oliver, "Baptist Confession Making," 12–13.

12 Cited in Barry Reay, *The Quakers and the English Revolution* (New York: St. Martin's Press, 1985), 33. For a discussion of Fisher's approach to Scripture, see Dean Freiday, *The Bible: Its Criticism, Interpretation and Use in 16th and 17th Century England* (Pittsburgh, PA: Catholic and Quaker Studies, 1979), 97–102.

13 Cited in Geoffrey F. Nuttall, *The Holy Spirit in Puritan Faith and Experience*, 2nd ed. (Oxford: Basil Blackwell, 1947), 32.

14 Cited in Reay, *Quakers*, 34.

oddest has to have been the practice of "going naked as a sign"![15] One Quaker who appears to have been something of an "expert" in this type of behavior was Solomon Eccles (*c.* 1618–1683). When he first went naked in 1659, he asserted that he did so because by "the same spirit [which moved Isaiah and Ezekiel] hath the Lord raised me up, to go as a Sign to this dark Generation." While the practice of "going naked as a sign" was a relatively infrequent occurrence after 1662—though Eccles was still engaged in it as late as 1669—the phenomenon well illustrates the tendency inherent in Quakerism to exalt the Spirit at the expense of the Word.

Isaac Penington the Younger (1616–1679) is one early Quaker author who well illustrates this tendency to make the indwelling Spirit rather than the Scriptures the touchstone and final authority for thought and practice. Converted to Quakerism in 1658 after hearing George Fox preach the previous year, Penington became an important figure in the movement. In the words of historian J. W. Frost, Penington "remains a prime example of the intellectual sophistication of the second generation of Quaker converts."[16] In a letter that he wrote a fellow Quaker by the name of Nathanael Stonar in 1670, Penington told his correspondent that there was "a great dispute . . . concerning the rule" between themselves and other "professors," namely, various Dissenting bodies including the Particular Baptists. While the latter asserted that the Scriptures were the rule by which men and women ought to direct their lives and thinking, Penington was convinced that the indwelling Spirit of life is "nearer and more powerful, than the words, or outward relations concerning those things in the Scriptures." Penington noted,

> The Lord, in the gospel state, hath promised to be present
> with his people; not as a wayfaring man, for a night, but to
> dwell in them and walk in them. Yea, if they be tempted
> and in danger of erring, they shall hear a voice behind them,
> saying, "This is the way, walk in it." Will they not grant

15　For an excellent study of this phenomenon, see Kenneth L. Carroll, "Early Quakers and 'Going Naked as a Sign'," *Quaker History* 67 (1978): 69–87. The following paragraph is indebted to this study. See also Richard Bauman, *Let Your Words Be Few: Symbolism of Speaking and Silence among Seventeenth-Century Quakers* (Cambridge: Cambridge University Press, 1983), 84–94.

16　"Penington, Isaac (the Younger)" in Richard L. Greaves and Robert Zaller, ed., *Biographical Dictionary of British Radicals in the Seventeenth Century* (Brighton, Sussex: The Harvester Press, 1984), 3:23.

this to be a rule, as well as the Scriptures? Nay, is not this a more full direction to the heart, in that state, than it can pick to itself out of the Scriptures? ... And the Spirit, which gave forth the words, is greater than the words; therefore we cannot but prize Him himself, and set Him higher in our heart and thoughts, than the words which testify of Him, though they also are very sweet and precious to our taste.[17]

Penington here affirmed that the Quakers esteemed the Scriptures as "sweet and precious," but he was equally adamant that the indwelling Spirit was to be regarded as the supreme authority when it came to direction for Christian living and thinking.[18]

The Quakers especially preyed on Baptist congregations, shattering many of them in the process of winning converts. While the General Baptists were more susceptible to the views of the Quakers, the Particular Baptists were by no means immune. For instance, a member of the Petty France Particular Baptist Church, a Sister Hattam, was, after being admonished, excommunicated in October of 1676 for joining the Quakers. Another good example was Luke Howard, who was instrumental in persuading Samuel Fisher to become a Quaker. Howard had been baptized by William Kiffen in either 1643 or 1644, but subsequently went over to the Quakers.[19] In the West Country, several leading Quakers had been Baptists prior to their change of mind. Thomas Budd, known once as a "Baptist teacher," opened up his property for large Quaker gatherings. William Ames, who had been a Baptist minister in Somerset, became a Quaker while serving as a soldier in Ireland. Jasper Batt (d. 1702), who later preached at George Fox's funeral, had also once been a Baptist.[20] To help minimize such Particular Baptist losses to

---

17 Isaac Penington, Letter to Nathaniel Stonar, September 24, 1670, in *Letters of Isaac Penington*, 2nd ed. (London: Holdsworth and Ball, 1829), 202–203. I am indebted to Heinz G. Dschankilic of Cambridge, ON, for access to this letter.

18 See also the remarks by Richard Dale Land, "Doctrinal Controversies of English Particular Baptists (1644–1691) as Illustrated by the Career and Writings of Thomas Collier" (DPhil thesis, Regent's Park College, University of Oxford, 1979), 205–211. In the words of Richard Bauman, "the Quakers were intensely devoted to the Bible, not as a source of traditional authority, but as historical validation of the patterns and dynamics of their own charismatic prophetic mission," (*Let Your Words Be Few*, 38).

19 B. R. White, "The Frontiers of Fellowship Between English Baptists, 1609–1660," *Foundations*, 11 (1968): 250.

20 Dowley, "London Congregation," 237; Land, "Doctrinal Controversies," 191–192.

the Quakers, it was clear that a more comprehensive statement on the nature of the authority of Scripture was needed than the various remarks found here and there in the First London Confession.

"This Collier is a great sectary"

Probably the most pressing doctrinal reason for a new confession was the defection of Thomas Collier (fl.1634?–1691).[21] Collier, a member of William Kiffen's church, had served as a chaplain with the parliamentary troops in the final years of the Civil War. In 1651 he became an itinerant evangelist in the southwest of England, where he labored for the next fifteen years. During this period, he became a well-known leader among the Particular Baptists. Testimony to Collier's importance comes from Thomas Edwards (1599–1647), a Presbyterian and Puritan in theology, but one who had a deep-seated antipathy toward the Baptists. He described Collier thus: "This Collier is a great sectary in the west of England, a mechanical fellow [i.e., a vulgar fellow belonging to the lower classes], and a great emissary, a dipper who goes about Surrey, Hampshire, and those countries, preaching and dipping."[22]

In 1674, however, Collier published a work entitled *A Body of Divinity*, which sent shock waves throughout the Particular Baptist community, for in this book Collier denied the Calvinistic doctrine of original sin, argued that Christ had died for all men and women, and maintained that Christ's humanity was eternal.[23] Due to Collier's standing among the Particular Baptists, it was imperative that his views be dealt with. A meeting was arranged between Collier and five Baptist ministers from London, including Kiffen and Nehemiah Coxe.[24] Collier, though, refused to renounce his new views and he was duly accused of heresy. After the first publication of what has become known as the Second London Confession, Collier issued his

---

21 Oliver, "Baptist Confession Making," 13. For a full examination of Collier's ministry and writings, see Land, "Doctrinal Controversies." See also James M. Renihan, "Thomas Collier's Descent Into Error: Collier, Calvinism, and the Second London Confession," *Reformed Baptist Theological Review* 1, no.1 (January 2004): 67–83.

22 Cited in Thompson Cooper, "Collier, Thomas," *The Dictionary of National Biography* (1887, Oxford: Oxford University Press, 1963–1964), 4:810–811.

23 Oliver, "Baptist Confession Making," 13.

24 For biographical details of Nehemiah Coxe, see Dowley, "London Congregation," 238n12; Joseph Ivimey, *A History of the English Baptists* (London, 1814), 2:403–407.

own confessional statement. He took great pains to affirm again that Christ died for all of mankind, for it was both "irreligious and irrational" to believe otherwise." He also upheld the freedom of the human will—"all Men have a power and liberty of Will"— and this meant that "the Doctrine of impossibility of falling from Grace . . . [was] contrary to the Doctrine of Christ and his Apostles." According to Collier, the perseverance of the saints was "a graceless and dangerous Doctrine." In this statement of his faith, Collier also devoted considerable space to an eschatological vision of the future which affirmed a universal restoration of the entirety of mankind.[25] In all three of these areas of doctrine, Collier was purposely and explicitly rejecting theological sentiments expressed by the Particular Baptists.[26]

Although Coxe had published an extensive rebuttal of Collier's views in 1677, the controversy threatened to call into question the commitment of the Particular Baptists to Calvinism. A fresh statement of their commitment to Calvinism was needed.

"Those important Articles of the Christian Religion"

William Collins and his fellow pastor Nehemiah Coxe published the new confession anonymously in 1677.[27] Collins had studied in France and Italy, and had then taken a BD in England. Efforts were made to induce him into conforming to the Church of England, but he resisted them and in 1675 he accepted a call to pastor the Petty France Church. Coxe had originally been a member of John Bunyan's (1628–1688) church in Bedford, had spent time with Bunyan in prison for preaching the gospel, and had been ordained to the ministry at the same church meeting which called Bunyan to be the pastor of the church.[28]

As has been noted, Collins and Coxe used the Westminster Confession and the Savoy Declaration in their preparation of the Second London Confession. Nevertheless, they did not reproduce these confessions holus-bolus. As they stated in the preface: "Some things, indeed, are in some places added, some terms omitted, and

25 Thomas Collier, *A Confession of Faith, Published on Special Occasion* (London: Francis Smith, 1678), 5–15, 19, 21, 22–41.
26 See the postscript in Collier, 42–44.
27 On William Collins, see Ivimey, *History*, II, 397–403.
28 Christopher Hill, *A Turbulent, Seditious and Factious People: John Bunyan and His Church, 1628–1688* (Oxford: Clarendon, 1988), 122.

some few changed."[29] These changes related to not only such obvious things as baptism and church government, but also included
modification in other less obvious areas. The statement of reprobation, for example, in both the Westminster Confession and the
Savoy Declaration described the reprobate as being "foreordained to
everlasting death."[30] The Second London Confession has softened
this somewhat by stating that the reprobate are "left to act in their
sin to their just condemnation."[31] Moreover, in the same article an
entire paragraph on reprobation that is found in the Westminster
Confession and the Savoy Declaration has been deleted from the
Second London Confession. Another change appears in the article
relating to worship. In the Westminster Confession and the Savoy
Declaration singing is restricted to the "singing of psalms." But in
the Second London Confession "Hymns and Spiritual Songs" were
included alongside the Psalms as fit material for singing.[32] Yet, as
Robert W. Oliver notes: "These differences must not be allowed to
obscure the overwhelming agreement between the Second London
Confession and those of Westminster and Savoy. The Baptist
Confession can be clearly seen to be in the stream of evangelical
theology, which flowed from the Westminster Assembly."[33]

Eleven years after the anonymous publication of the confession by Coxe and Collins, it was issued again in a second edition
in 1688. This second edition also included an appendix that had
been appended to the first edition and that sought to resolve a
controversy over the relationship of baptism to the Lord's Supper
that had been rumbling around Particular Baptist circles for fifteen
years or so. The second edition of the First London Confession had
clearly made believer's baptism requisite for fellowship at the Lord's
Table.[34] However, in the 1670s and early 1680s, William Kiffen had
been involved in a lengthy controversy with none other than John
Bunyan over this very matter. In fact, this controversy drew forth

---

29 "To the Judicious and Impartial Reader" in *Confession of Faith* (1688), [A6
verso–A7 recto].

30 Westminster Confession 3.3; Savoy Declaration 3.3.

31 Confession of Faith (1688) 3.3.

32 Westminster Confession 21.5; Savoy Declaration 22.5; Confession of Faith
(1688) 22.5.

33 Oliver, "Baptist Confession Making," 21.

34 See *A Confession of Faith Of seven Congregations or Churches of Christ in London,
which are commonly (but uniustly) called Anabaptists*, 2nd ed. (London: Matthew
Simmons, 1646), Article 39.

from Kiffen his most important work, *A Sober Discourse of Right to Church-Communion* (1681), a studied and heartfelt response to a series of treatises by John Bunyan in favor of open communion and open membership. Although Bunyan is currently one of the most celebrated Christian authors of the seventeenth century, in his own day he had little influence amongst his fellow Baptists.[35] His strong commitment to open communion and open membership put him out of step with most seventeenth-century Calvinistic Baptists, who favored closed communion and closed membership. Kiffen's *Sober Discourse* was characterized by "clear logic and crisp presentation," and was undoubtedly aimed at Bunyan, although the Bedford pastor is never explicitly named in the work. From Kiffen's perspective, the practice of open communion and open membership "destroys Order and flatly contradicts the Practice of the Primitive Christians." The "right Gospel Order" is laid down in Acts 2:41–42, where believers are first baptized, then "received into Church-fellowship," and only then share in the Lord's Table.[36]

This requirement of closed communion, though, is totally absent from the Second London Confession. In the appendix attached to the confession when it was first issued in 1677, it was stated:

We are not insensible that as to the Order of God's House, and entire Communion therein, there are some things

---

35 On the controverted question about whether or not Bunyan actually was a Baptist, see Thomas Armitage, *A History of the Baptists* (New York, NY: Bryan, Taylor, & Co., 1887), 529–539; John Brown, *John Bunyan (1628–1688): His Life, Times, and Work*, revised Frank Mott Harrison (London/Glasgow/Birmingham: The Hulbert Publishing Co., 1928), 221–225, 236–238; Joseph D. Ban, "Was John Bunyan a Baptist? A Case-Study in Historiography," *The Baptist Quarterly* 30 (1983–1984): 367–376. I would agree with the estimation of Richard L. Greaves when he states that "Bunyan is rightly regarded as an open-membership Baptist" ("Conscience, Liberty, and the Spirit: Bunyan and Nonconformity" in N. H. Keeble, ed., *John Bunyan: Conventicle and Parnassus. Tercentenary Essays* (Oxford: Clarendon Press, 1988], 35). In this regard, see also Kenneth Dix, *John Bunyan: Puritan Pastor* ([Dunstable, Bedfordshire].: The Fauconberg Press for The Strict Baptist Historical Society, 1978), 8.

36 William Kiffen, *A Sober Discourse of Right to Church-Communion* (London, 1681), 16–17. The description of this treatise is taken from T.L. Underwood, " 'It pleased me much to contend': John Bunyan as Controversialist," *Church History* 57 (1988): 468. For this controversy, see especially Michael A. G. Haykin and C. Jeffrey Robinson, "Particular Baptist Debates about Communion and Hymn-Singing" in Michael A. G. Haykin and Mark Jones, ed., *'Drawn into Controversie': Reformed Theological Diversity and Debates Within Seventeenth-Century British Puritanism*, Reformed Historical Theology (Göttingen: Vandenhoeck & Ruprecht, 2011), 17:285–296.

wherein we (as well as others) are not at a full accord among ourselves; as for instance, The known principle, and state of the Consciences of diverse of us, that have agreed in this Confession is such, that we cannot hold Church-communion, with any other than baptized Believers, and Churches constituted of such; yet some others of us have a greater liberty and freedom in our spirits that way; and therefore we have purposely omitted the mention of things of that nature, that we might concurr, in giving this evidence of our agreement, both among Ourselves, and with other good Christians, in those important Articles of the Christian Religion, mainly insisted on by us.[37]

One of the reasons for this difference between the two confessions is that Nehemiah Coxe, who was intimately involved in drawing up the Second London Confession, had been called to the ministry in 1672 by the open-Communion, open-membership church in Bedford that John Bunyan pastored from 1672 till his death sixteen years later.[38] Moreover, Petty France Church in London, which Coxe later pastored, regularly received into its membership believers from open-communion Particular Baptist churches.[39] Even more significant was the fact that by 1677, both open and closed Communion Particular Baptist churches had experienced seventeen years of persecution. In Robert Oliver's words, "disunity was a luxury that they could ill afford."[40]

The accession of William III (1650–1702) to the throne of England with his wife Mary II (1662–1694), when the so-called Glorious Revolution of 1688 removed the Roman Catholic James II (1633–1701), led to a genuine measure of religious toleration. William and Mary were declared the rightful sovereigns of England on February 13, 1689, and on May 24 the Act of Toleration, which secured religious toleration for all Trinitarian bodies outside of the Church of England apart from Roman Catholic churches, was passed into law. On July 22, Kiffen, Hanserd Knollys, Benjamin Keach (1640–1704), and a number of other Particular Baptist leaders in London invited churches throughout England and Wales to

---

37　"An Appendix" in *Confession of Faith* (1688), 136.
38　Oliver, "Baptist Confession Making," 17.
39　Dowley, "London Congregation," 233–234.
40　Oliver, "Baptist Confession Making," 20.

send messengers to the first national assembly of the denomination that September in London.[41] Messengers from 107 churches were sent and affirmed the Second London Confession as the doctrinal standard of their denomination as the assembly met from September 3–12. In their words, it was the "confession we own, as containing the doctrine of our faith and practice."[42]

This assembly also passed a resolution to the effect that the churches were to be given the liberty to follow their own judgment when it came to open or closed Communion. This resolution read as follows: "In those things wherein one church differs from another church in their principles or practices, in point of communion, . . . we cannot, shall not impose upon any particular church therein, but leave every church to their own liberty to walk together as they have received from the Lord."[43] A. C. Underwood and Joshua Thompson, both twentieth-century Baptist historians, have understood this resolution to mean that while fellowship and recognition was to be extended to open-communion churches with closed membership, it was not to be extended to those churches which, like Bunyan's, held to both open communion and open membership.[44] Yet, as B. R. White has pointed out, there was at least one open-membership church which sent a representative to this Particular Baptist Assembly in 1689, namely, Broadmead Church in Bristol.[45] Believer's baptism and a personal profession of faith before the church were the normal requirements for admission to membership in this church, but on occasion some were received into membership solely on the basis of a personal testimony.[46] The fact that just eight years after Kiffen had published a stout defense of closed Communion and closed membership he

---

41 W. J. McGlothlin, *Baptist Confessions of Faith* (Philadelphia, PA: American Baptist Publication Society, 1911), 217.

42 Cited in McGlothlin, *Baptist Confessions of Faith*, 218.

43 Quoted in Ivimey, *History*, I, 490.

44 A. C. Underwood, *A History of the English Baptists* (London: The Baptist Union Publication Dept. (Kingsgate Press), 1947), 129; Joshua Thompson, "The Communion Controversy and Irish Baptists," *Irish Baptist Historical Society Journal* 20 (1987–1988): 29–30.

45 B. R. White, "Open and Closed Membership among English and Welsh Baptists," *The Baptist Quarterly*, 24 (1971–1972): 332; *idem*, B. R. White, *The English Baptists of the Seventeenth Century*, Rev. ed. (London: The Baptist Historical Society, 1996), 10–11.

46 *The Records of a Church of Christ in Bristol, 1640–1687*, ed. Roger Hayden (Bristol: Bristol Record Society, 1974), 52–53. Kiffen's relationship with the Broadmead Church appears to have been cordial; see White, *English Baptists*, 113–115.

signed the Second London Confession indicates that by 1689 the London Baptist leader was clearly willing to agree to disagree on the issue. The desire for a harmonious relationship with other Puritan bodies, so evident in the employment of the Westminster and Savoy confessions in the Second London Confession, had borne this added fruit: a catholic attitude with regard to fellow Baptists who differed on the relationship of the ordinances.

5

"The Word of God which is Here Mapped Out"

The Theology of the Second London Confession

Michael A. G. Haykin[1]

A THOROUGH STUDY OF THE THEOLOGY of the Second London Confession in its historical context requires nothing less than a major monograph.[2] What follows in this chapter is obviously not that and much more modest in its aims. It is focused on three issues that were utterly central to seventeenth-century Particular Baptist life: the final authority of the Scriptures, which gave them theological ballast in the turbulence of the seventeenth century; a Reformed soteriology, which bound them to the theological tradition that came from the Reformation and gave them a firm identity within that tradition; and the Lord's Supper, which, seen as a vital means of grace in the Christian life, deeply enriched their spirituality.

---

1 Much of this chapter first appeared as a chapter in my *Kiffen, Knollys, and Keach: Rediscovering our English Baptist Heritage*, 2nd ed. (Peterborough, ON: H&E, 2019). Used by permission of the publisher. The material has been largely rewritten and expanded, and the footnotes updated throughout.

2 See the popular study by Samuel E. Waldron, *A Modern Exposition of the 1689 Baptist Confession of Faith* (Darlington, Co. Durham, England: Evangelical Press, 2016).

"The infallible Truth"

Following the order of the Westminster Confession and the Savoy Declaration, the Second London Confession of Faith began with a lengthy chapter on Scripture. In the words of American Baptist authors L. Russ Bush and Tom J. Nettles, this chapter "contains the clearest confessional statement on Scripture in all of Christendom."[3] Apart from an introductory sentence and a concluding phrase, it virtually reproduced the parallel chapters of the Westminster Confession and the Savoy Declaration. The introductory sentence, though, was highly significant and a valuable gauge as to where the seventeenth-century Particular Baptists stood with regard to the nature of Scripture.

"The Holy Scripture," it stated, "is the onely sufficient, certain, and infallible Rule of all Saving Knowledge, Faith, and Obedience."[4] This sentence described the nature of Scripture by four carefully chosen terms. The first term, "onely," emphasized that apart from the Scriptures there is no other source of ultimate religious authority. Further on in its statement on Scripture, the Second London Confession elaborated on this claim by stating that nothing is to be added to Scripture, "whether by new Revelation of the Spirit, or Traditions of Men."[5] In the historical context of the confession, this statement would especially rule out the revelations of the Quakers, which their opponents felt were being elevated to authoritative status alongside Scripture.

Then this opening sentence of the confession asserted that, while God did reveal himself in ways other than the Scriptures, for instance through the created realm, only Scripture was "sufficient" to "give that knowledge of God and his Will which is necessary unto Salvation."[6] Or in the words of the chapter 1, paragraph 6: "The whole Councel of God concerning all things necessary for his own Glory, Man's Salvation, Faith and Life, is either expressly set down or necessarily

---

3 L. Russ Bush and Tom J. Nettles, *Baptists and the Bible: The Baptist Doctrines of Biblical Inspiration and Religious Authority in Historical Perspective* (Chicago: Moody, 1980), 62.

4 *A Confession of Faith Put Forth by the Elders and Brethren Of many Congregations of Christians (Baptized upon Profession of their Faith) in London and the Country 1.1* (London: John Harris, 1688). References to the Second London Confession will be cited thus: "Confession of Faith (1688)" with the appropriate chapter and paragraph numbers. The analysis of the opening sentence is indebted to Bush and Nettles, *Baptists and the Bible*, 65–72.

5 Confession of Faith (1688) 1.6.

6 Confession of Faith (1688) 1.1.

contained in the Holy Scripture."[7] The written Scriptures are necessary for God to be properly glorified by men and women, as well as being vital for men and women to come to a saving knowledge of God, and then to develop a worldview (so Bush and Nettles interpret "faith"[8]) and lifestyle that is in accord with their salvation.

The next two terms of the opening sentence of this article on Scripture are similar, but not identical, in their import. Scripture is "certain," that is, it does not contain error. Bush and Nettles consider this term to be equivalent to the word "inerrant" as it is currently used in evangelical circles to mean that which is totally truthful. Scripture is also said to be "infallible," a term that has a long history of usage in Christian theology, and which identifies Scripture as possessing the quality of being entirely trustworthy and reliable.[9]

Given the very real threat posed by the Quaker movement to Particular Baptist churches, it seems most probable that the strengthening of this statement on Scripture is a definite response to this situation. In their emphasis on Scripture as the supreme arbiter for the Christian life, the Particular Baptists were reflecting their Puritan heritage, for "Puritanism was first and foremost a movement centred in Scripture."[10] Thus, from the Particular Baptist point of view, the Quakers were guilty of making an unbiblical cleavage between the Spirit and the Word. As Benjamin Keach declared in 1681, in a direct allusion to the Quakers: "Many are confident they have the Spirit, Light, and Power, when 'tis all meer Delusion. The Spirit always leads and directs according to the written Word: 'He shall bring my Word,' saith Christ, 'to your remembrance' [John 14:26]."[11]

Lest it be thought that the seventeenth-century Particular Baptists, in their desire to emphasize the authority of the Scriptures,

7 Confession of Faith (1688) 1.6.

8 Bush and Nettles, *Baptists and the Bible*, 68.

9 Bush and Nettles, 70. For this definition of the terms "inerrant" and "infallible," see J. I. Packer, "Infallibility and Inerrancy of the Bible" in Sinclair B. Ferguson, David F. Wright, and J. I. Packer, ed., *New Dictionary of Theology* (Downers Grove, IL: InterVarsity Press, 1988), 337. See also J. I. Packer, *'Fundamentalism' and the Word of God. Some Evangelical Principles* (London: Inter-Varsity Fellowship, 1958), 94–96.

10 Richard Dale Land, "Doctrinal Controversies of English Particular Baptists (1644–1691) as Illustrated by the Career and Writings of Thomas Collier" (DPhil thesis, Regent's Park College, University of Oxford, 1979), 205.

11 Benjamin Keach, *Tropologia: A Key to Open Scripture Metaphors* (London: Enoch Prosser, 1681), 2:312.

went to the opposite extreme and depreciated the importance of the work of the Spirit in the Christian life, one needs to note the words of the confession 1.5, where it is stated that "our full perswasion, and assurance of the infallible Truth" of the Scriptures comes neither from "the testimony of the Church of God" nor from the "heavenliness of the matter" of the Scriptures, the "efficacy of [their] Doctrine," and "the majesty of [their] Stile." Rather it is only "the inward work of the Holy Spirit, bearing witness by and with the Word in our Hearts" that convinces believers that God's word is indeed what it claims to be.[12]

"An effectual insuperable Work of the Holy Spirit"

In light of the documents that were used in the preparation of the Second London Confession, as well as some of the reasons for its publication, it is only to be expected that the distinguishing tenets of Calvinism are highly visible in the confession. Each of what are described as "the five points of Calvinism" is treated clearly and comprehensively. Now, an excellent window for observing the Calvinism of this text is its doctrine of the work of the Holy Spirit.

It was Benjamin B. Warfield (1851–1921), the early twentieth-century Presbyterian theologian, who once stated that the greatest contribution of John Calvin to the science of theology was his systematic exposition of the work of the Holy Spirit. In Warfield's words, it was Calvin "who first related the whole experience of salvation specifically to the working of the Holy Spirit, worked it out into its details, and contemplated its several steps and stages in orderly progress as the product of the Holy Spirit's specific work in applying salvation to the soul. Thus he gave systematic and adequate expression to the whole doctrine of the Holy Spirit and made it the assured possession of the Church of God."[13]

And of Calvin's theological heirs, it was the Puritans and the Particular Baptists who shared this great interest of the French Reformer.[14] It is thus quite appropriate to examine the Calvinism of

---

12 Confession of Faith (1688) 1.5. For the importance of balance in this area, see the remarks of D. Martyn Lloyd-Jones, *Authority* (1958, Edinburgh: Banner of Truth, 1984), 62–64.

13 Benjamin B. Warfield, "John Calvin the Theologian" in his *Calvin as a Theologian and Calvinism Today* (London: Sovereign Grace Union, [1951]), 9.

14 Benjamin B. Warfield, "Introductory Note" to Abraham Kuyper, *The Work*

the Second London Confession through its discussion of the work of the Holy Spirit in salvation.[15]

For a man or woman to repent and turn to God, it was necessary that there be a prior work of the Spirit. As Confession 10.1 put it:

> Those whom God hath predestinated unto Life, he is pleased, in his appointed, and accepted time, effectually to call by his Word, and Spirit, out of that state of Sin, and Death, in which they are by Nature, to Grace and Salvation by Jesus Christ; enlightening their minds, spiritually, and savingly to understand the things of God; taking away their heart of stone, and giving unto them an heart of flesh; renewing their wills, and by his Almighty Power determining them to that which is good, and effectually drawing them to Jesus Christ; yet so as they come most freely, being made willing by his Grace.[16]

Due to the fact that those outside of Christ were dead spiritually, blind to the things of God, unresponsive to his appeals, and in bondage to sin, God had to undertake on their behalf if they were ever to be saved. This he did for those sinners he had elected to save by remodeling their wills and giving them new affections. In the same action, God quickened them and gave them new life through his Spirit. They were now able to respond to God and embrace all that Christ had done for them.

The same truth was emphasized in a later article entitled "Of the Gospel, and of the extent of the Gospel thereof." This article is not to be found in the Westminster Confession but appears first in the Savoy Declaration, which is the source for its inclusion in the Second London Confession.[17] In the fourth paragraph of this article we read that "although the Gospel be the only outward means, of revealing Christ, and saving Grace, and is, as such, abundantly sufficient

---

of the Holy Spirit, trans. Henri De Vries (1900, Grand Rapids: Eerdmans, 1956), 33, 35.

15 Of the forty-five or so explicit references to the Holy Spirit in the Confession, the majority focus on the Spirit's role in applying God's saving work to believers. See the remarks of Douglas J. W. Milne regarding the pneumatology of the Westminster Confession: "The Doctrine of the Holy Spirit in the Westminster Confession," *The Reformed Theological Review* 52 (1993): 121.

16 Confession of Faith (1688) 10.1.

17 For a discussion of this article from somewhat differing positions, see Peter Toon, *Puritans and Calvinism*, 80–83; Alan P. F. Sell, *The Great Debate, Calvinism, Arminianism and Salvation* (1982, Grand Rapids: Baker Book House, 1983), 39–40.

thereunto; yet that Men, who are dead in Trespasses, may be Born again, Quickened or Regenerated; there is moreover necessary, an effectual insuperable Work of the Holy Spirit, upon the whole Soul, for the producing in them a new Spiritual Life; without which no other means will effect their Conversion unto God."[18] For a person to be converted it was not enough for him or her to simply hear the gospel and seek to respond to it in his or her own strength. Positive response to the gospel could only come about when the Spirit worked with unconquerable power in the heart of the unbeliever, irresistibly giving to him or her the wherewithal to turn to God.

Passages like Ezekiel 36:26–27 ("A new heart also will I give you, and a new spirit will I put within you: and I will take away the stony heart out of your flesh, and I will give you an heart of flesh. And I will put my spirit within you, and cause you to walk in my statutes, and ye shall keep my judgments, and do them" [KJV]) led those who issued this Confession to see that God has promised "to give unto all those that are ordained unto eternal Life, his holy Spirit, to make them willing, and able to believe."[19] It should come as no surprise, therefore, that saving faith was also recognized by the confession to be the work of the Spirit. "The Grace of Faith," we read in chapter 14.1, "whereby the Elect are enabled to believe to the saving of their Souls, is the work of the Spirit of Christ in their hearts."[20] In this connection, it is also noteworthy that the Second London Confession emphasizes a close link between the Spirit's work in salvation and the Word of God. Effectual calling, for instance, is by the "Word and Spirit." Also, the "Grace of Faith," described above as a "work of the Spirit of Christ" in the heart, is normally given through "the Ministry of the Word."[21]

Furthermore, those whom the Spirit regenerated he also sanctified: "They who are united to Christ, effectually called, and regenerated, having a new Heart, and a new Spirit created in them, through the vertue of Christ's Death and Resurrection; are also farther sanctified, really, and personally, through the same vertue, by

---

18 Confession of Faith (1688) 20.4.
19 Confession of Faith (1688) 7.2. The text from Ezekiel is one of the marginal Scripture references at this point.
20 Confession of Faith (1688) 14.1.
21 Confession of Faith (1688) 10.1; 14.1. See also Milne, "Doctrine of the Holy Spirit," 126.

his Word and Spirit dwelling in them."[22] The confession especially emphasized that in this life, the sanctification of any believer was "yet imperfect," since within every child of God there was "a continual, and irreconcilable war; the Flesh lusting against the Spirit, and the Spirit against the Flesh," a clear reference to Paul's word in Galatians 5:17. Though the flesh, or "the remaining corruption for a time may much prevail; yet through the continual supply of strength, from the sanctifying Spirit of Christ, the regenerate part doth overcome."[23] In other words, despite setbacks and failures the ultimate outcome of the believer's struggle against the flesh would be victory for the believer. But such a victory was only possible because of the power given to the believer by the indwelling Holy Spirit.

This perspective on the Christian life was essentially that of the Puritans. John Owen, for instance, in a series of sermons on Romans 8:13, had argued that the believer has a constant duty to engage in putting to death the sin that still indwells his or her mortal frame. But such a duty is only possible in the strength supplied by the Holy Spirit, who alone is "sufficient for this work."[24] An earlier Puritan author, Richard Sibbes (1577–1635), could state that to those whom God forgives, "he gives his Spirit to sanctify them. The same Spirit that assures me of the pardon of my sin, sanctifies my nature."[25] Owen's argument, Sibbes's comment, and the paragraph from the Particular Baptist Confession stand as a proper corrective to those evangelical quarters today which maintain that regeneration need not be followed by sanctification, that one can, in popular parlance, have Jesus as one's Savior and not as one's Lord. The early Particular Baptists, like the Puritan movement out of which it had sprung, would have regarded such sentiments as both misguided and unbiblical. Those in whom the Spirit worked saving faith, he came to indwell, and as the indwelling Holy Spirit he never abode without his holy and moral character reshaping the lives of those in whom he dwells.[26]

---

22 Confession of Faith (1688) 13.1.
23 Confession of Faith (1688) 13.2–3. For other references to the Holy Spirit as a sanctifying Spirit, see, for instance, Confession of Faith (1688) 15.3; 16.3; 17.1. See also the remarks of Milne, "Doctrine of the Holy Spirit," 127.
24 John Owen, *Of the Mortification of Sin in Believers* in *The Works of John Owen*, ed. William H. Goold (1850–1853, Edinburgh: The Banner of Truth Trust, 1965), VI, 16.
25 Cited in J. I. Packer, "The Puritan Treatment of Justification by Faith," *The Evangelical Quarterly* 24 (1952): 143.
26 For the way in which this particular sentence is phrased, I am indebted to George Verwer, *Revolution of Love and Balance*, Rev. ed. (Bromley, Kent; Waynes-

The confession went on to indicate that the Spirit, along with the Father and Son, was vitally involved in enabling believers to persevere in the faith. "Those whom God hath accepted in the Beloved," we read, "effectually called and sanctified by his Spirit, and given the precious Faith of his Elect unto, can neither totally nor finally fall from the state of Grace; but shall certainly persevere therein to the end and be eternally saved." The believer's perseverance ultimately depends not on the exercise of his or her own free will, but, among other things, upon "the abiding of his Spirit, and the Seed of God within" the believer.[27]

Perseverance ultimately issued in glorification; and here too, the confession indicated, the Holy Spirit was active. As it stated in chapter 31.3: "The Bodies of the unjust shall, by the power of Christ, be raised to dishonour; the bodies of the just by his Spirit, unto honour."[28] The text to which the confession turns to justify its inclusion of "by his Spirit" here is Philippians 3:21—"[The Lord Jesus Christ] shall change our vile body, that it may be fashioned like unto his glorious body, according to the working whereby he is able even to subdue all things unto himself" (KJV)—a verse which contained no explicit mention of the Spirit. Evidently those who issued the confession understood the phrase "according to the working" as an oblique reference to the Holy Spirit. Probably a better proof text at this point would have been Romans 8:11, where the Holy Spirit's involvement in the resurrection of believers is clearly indicated. It is also patent that the pneumatology of the Second London Confession is in fundamental opposition to the soteriology of Collier and would have assured those outside of Particular Baptist circles that the sentiments of Collier were not representative of the communities within this Christian denomination.

It should be pointed out that this sturdy Calvinism of the Second London Conference is also a firmly evangelical Calvinism. For instance, in chapter 7.2 it is stated unequivocally that "Man having brought himself under the curse of the Law by his fall, it pleased the Lord to make a Covenant of Grace, wherein he freely offereth unto Sinners, Life and Salvation by Jesus Christ, requiring of them Faith

---

boro, GA: STL Books, 1980), 19.
27 Confession of Faith (1688) 17.1, 2. See also Milne, "Doctrine of the Holy Spirit," 128.
28 Confession of Faith (1688) 31.3.

in him, that they may be saved."[29] The statement that God "freely offereth unto Sinners, Life and Salvation by Jesus Christ" envisages an unencumbered preaching of the gospel to all and sundry.[30] Numerous statements could be culled from the writings of those who issued this Confession that made the same point. For instance, Hanserd Knollys stated unambiguously: "The ordinarie meanes which God hath in his infinite wisdome appointed to convert sinners, and also to build them up in Christ, is the Word preached, Rom. 10:8, 17. This word of the Gospel God will have preached to every creature in all parts of [the] world, Mark 16:15. None are exempted or prohibited from hearing the Gospel preached, but everyone that hath an eare is required to heare, Revel. 2:7."[31]

Benjamin Keach similarly maintained that the Holy Spirit is "a River that lieth open to all poor Sinners; whoever will may come to these Waters," and that "Christ is sent to all, to Jews and Gentiles, to the Small as well as the Great, to the Poor as well as the Rich; none are excluded."[32]

"Spiritually present to the faith of Believers"

The chapter in the confession dealing with the Lord's Supper, chapter 30, is a good example of the way in which the Particular Baptists sought to demonstrate their fundamental solidarity with other Calvinists. Following the Westminster Confession and the Savoy Declaration, the Baptist Confession denounces as unbiblical the Roʄ man Church's doctrine of the mass, its practice of private masses, its refusal to allow any but a priest to partake of the cup, and its dogma of transubstantiation.[33] Having noted such errors regarding the Lord's Table, a right understanding of this ordinance is then inculcated: "Worthy Receivers, outwardly partaking of the visible Elements in this Ordinance, do then also inwardly by Faith, really and indeed, yet not carnally, and corporally, but spiritually receive, and feed upon Christ crucified & all the benefits of his Death: the

29 Confession of Faith (1688) 7.2.

30 Robert William Oliver, "The Emergence of a Strict and Particular Baptist Community Among the English Particular Baptists, 1770–1850" (PhD thesis, London Bible College, 1986), 16.

31 Hanserd Knollys, *Christ Exalted: A Lost Sinner Sought, and Saved by Christ* (London, 1646), 12.

32 Keach, *Tropologia*, 2:313, 2:140.

33 Confession of Faith (1688) 30.2–6.

Body and Blood of Christ, being then not corporally, or carnally, but spiritually present to the faith of Believers, in that Ordinance, as the Elements themselves are to their outward senses."[34]

Close comparison of this statement with the parallel statements in the Westminster Confession and the Savoy Declaration reveals two main areas of difference. The two earlier confessions used the term "sacrament" to describe the Lord's Supper, whereas in the Second London Confession this was altered to "ordinance."[35] Neither term is actually used in the New Testament, but the term "ordinance" appears to have been adopted to stress the divine institution of the Lord's Supper.[36]

The second change was an omission. The omission is best seen by displaying the relevant passages side by side in the following table, with the omitted words in italics.

Westminster Confession/ Savoy Declaration[37]	Second London Confession[38]
The body and blood of Christ being then not corporally or carnally, *in, with, or under the bread and wine; yet, as really,* but spiritually present to the faith of believers in that ordinance, as the elements themselves are to their outward senses.	The Body and Blood of Christ being then not corporally or carnally, but spiritually present to the faith of Believers in that Ordinance, as the Elements themselves are to their outward senses.

34 Confession of Faith (1688) 30.7.

35 It should be noted that both the Westminster Confession and the Savoy Declaration did use the term "ordinance" in later paragraphs to describe the Lord's Supper.

36 W. Morgan Patterson, "The Lord's Supper in Baptist History," *Review and Expositor* 66, no.1 (Winter, 1969): 26. Cf., however, Erroll Hulse's discussion of these two terms in "The Implications of Baptism" in his *et al.*, *Local Church Practice* (Haywards Heath, Sussex: Carey Publications, 1978), 46–47.

37 Westminster Confession of Faith 29.7 (The Confession of Faith of the Assembly of Divines at Westminster, ed. S.W. Carruthers [Glasgow: Free Presbyterian Publications, 1978], 22–23); Savoy Declaration 30.7 (The Savoy Declaration of Faith and Order 1658 [London: Evangelical Press, 1971], 41). There is one slight difference between the Westminster Confession and the Savoy Declaration. Where the former reads "in, with, or under the bread and wine," the latter has "in, with, or under the bread or wine" [italics added].

38 Confession of Faith (1688) 30.7.

The phrase which has been omitted in the Second London Confession was intended to reject the Lutheran explanation of how Christ is present in the Lord's Supper.[39] In the view of Martin Luther (1483–1546), Christ's body and blood are present "in, with, and under" the bread and the wine. Contrary to the Roman dogma of transubstantiation, the bread remains bread; yet, in some way, it also contains Christ's body after the prayer of consecration. Likewise, the wine is his blood, but remains wine. Why the Second London Confession omitted this phrase is not at all clear. Possibly Luther's view was not entertained by any in the Particular Baptist community during the seventeenth century, and it was thus omitted so as to avoid encumbering the confession with needless statements.

The differences between the three confessions, however, were minimal compared to what they had in common. All three affirmed that as believers partake of the bread and the wine, they were actually feeding upon Christ crucified. Contrary to the dogma of the Roman Church, this feeding does not entail eating the physical body of Christ and drinking his physical blood. It is a spiritual feeding; Christ is "spiritually present" to believers in the Lord's Supper. What did those who approved this Confession understand by this expression "spiritually present"? One of those who gave his approval to the confession was Hercules Collins (1646/7–1702), pastor of Wapping Baptist Church in London, who was a key Particular Baptist leader in the capital and much in demand as a preacher. According to John Piggott (d. 1713), who preached his funeral sermon: "If he had not some men's accuracy, yet it was made up by a constant flame: for no man could preach with a more affectionate regard to the salvation of souls."[40] In his *An Orthodox Catechism* (1680) Collins stated that in the Lord's Supper we are "verily Partakers of his Body and Blood through the working of the Holy Ghost."[41] From Collins's perspective it is the Holy Spirit who makes Christ present in the Lord's Supper. Although Christ's body is in heaven, through the Spirit we can have

---

39 For the Puritan rejection of Luther's position, see John F. H. New, *Anglican and Puritan. The Basis of Their Opposition, 1558–1640* (Stanford, CA: Stanford University Press, 1964), 60.

40 Quoted in Ernest F. Kevan, *London's Oldest Baptist Church: Wapping 1633–Walthamstow 1933* (London: The Kingsgate Press, 1933), 68. On Collins and his ministry, see Kevan, *London's Oldest Baptist Church*, 38–50, 64–68.

41 Cited in E. P. Winter, "Calvinist and Zwinglian Views of the Lord's Supper Among the Baptists of the Seventeenth Century," *The Baptist Quarterly* 15 (1953–1954): 327.

communion with the risen Christ. Again, William Kiffen, in his response to John Bunyan in their debate over the question of open and closed communion, could state that "the [Lord's] Supper is a Spiritual participation of the Body and Blood of Christ by Faith."[42]

These views are essentially those of John Calvin. As G. S. M. Walker summarized Calvin's view of Christ's presence in the Supper: "Although communion is a spiritual act, it involves an actual sharing in Christ's flesh and blood, and although his body has now ascended physically into heaven, we are none the less able to make contact with it through the Spirit. How these things can be remains a mystery, to be treated with reverence and accepted in faith."[43] The Particular Baptist Confession shares Calvin's perspective to the full. When it declared that Christ was "spiritually present" in the Lord's Supper, it was maintaining that Christ's presence in the Supper was one that was effected by the Holy Spirit.

A more detailed discussion of the importance of the Lord's Supper for the Christian life was provided in the first paragraph of chapter 30. There it is stated that the

> Supper of the Lord Jesus, was instituted by him, the same Night wherein he was betrayed, to be observed in his Churches unto the end of the World, for the perpetual remembrance, and shewing forth the Sacrifice of himself in his Death, confirmation of the Faith of Believers in all the benefits thereof, their spiritual nourishment, and growth in him, their further ingagement in, and to, all Duties which they owe unto him; and to be a Bond and Pledge of their Communion with him, and with each other.[44]

In this enumeration of the reasons for the Lord's Table, the Second London Confession followed closely the Westminster Confession and the Savoy Declaration. Christ instituted the Lord's Supper for five reasons according to this paragraph. The Supper served as a vivid reminder of and witness to the sacrificial death of

---

42   William Kiffen, *A Sober Discourse of Right to Church-Communion*, 25.

43   G. S. M. Walker, "The Lord's Supper in the Theology and Practice of Calvin" in G. E. Duffield, ed., *John Calvin* (Grand Rapids: Eerdmans, 1966), 133–134. Another good discussion of Calvin's treatment of the Lord's Supper is John D. Nicholls, " 'Union with Christ': John Calvin on the Lord's Supper" in *Union and Communion, 1529–1979* (London: The Westminster Conference, 1979), 35–54.

44   Confession of Faith (1688) 30.1.

Christ. Then, participation in the Lord's Supper enabled believers to more firmly grasp all that Christ had done for them through his death on the cross. In this way the Lord's Supper was a means of spiritual nourishment and growth. Fourth, the Lord's Supper served as a time when believers could recommit themselves to Christ. Finally, the Lord's Supper affirmed the indissoluble union which existed, on the one hand, between Christ and believers, and, on the other, between individual believers.

One cannot come away from reading these paragraphs on the Lord's Supper without the conviction that those who issued this Confession were deeply conscious of the importance of the Lord's Supper for the Christian life. Benjamin Keach spoke for his fellow Baptists when he stated, probably with reference to the Quakers, who had discarded the observance of both baptism and the Lord's Supper: "Some men boast of the Spirit, and conclude they have the Spirit, and none but they, and yet at the same time cry down and villify his blessed Ordinances and Institutions, which he hath left in his Word, carefully to be observed and kept . . . The Spirit hath its Bounds, and always run[s] in its spiritual Chanel, viz. the Word and Ordinances."[45]

In this hearty appreciation of the Lord's Supper these early Baptists were once again in the mainstream of Puritan thought. The Puritans generally regarded the Supper as a vehicle which the Spirit employed as an efficacious means of grace for the believer. And for the most part they opposed the view associated with the name of the Swiss Reformer Huldreich Zwingli (1484–1531), which looked upon the bread and the wine as simply signs and the Supper as chiefly a memorial.[46] In recent discussions of Zwingli's perspective on the Lord's Supper it is often maintained that Zwingli was not really a Zwinglian, that is, he saw more in the Lord's Supper than simply a memorial.[47] Be this as it may, a tradition did take its start from aspects of his thought, which stressed primarily the memorial nature of the Lord's Supper. In Particular Baptist circles, this Zwinglian

---

45 Keach, *Tropologia*, 2:312.
46 For the Puritan view of the Lord's Table, see Nuttall, *The Holy Spirit in Puritan Faith and Experience*, 90–101; New, *Anglican and Puritan*, 59–76; Hywel W. Roberts, " 'The Cup of Blessing': Puritan and Separatist Sacramental Discourses" in *Union and Communion*, 55–71.
47 See Derek R. Moore-Crispin, " 'The Real Absence': Ulrich Zwingli's View of the Lord's Supper" in *Union and Communion*, 22–34.

perspective on the Lord's Supper would eventually come to be the overwhelming consensus in the late eighteenth and nineteenth centuries. And it would be forgotten that the early Particular Baptists were of quite a different mind. The seventeenth-century Baptists would have judged the Zwinglian view of the Lord's Supper as far too mean a perspective on what was for them such a rich means of grace. Indeed, in seeking to articulate a more balanced view of the Lord's Table, contemporary Baptists can do no better than to listen afresh to what their Baptist forebears wrote in chapter 30 of the Second London Confession.

Coda

There were new editions of this confession in 1699, 1719, and 1720, which was the fifth edition.[48] No new edition appeared after that point until 1791. Robert Oliver has commented: "This long eclipse of a *Confession*, which had received the commendation of a representative Assembly in 1689, creates the suspicion that its theology was not completely acceptable for much of the eighteenth century."[49] Oliver points to the fact that a number of Particular Baptist preachers in the long eighteenth century rejected the evangelical Calvinism of the confession. Embracing Hyper-Calvinism, they had little or nothing to say to the unconverted. Their view of salvation cut the nerve of aggressive Baptist evangelism, and not surprisingly led to a neglect of the Second London Confession among these Hyper-Calvinistic Baptists.

And yet the Second London Confession was not even used by those Baptists opposed to Hyper-Calvinism. For instance, when the evangelical Calvinist Alvery Jackson (1700–1763), pastor of the Baptist cause in Barnoldswick, Lancashire, needed to draft a

---

48 *A Confession of Faith, Put forth by the Elders and Brethren Of many Congregations of Christians (Baptized upon Profession of their Faith) in London and the Countrey*, 3rd ed. (London: Ebenezer Tracy, William Marshall, and John Marshall, 1699). Opposite the title page of this edition is the list of signatories, headed by Hanserd Knollys and William Kiffen (spelled *Kiffin* in the list); *A Confession of Faith, Put forth by the Elders and Brethren Of many Congregations of Christians (Baptized upon Profession of their Faith) in London and the Country*, 4th ed. (London: John Marshall, 1719); *A Confession of Faith, Put forth by the Elders and Brethren Of many Congregations of Christians (Baptized upon Profession of their Faith) in London and the Country*, 5th ed. (London: John Marshall, 1720).

49 Oliver, "Strict and Particular Baptist Community," 20–21.

confession for his church, he did not employ that of 1688.[50] And when Particular Baptist pastors were ordained within the denomination, they drafted their own individual statements of faith, such as that written by Caleb Evans (1737–1791), the President of Bristol Baptist Academy, or that drawn up by the London Baptist Abraham Booth (1734–1806).[51] The Second London Confession was reprinted in 1855 by C. H. Spurgeon (1834–1892) for use within his congregation, but it was not until the second half of the twentieth century that the confession was once again widely used as numerous Baptists in the Anglophone world rediscovered the doctrines of grace. And as they employed this Confession in the life of their churches, they realized the truth of these words of Spurgeon about the utility of the confession: "This little volume is not . . . an authoritative rule, or code of faith, whereby you are to be fettered, but . . . an assistance to you in controversy, a confirmation in faith, and a means of edification in righteousness. . . . Cleave fast to the Word of God which is here mapped out for you."[52]

50 For the confession that was drafted, see Evan R. Lewis, *History of the Bethesda Baptist Church, Barnoldswick, Yorks* (Cwmavon, Wales: L. I. Griffiths, 1893), 45–52.

51 Caleb Evans, "A Confession of Faith" in *A Charge and Sermon Together with an Introductory Discourse and Confession of Faith Delivered at the Ordination of the Rev. Mr. Caleb Evans* (Bristol: S. Farley, 1767), 12–35; and Abraham Booth, "A Confession of Faith" in *A Charge and Sermon Together with an Introductory Discourse and Confession of Faith Delivered at the Ordination of the Rev. Mr. Abraham Booth* (London: G. Keith; J. Buckland; W. Harris; B. Tomkins; J. Gurney, 1769), 12–26.

52 Cited in the foreword to *The Baptist Confession of Faith with Scripture Proofs* (Choteau, MT: Gospel Mission, n.d.), 6. For further comment on the usefulness of the Second London Confession, see Erroll Hulse, "The Reformed Confessions of 17th Century England," *The Evangelical Library Bulletin* 83 (August 1989): 7; Hulse, "The 1689, Why Another Confession?" (Unpublished paper, n.d.), 17–19.

6

The New Hampshire Confession

Tom J. Nettles

T HE NEW HAMPSHIRE CONFESSION OF FAITH was written after the first third of the nineteenth century. Evangelicalism
in the United States, and particularly New England, was
bursting with energy and with controversy. The legacy of Jonathan
Edwards was evocative and energetic, and it had spawned move-
ments devoted to the idea of "disinterested benevolence," as well as
rigorous thinking about the relationship between divine purpose and
human volition. This confession arose initially from the determination of the Baptist Convention of New Hampshire that a confession
more adapted to the language of their context was needed. This care
in language is seen throughout.

Beginning with a committee of three, after several persons and
at least two committees had worked on the confession, the state
convention of New Hampshire in 1833 recommended its adoption
by the Baptist churches in the state. It gained national attention two
decades later when J. Newton Brown published it in the *Baptist
Church Manual*, having added two articles: "Of Repentance and
Faith" (8) and "Of Sanctification" (10). J. M. Pendleton published
the confession in his *Church Manual*, spreading its influence among
churches that were suspicious of the doctrine of a universal church.

Edward T. Hiscox (1814–1901) also included it in his *Standard Manual* and *New Directory*. It became the basis for the family of three confessions known as *the Baptist Faith and Message* (1925, 1963, and 2000).

Historical Provocations

Anti-Missionism

One factor that prompted the particular language of the New Hampshire Confession was the development of the Anti-mission Society movement. Adoniram Judson, Ann Judson, and Luther Rice were missionaries sent out by the American Board of Commissioners, a Congregational missionary agency, in 1812. Each of them converted to the doctrine of believers' baptism by immersion, rejecting the instruction received to baptize "credible believers and their households."[1] This led to a series of events that formed the missionary body among Baptists, the General Missionary Convention. By the mid-1820s a reaction was in progress against the Convention and other missionary societies over ecclesiological matters in the main. Some, however, began to raise doctrinal resistance, considering the effort to be tinged with Arminian assumptions.

Among the leaders of this reaction was a Baptist Association in North Carolina. In writing a history of the "Primitive Baptists," Sylvester Hassell commented on a report received from the General Missionary Convention in 1818 by the Kehukee Association. "This showed the age of the Baptist Board of Foreign Missions to be four years," he observed, and added, "It was born of spurious philanthropy and false zeal in 1814." He queried, "How did the churches and the people of God in America get along without it till this auspicious year dawned upon the world?" Nothing of such a kind had been promoted in prior decades in America, so why the necessity and contrived urgency now? In addition, there is "nothing of it in England previous to the days of Fuller and Carey." He drew the conclusion that "the modern missionary system is an innovation and a human appendage to the church of Christ, worldly in character and insulting in its nature to the King of Zion."[2]

---

1   Robert A. Baker, *A Baptist Sourcebook* (Nashville: Broadman Press, 1966), 54.
2   C. B. Hassell and Sylvester Hassell, *History of the Church of God from the Cre-*

By 1827, this Association adopted a resolution that stated the agreement of its churches to "discard all Missionary Societies, Bible Societies and Theological Seminaries, and the practices heretofore resorted to for their support, in begging money from the public." Any agents of such institutions were to be discountenanced and excluded from the pulpits of churches in the Association. They believed "these societies and institutions to be an invention of men, and not warranted from the word of God." They believed that any attempt to form a means by which the gospel might be preached beyond its present concentration of churches was unwarranted and an invasion of the divine prerogative in his providential operations to send the gospel where he pleased.[3]

In addition, they adopted the strict Hyper-Calvinist viewpoint that an unrestricted call on the part of a gospel-proclaimer to repentance and faith for all that heard was not warranted by Scripture. The true biblical preachers, "though they proclaimed to sinners that they were in danger and on the high road to perdition, they did not call upon all men, whether spiritually concerned or not, to repent and believe the gospel."[4]

They attributed the idea of a universal call on the basis of universal obligation to repent and believe to the influence of Andrew Fuller, who, though he was personally a strict Calvinist and fully dependent in his mind and experience on sovereign grace, was inconsistent and engineered a change in historic Baptist methods of gospel work. "Mr. Fuller began to ponder upon the expediency of making a change in Baptist tactics, and offering salvation freely to all sinners without distinction." They saw Fuller as the cause of a declining spirituality in Baptist Churches for, "The actual result of Mr. Fuller's methods has been, not to effectuate the eternal salvation of a single sinner (for Christ is the only and complete Savior of His people), but to increase largely the number of those professing, while unhappily not possessing, true religion."[5]

Another association that answered the anti-mission-society call was the Black Rock Association in Maryland. As the supposed "Fullerite" doctrine advanced, the Black Rock Church published

ation to A. D. 1885 (Middletown, NY: Gilbert Beebe's Son, 1886), 731.

3 Hassell and Hassell, 737.

4 Hassell and Hassell, 337.

5 Hassell and Hassell, 340–341.

opposition to it. Gilbert Beebe wrote, "When the Fullerite heresies
had been introduced among the Baptists, and produced great dis-
cord and turmoil, some of the old veterans of the cross met at Black
Rock, Maryland, in 1832, and published a solemn protest against all
the newly introduced innovations upon our former faith and order,
and made the rejection of the new departure a test of fellowship."[6]

In light of this growing Primitive Baptist resistance, the missionary
Baptists of New England felt they needed a statement of faith that
would affirm the doctrines of grace while manifesting a confidence
that such doctrines were fully consistent with human responsibility. Our dependence on grace did not diminish the commensurate
necessity of the means that were the divinely ordained channels of
saving truth and power.

Charles Finney

Simultaneous with the rise of the Primitive Baptist resistance to what
they perceived as an Arminianizing of Baptist life, Baptists saw the
growing impact of Charles Finney on New England theology. Converted in 1821, Finney began his revival activities in small towns and
villages in western and central New York. Soon he was being asked
to places in Pennsylvania, New Jersey, New Hampshire, and Massachusetts. Even Lyman Beecher, at one time an ardent opponent
of Finney, consented to issue him an invitation to preach in Bos-
ton. Baptists often attended his meetings and he sometimes spoke in
Baptist churches. His opposition to historical confessional Calvinism
was deep-seated and aggressive. Two points are important for us to
consider as influences on the language of the New Hampshire Confession.

Finney preached with acute logic and intensity on the inviola-
bility of the voluntary nature of all human decision in a divinely
ordained moral order. "God cannot save men without their concurrence; in the nature of the case, they could not be holy without their
own concurrence," and could not, therefore "be happy without it."
Every moral agent as a subject of moral government cannot, in any
point of view, be saved "unless they will turn from their sins." As a
Moral Governor, God can do nothing "inconsistent with its moral
nature" and must therefore, confine himself to persuasion. "If, then,

---

6 Hassell and Hassell, 356.

God works upon the sinner by means of his providence and his spirit, to the utmost extent he wisely can, and all in vain, there remains nothing more which, as a moral governor, he can do to save him."[7] Regeneration consists in a voluntary change.

Finney considered the concept of moral inability an absurdity because commands always imply present ability. Any idea of natural ability, when considered in the framework of human choice, must include moral ability to perform the command. Any distinction between natural and moral inability is nonsensical.[8]

Christian conversion, therefore, consists of four confluent causes. First, the Spirit of God is the "agent who induces" the sinner to see his danger, who prompts him to consider the truth of his condition and its remedy in repentance. Second, "The truth is the instrument, or motive, which the Spirit uses to induce the sinner to turn." Third, the preacher is a secondary agent who presents the truth, and he must use every persuasion warranted by Scripture, consistent with the gravity of the sinner's condition and the reality of the necessity of his converting himself. Finney began to emphasize the necessity of pressing for the sinner's conversion as the preacher sets forth such a necessity. "Not only does the preacher cry 'Stop,' but, through the living voice of the preachers, the Spirit cries 'Stop.' " But all these factors finally are ineffectual to conversion apart from the free consent of the sinner himself who is bound to change his own heart. While these other factors necessarily contribute, "The fact is, that the actual turning, or change, is the sinner's own act." The sinner himself is the final effective agent of change and "is, therefore himself, in the most proper sense, the author of the change." Finney emphasized relentlessly, "God commands you to do it, expects you to do it, and if it ever is done, you must do it." The sinner himself finally produces "the actual turning, or change." Conversion is indeed "the sinner's own act."[9]

Finney believed that only moral suasion and providential arrangement are consistent with the free moral agency of men in seeking to

---

7   Charles Finney, "God has no Pleasure in the Sinner's Death," in *The Way of Salvation* (London: R. D. Dickinson, 1896), 267.

8   Charles Finney, *Finney's Systematic Theology*, ed. J. H. Fairchild (Minneapolis: Bethany Fellowship, 1964), 256–277.

9   Charles Finney, "Sinners Bound to Change Their Own Hearts," The Gospel Truth, accessed January 21, 2020, https://www.gospeltruth.net/1836SOIS/01sois_sinners_bound.htm.

bring about conversion. In order to make his understanding of the voluntaristic character of all moral action consistent, Finney had to deny imputed guilt from a covenant head. Likewise, the resulting corruption of nature as a manifestation of the death threatened upon disobedience went away. Having rejected covenant headship, he then denied the substitutionary nature of Christ's work. This rendered void his active obedience and the resulting imputation of righteousness as well as Christ's shouldering the punishment for the sins of others with the resultant forgiveness of sins for all of those for whom Christ was covenant head. He considered this entire system one elongated irrationality, immorality, and insult to the universal consent of the nature of true justice. Regeneration, therefore, is "something over which we have control, for which we are responsible." It consists of the "supreme ultimate intention of the soul," a change of character resulting from an "executive volition" producing a "benevolent ultimate choice." Given the finality of the human intelligence and will in this change, Finney says, "Regeneration then is a radical change of ultimate intention and, of course, of the end or object of life."[10]."

How effectual calling, as set within historical Baptist confessions, violates the true moral agency of the creature he does not explain, other than to assert that compulsion is wrong and that the nature of the influence must be moral. If by moral, he means that impetus to holiness, that is, the attempt to convince one to be holy, can come only from the outside, then he denies the nature of true biblical morality, or holiness. Such moral actions as are truly moral, that is, in accord with the divine law in its letter and in its intention, must arise from the heart. As long as a person remains in the "flesh," that is, in the condition he received at his natural birth, he can produce nothing truly moral for he has only selfishness and inveterate resistance to God and his holiness as the principle of moral action. "It is the Spirit who gives life; the flesh profits nothing" (John 6:63). "Flesh gives birth to flesh; Spirit gives birth to Spirit" (John 3:6). "Having purified your souls by your obedience to the truth for a sincere brotherly love, love one another earnestly from a pure heart, since you have been born again, not of perishable seed but of imperishable, through the living and abiding word of God" (1 Peter 1:23).

---

10 *Finney's Systematic Theology*, 222, 223.

Effectual calling, in the confessional Reformed understanding of it, establishes the "concurrence" of man's moral nature with the moral perfections as set forth in the gospel. Effectual calling honors man as a moral agent, even if his sinfulness is much more radical than admitted by Finney and imposes no loyalty or response of repentance and faith that is not fully concurrent with a heart made holy. "Effectual calling is a work of God's Spirit, whereby, convincing us of our sin and misery, enlightening our minds in the knowledge of Christ, and *renewing our wills*, he doth persuade and enable us to embrace Jesus Christ freely offered to us in the gospel."[11] Finney wanted only the persuasion, not the enabling. The New Hampshire Confession in stark contrast states, "That in order to be saved, we must be regenerated or born again; that regeneration consists in giving a holy disposition to the mind; and is effected in a manner above our comprehension or calculation, by the power of the Holy Spirit [in connection with divine truth] *so as to secure our voluntary obedience to the gospel*; and that its proper evidence is found in the holy fruit which we bring forth to the glory of God." Finney's characterization as absurd and nonsensical the idea that no contradiction exists between free acts of the will and the determining quality of character creates several inconsistencies in his theology. This is seen clearly in his response to the historic Reformed, and specifically Edwardsean, distinction between moral ability and natural ability.

Free Will Baptists

Most immediately pertinent to the development of the New Hampshire Confession is the emergence of Free Will Baptists under the influence of Benjamin Randall. Benjamin Randall was converted in 1770 after hearing of the death of George Whitefield, whom he had opposed as a mere enthusiast. "I felt enough of the spirit of persecution, to have had all such preachers whip'd out of town."[12] But on hearing of his death, Randall thought, "Whitefield is now in heaven; and I am on the road to hell. I shall never hear his voice any more. I have despised him—He was a man of God, and I have reviled, and spoke reproachfully of him. He has taught me that way to heaven;

---

11 Westminster Confession, Q.31
12 Scott Bryant, *The Awakening of the Freewill Baptists: Benjamin Randall and the Founding of an American Religious Tradition* (Macon: Mercer University Press, 2011), 67.

and I regarded it not.[13] Randall was converted in an extraordinary struggle that culminated in a deep encounter with Hebrews 9:26, "But now once for all at the end of the ages has he appeared to put away sin by the sacrifice of himself." At first, he was alarmed at the peace that flooded his soul, but on contemplation believed that this is what the Scripture meant by the new birth. From his sense of the surprising freeness of God's redeeming action toward him, he extrapolated three ideas from which he never departed. He wrote, "I saw in him a universal love, a universal atonement, a universal call to mankind, and was confident that none would ever perish, but those that refused to obey it."[14] Amazingly, despite the apparent sovereignty of divine grace in his own conversion, these three extrapolations eventually worked themselves into a full-blown Arminianism.

When Randall discovered that other pastors had a different theological scheme from his, he engaged in several public disputations. These debates with Calvinists brought to his attention two Scriptures he had great difficulty in reconciling to his system—Romans 8:29 and Ephesians 1:4. In a great struggle that he described in gripping terms, he believed he received a direct revelation from God that all the Scriptures with which he had problems were perfectly consistent with his viewpoint. He narrated this experience, in which he saw himself, as an outside observer, robed in a garment as white as snow.

> I saw all the scriptures in perfect harmony; and those texts, about which my opposers were contending were all opened to my mind; and I saw that they ran in perfect connection with the universal love of God to men and the universal atonement in the work of redemption, by Jesus Christ, who tasted death for every man—the universal appearance of grace to all men, and with the universal call of the gospel; and glory to God! My soul has never been in any trials about the meaning of those scriptures since.[15]

Randall never gave an exposition of how, exegetically, he reconciled those texts with his system, but only asserted that the reconciliation had been made. His most recent biographer never gives that explanation either but wrote: "Randall's trance-like spiritual

---

13 Bryant, 68.
14 Bryant, 71.
15 Bryant, 95.

revelation serves as a prime example of the power of a visionary experience, as Randall placed greater authority in the direct revelation from God than in the logic and arguments of his opponents. The revelation he experienced provided Randall all the authority he needed to remove his doubts regarding the doctrines of Calvin."[16]

Randall labored incessantly and founded many churches in New Hampshire and Maine. The Free Will Baptist movement was virtually governed by him in both procedure and doctrine during his lifetime and, following his desire, kept aloof from any fraternal relation with Calvinists. "I found great freedom," he wrote, "in preaching—the truth prevailed, and the people through all that country appeared to be awakened, the Calvinistic vail which had been so long over their hearts, seemed to be rent in twain from the top to the bottom, and the people were able to look into the perfect law of liberty."[17]

Randall died in 1807. The Free Will Baptist movement grew and in 1826 began publishing *The Free Will Baptist Magazine.* By 1833 they initiated a foreign mission outreach. In 1832 the General Conference approved the writing of a confession of faith, an action that Benjamin Randall never would have approved. This confession was adopted in 1834. This probably was in response to the action of the New Hampshire Baptist Association's adoption of the New Hampshire Confession in 1833. They had begun the process of adopting a confession in 1830.

That the confluence of Randall's ideas with the growth of Finney's concepts of moral government and radical voluntarism was giving status to a non-Calvinist approach to gospel preaching is seen in several statements of the Free Will confession. It must be said that the Free Will Baptists were much more consistently evangelical in their overall theology than was Finney.[18]

Chapter 3, entitled "Divine Government and Providence," says in paragraph 2, "God has endowed man with power of free choice, and governs him by moral laws and motives; and this power of free choice is the exact measure of man's responsibility." It continues in paragraph 3, "All events are present with God from everlasting to

---

16 Bryant, 98.
17 Bryant, 123, 124.
18 Lumpkin, *Baptist Confessions of Faith*, 369–376. All quotes from the confession are from this source.

everlasting; but His knowledge of them does not in any sense cause them, nor does He decree all events which He knows will occur." Chapter 8, entitled "The Gospel Call," affirms, "The call of the gospel is co-extensive with the atonement to all men, both by the word and strivings of the Spirit, so that salvation is rendered equally possible to all; and if any fail of eternal life, the fault is wholly his own." They affirm that due to Adam's fall, people "have not that righteousness and purity which Adam had before the fall." Consequently, "none, by virtue of any natural goodness and mere work of their own, can become the children of God; but they are all dependent for salvation upon the redemption effected through the blood of Christ, and upon being created anew unto obedience through the operation of the Spirit; both of which are freely provided for every descendent of Adam." The doctrine of regeneration focuses on the preeminence of the work of the Spirit but mildly implies that penitence precedes this working of the Spirit: "As man is a fallen and sinful being, he must be regenerated in order to obtain salvation. This change is an instantaneous renewal of the heart by the Holy Spirit, *whereby the penitent sinner receives new life*, becomes a child of God, and is disposed to serve Him" (italics mine). Perseverance is not certain, for the will of man, even in the regenerate, still may assert itself to the contrary: "There are strong grounds to hope that the truly regenerate will persevere unto the end, and be saved, through the power of divine grace which is pledged for their support; but their future obedience and final salvation are neither determined nor certain, since through infirmity and manifold temptations they are in danger of falling; and they ought, therefore, to watch and pray lest they make shipwreck of their faith and be lost."[19]

The New Hampshire Confession

In light of the varied theological dynamics providing the context for this confession, it seems that it was designed to give an answer to several atmospheric queries. "If election is true, is there sufficient moral justification for the condemnation of sinners? Can men actually be seen as responsible if a divine decree rules their eternity and moral inability rules their present? Does not this render the preaching of the gospel a futile, irrelevant, and unnecessary exercise? Or,

19 Lumpkin, 374.

since the divine decree determines all things, notably the salvation or condemnation of individuals and the providential means by which they come to hear the gospel, is it not an intrusion on the divine prerogative and honor to impose extraordinary human effort in going to the unconverted?"

Some historians have viewed this confession as a capitulation to the Free Will movement, giving only minimal assertions of the former strong Calvinism of the New Hampshire Baptists. The Free Will movement, combined with the revivalism of the age, had worn away the sharp edges of their Calvinistic persuasion. William Lumpkin surmised, "In point of fact, the theological views of Calvinistic Baptists in the New Hampshire area had been considerably modified after 1780. . . . The Free Will Baptist message was welcomed with enthusiasm by the great middle class in New England and its warm evangelism produced a revolt against the rigid theological system of some Calvinistic Baptists. The New Hampshire Convention thus sought to restate its Calvinism in very moderate tones."[20] In an article on J. Newton Brown, Cathcart's *The Baptist Encyclopedia* states, "He was the author of the little creed so commonly adopted in newly organized Baptist churches, and known as *The New Hampshire Confession.* Like mild Dr. Brown it is gently Calvinistical." O. C. S. Wallace wrote an exposition of the confession and in his introduction referred to the "non-commital character of certain parts of the declaration." William J. McGlothlin in his introduction to the confession stated, "The only Confession of any note produced by American Calvinistic Baptists is the so-called *New Hampshire Confession of Faith.* Indeed, it is doubtful if it ought to be called Calvinistic, since it is non-commital on every point of difference between the Calvinistic and Arminian systems. It is very brief and very moderately Calvinistic. It emanated from the region where Arminian influences among American Baptists have always been strongest, and it faithfully reflects the modifying tendency of their presence."[21]

My personal investigation of the theology and historical context does not yield the same judgment. I view this confession as fundamentally loyal to the Calvinistic tradition, not a capitulation to any view

---

20 Lumpkin, 360.
21 William J. McGlothlin, *Baptist Confessions of Faith* (Philadelphia: American Baptist Publication Society, 1910), 279.

that they had historically viewed as inconsistent with the expressed biblical faith of Baptists. It employs, however, words, phrases, and carefully constructed ideas relevant to the tensions of its context. What McGlothlin called, "the modifying tendency" of the presence of Arminianism only involves a noble apologetic for Calvinism in light of implied absurdities. The growing impact of Charles Finney on vocabulary and concepts was remarkable. Add to that the rigorously arminianized arguments of Benjamin Randall and the Free Will Baptists juxtaposed to the developing hyper-Calvinism among anti-mission society Baptists. The framers of the New Hampshire Confession had to stress the existence of ideas in the Calvinistic doctrines that were not explored sufficiently by the Primitives, on the one hand, or represented accurately by the Arminians, on the other.

The confession consists, in its 1853 rendition, of eighteen articles. Each of these is carefully worded in light of the theological context within which they were written. The first article on Scripture gives a strong affirmation of the authority of Scripture as inspired—"a perfect treasure of heavenly instruction"—and containing the famous statement "That it has God for its author, salvation for its end, and truth, without any mixture of error, for its matter."

Article 2, "Of the True God," affirms a robust monotheism ["inexpressibly glorious in holiness"] with an orthodox understanding of the Trinity—"that in the unity of the Godhead there are three persons, the Father, the Son, and the Holy Ghost; equal in every divine perfection and executing distinct but harmonious offices in the great work of redemption." The sameness of essence, integrity of personhoods, and perfect harmony of operations are affirmed.

The article "Of the Fall of Man" uses vocabulary that aligns it with some of the concerns about the voluntary nature of all sin while not diminishing the effects of the fall on the moral corruption and its necessary connection with condemnation. It begins, "We believe that man was created in holiness, under the law of his Maker, but by *voluntary transgression* fell from that holy and happy state." The language, "voluntary transgression," is important for resisting any misperception that divine decree bypasses the reality of the voluntary nature of human action. It continues, "in consequence of which all mankind are now sinners, *not by constraint, but by choice*; being *by nature utterly void of that holiness required by the law of God, positively inclined to evil*; and therefore under just condemnation to eternal ruin, without defense or excuse." Again, even in the fallen state with a positive inclination to evil, sin still is "by choice." That element of choice, moreover, is seen as perfectly consistent with a state of being "utterly void of . . . holiness."

Article 4, "Of the way of Salvation," affirms that salvation is all of grace made possible only by the "Mediatorial Offices of the Son of God." The confession points to the Christ in his complex person as having fulfilled all that was necessary for salvation. His perfect obedience to the law and substitutionary death "made a full atonement for our sins." His resurrection consummated his saving work and, in his complex personhood he combines "the tenderest sympathies with divine perfections" and thus is qualified in every way to be "a suitable, a compassionate, and an all-sufficient Saviour."

The article "Of Justification" sets forth a clear rejection of works righteousness, and affirms the pardon of sin, the promise of eternal life "on principles of Righteousness." This means "not in consideration of any works of righteousness which we have done, but solely through faith in the Redeemer's blood; by virtue of which faith his perfect righteousness is freely imputed to us of God; that it brings us into a state of most blessed peace and favor with God, and secures every other blessing needful for time and eternity." This affirmation of imputed righteousness in the 1853 version was added by J. Newton Brown. It sets a position in favor of that Reformation doctrine as a corrective to the Finneyite doctrine and certain elements of New England Theology that dismissed imputation as a morally impossible concept.

Article 6, entitled "Of the Freeness of Salvation," is aimed to show the Free Will folk that Calvinists believe in universal offer based on universal *duty*, not necessarily universal *provision*. It also positions them as opposed to the Primitives and fully in accord with what the Primitives opprobriated as "Fullerism." "We believe that the blessings of salvation are made free to all by the gospel; that it is the immediate duty of all to accept them by a cordial penitent, and obedient faith; and that nothing prevents the salvation of the greatest sinner on earth, but his own inherent depravity and voluntary rejection of the gospel; which rejection involves him in an aggravated condemnation." Note the maintenance of "inherent depravity" put alongside "voluntary rejection." Depravity does not eliminate the voluntary nature of all human moral action but is in complete accord with the biblical reality that all moral action arises from the heart. God may bring just aggravation of the human hostility to divine holiness, but election is not a doctrine of prohibition, but a doctrine of covenantal faithfulness that infrustrably leads to salvation. A refusal to receive a love of the truth and thus believe the truth is the prohibitive factor in continuing unbelief (2 Thess. 2:10–12).

"Of Grace in Regeneration," article 7, sets forth a clearly Calvinistic understanding of this doctrine while appropriating language that would catch the attention of Arminians and Finneyites and hopefully convince the hyper-Calvinists that they had not forsaken the necessity of efficacious grace for salvation. Regeneration does not come on the basis of a prior disposition but establishes the necessary disposition of mind consistent with salvation. "We believe that in order to be saved, sinners must be regenerated, or born again; that *regeneration consists in giving a holy disposition to the mind.*" Note that the "holy disposition" must be granted. Also, note the connections of means in this work of grace—"that it is effected in a manner above our comprehension by the power of the Holy Spirit, in connection with divine truth, so as to *secure our voluntary obedience to the gospel*; and that its proper *evidence* appears in the holy fruits of repentance and faith and newness of life" (italics mine). Note that the elements—Spirit, truth, some medium for the presentation of truth, and voluntary obedience—involved in Finney's discussion of the new birth all are present, but their ordering in cause-and-effect relationship is profoundly different.

It is theologically important that the article "Of Repentance and Faith" follows, in the 1853 edition, regeneration. To solidify the historical view consistent with effectual calling and yet fully in tune with the theological tensions within which they operated, Brown constructed this article as a reinforcement of the article on regeneration. "We believe that Repentance and Faith are *sacred duties*, and also *inseparable graces, wrought in our souls by the regenerating Spirit of God*; whereby, being deeply convinced of our guilt, danger, and helplessness, and of the way of salvation by Christ, we turn to God with unfeigned contrition, confession, and supplication for mercy; at the same time heartily receiving the Lord Jesus Christ as our

Prophet, Priest, and King, and relying on him alone as the only and all-sufficient Saviour."

Why are repentance and faith called "duties?" First, repentance and faith are duties because they are commanded in Scripture: *repent*—Luke 3:3 followed by an exhortation to bear fruit in keeping with repentance; Mark 1:15 (Jesus); Luke 24:46–47; Acts 2:38; 11:18; 17:30, 31; 26:18; 2 Peter 3:9, 10; *believe* is set forth as a duty to be obeyed—Rom. 1:5; 5:1, 2; 10:9, 10; 16:26; Acts 16:31; Heb. 4:2, 6, 11.

Repentance implies the excellence and immutable perfection of the moral law against which we have sinned and to which all mankind must be subject. To turn the mind and heart from disobedience and hatred toward love of law and joy in obeying it is the most fundamental of all duties of rebellious creatures. Faith implies the perfection of Christ as Savior in meeting all the demands of the law both in its punitive requirement and in its righteousness flowing from holiness. To consent to our reception before God only on the basis of just this kind of Savior is at once a complete submission to grace and the recognition of consummate duty. None of the dissenters in mind—Arminians, Finneyites, and Hyper-Calvinists—could affirm consistency between absolute dependence on grace as commensurate with absolute duty.

Note also that repentance and faith are called "inseparable graces." This is consistent with the Baptist Catechism that says, "Repentance unto life is a *saving grace* whereby a sinner, out of a *true sense of his sin*, and *apprehension of the mercy of God in Christ*, doth with *grief and hatred of his sin*, turn from it *unto God*, with full purpose of and endeavor after new obedience" (italics mine).

Note the use of the word "wrought." Though it is our duty, it is produced by another. Again the Baptist Catechism: "Effectual calling is a work of God's Spirit whereby, convincing us of our sin and misery, enlightening our minds in the knowledge of Christ, and renewing our will, he doth persuade and enable us to embrace Jesus Christ, freely offered to us in the gospel." This means that God, by the power in which he executes the entire scheme of salvation, operates in the moral nature of man to remake his moral perceptions and preferences (Phil. 2:12, 13; Eph. 1:19, 20; 2:4). The process within the human mind and heart is described in the confession:

"being deeply convinced of our guilt, danger, and helplessness, and of the way of salvation by Christ, we turn to God with unfeigned contrition, confession, and supplication for mercy." Such genuine repentance then, according to the confession, flows out into faith: "At the same time heartily receiving the Lord Jesus Christ as our Prophet, priest, and king, and relying on him alone as the only and all-sufficient saviour."

Article 9, "Of God's Purpose of Grace," emphasizes a robust affirmation of divine prerogative and power while also insisting on the immediate responsibility, or free agency, of man. It is important to observe the care and economy of language employed to make these highly distinctive points.

1. We believe that Election is the *eternal purpose of God*, [Not just his perfect foreknowledge of all things that will happen.]

2. according to which he graciously regenerates, sanctifies, and saves sinners, [God's eternal purpose culminates in the salvation of those he has elected. The grace of eternal election is first and on that basis he does everything else that is involved in the saving of sinners.]

3. that being perfectly consistent with the *free agency of man*, it comprehends *all the means in connection with the end*; [Nothing about election obliterates man's free agency but he maintains his status as a creature that is irreducibly a moral agent doing freely what he desires to do.]

4. glorious display of God's *sovereign goodness, being infinitely free, wise, holy and unchangeable;* [All of these words show how election reflects important aspects of the eternal attributes of God. Nothing about this is a capitulation to distinctive Arminianism or blurs the distinctions between the two viewpoints.]

5. that it encourages the *use of means in the highest degree*; [Election does not render means unnecessary but rather sets in motion those means that are necessary to accomplish the kind of salvation that God has decreed.]

6. ascertained by its effects in all who truly believe the gospel; [Election is not a granting of salvation to those who have no heart for godliness or love for the wisdom of God as displayed in the gospel, but produces those fruits.]

7. the foundation of Christian assurance; [Human certainty cannot transcend divine certainty but entirely depends on it.]

8. to ascertain it with regard to ourselves demands and deserves the utmost diligence. [Because eternal election is discerned by the presence of both its means and its fruits, the ascertaining of election involves the examination and pursuit of holy fruit.]

Sanctification (article 10) is progressive, is begun in regeneration, is carried on in the heart by the Holy Spirit with the use of appointed means. Since its order is in anticipation of perseverance, it is seen as a necessary constituent of that grace. Thus sanctification calls the believer to the "Word of God, self-examination, self-denial, watchfulness, and prayer."

Perseverance also gives a clear separation from the Free Will confession. "We believe that such only are real believers as endure unto the end; that their persevering attachment to Christ is the grand mark which distinguishes them from mere professors; that a special Providence watches over their welfare; and that they are kept by the power of God through faith unto salvation." For those elected, regenerated, and kept there is no "danger of falling" but their status will result, not in a careless life, but a life of grateful obedience.

"Of the Harmony of the Law and the Gospel" again emphasizes both moral inability and continuing responsibility because of the universal obligation to obey the moral law. This is a peculiarly Fullerite emphasis. God's law is the "eternal and unchangeable rule of his moral government" and is intrinsically "holy, just, and good." The sinner's inability to keep it is not because of a loss of moral agency but specifically comes from "their love of sin." Obedience to the moral law is one of the ends of salvation as well as the faithful use of the "means of grace connected with the establishment of the visible church."

Further articles emphasize the doctrine of the church, the ordinances, the Sabbath, civil government, judgment, and heaven and hell. The church is composed of regenerate persons, has two officers (pastors or bishops and deacons) and has only two ordinances, baptism of believers only and the Lord's Supper. Baptism necessarily precedes the right to receive the Lord's Supper. "The first day of the week is the Lord's Day or Christian Sabbath" to be kept to religious purposes including the "devout observance of all the means of grace."

It prepares us for the Sabbath rest yet to be attained for the people of God. Civil government is ordained of God, to be prayed for and obeyed except where laws violate the will of the Lord Jesus Christ, "who is the only Lord of the conscience." Only those justified and sanctified in Christ are deemed righteous; while all others are wicked in the sight of God and remain under his curse, a distinction that "holds among men both in and after death." After the resurrection, the wicked will be "adjudged to endless punishment" and the righteous "to endless joy." This righteous judgment will "fix forever the final state of men in heaven or hell." The final words emphasize the immutable character of God, the requirements of each component of the gospel, and the inescapable responsibility of all moral creatures before God: "on principles of righteousness."

Summary Evaluation

Though it does not have the quality of exposition found in the Second London Confession, the New Hampshire Confession is a noble confession, orthodox in its theology and Christology, uncompromised in its affirmation of the holy and wise sovereignty of God over his creation, the purely gratuitous character of salvation, clear in its baptistic understanding of the church, and firm in the reality of the eternal destinies of the righteous (esteemed so by the grace of God in the work of Christ) and the wicked, judged so by their continual transgression of the law and their wicked unbelief.

7

The Abstract of Principles

Tom J. Nettles

T HE ABSTRACT OF PRINCIPLES ORIGINATED in the vision that
J. P. Boyce had for theological education among Baptists. In
his justly acclaimed address, "Three Changes in Theological
Institutions," he called for a self-conscious commitment of Southern
Baptists to a theological education that would educate an abundant
ministry, a learned ministry, and a faithful ministry. Boyce delivered
the Abstract of Principles as an inaugural address for his professor-
ship at Furman University, and after having discussed the first two
principles of abundant ministry and learned ministry, he focused on
the issue of faithfulness in perpetuity.

Boyce's third "change" was "the adoption of a declaration of
doctrine to be required of those who assume the various professorships." His theological pilgrimage had riveted this conviction in his
conscience. Soon after his graduation from Brown, Boyce became
editor of *The Southern Baptist*. In that context he became familiar
with J. S. Mims's attack on confessions in his treatise *Orthodoxy*.
Also, Boyce read J. L. Reynolds's careful but compelling use of
Baptist confessional history in his articles on imputation. When
he attended Princeton, he experienced the benefits of a confes-
sion-based education. The subtlety with which both Campbellism
and Arminianism had infected segments of Baptist life led Boyce to
believe that "a crisis in Baptist doctrine is evidently approaching."
Given those influences, Boyce came to contend that those that held

to the "doctrines which formerly distinguished us" must not slack in their duty but contend for that same faith.[1]

Every doctrine of Scripture must be "determined and expressed," and those responsible for calling and ordaining ministers must ascertain that they are orthodox. Nothing could have been more reprehensible to Mims than this proposal of Boyce. Mims argued that orthodoxy is an attempt to "lord it over" others. His snarling response was thus: "In all countries, and at all times, there has existed a class of men who, if we may judge from their conduct, decided the question by teaching that he is the greatest who contends most earnestly for conformity to some standard of orthodoxy."[2]

Nevertheless, in Boyce's perception of Christian truth, confessional faithfulness should apply to every segment of Baptist life, although with different expectations of understanding and knowledgeable conformity. He set forth his view of expectations for church members, for ministers, and most stringently, for theological professors. He spoke of the "peculiar obligations" that rested on those invested with the teaching ministry to be preserved from corrupting the Word of God by "the crime of teaching a single error, however unimportant." Likewise, those that had authority over these professors, the boards of trustees, required "faithfulness to the trusts devolved upon them, that false doctrine, however trifling, may receive no countenance."[3]

Mims, however, had argued that the use of a confession to investigate orthodoxy was not a protection of the Word of God but amounted to a denial of the Bible. He said, in speaking of the enforcers of confessional orthodoxy, "If they undertake the grateful task of investigating the orthodoxy of any supposed heretic, they never appeal to the Bible, but only to their Standard." The Bible never changes, but supposed orthodoxy is a shifting shadow.[4]

Boyce wanted to remind his hearers, however, that Alexander Campbell flew under the banner of *no creed but the Bible*, and at the

1 J. P. Boyce, *Three Changes in Theological Institutions* (Greenville, SC: C. J. Elford's Book and Job Press, 1856), 33, 34.
2 James S. Mims, *Orthodoxy, An address delivered before the Board of Trustees of the Furman Theological Institution, on the Day of the Annual Commencement, June 19, 1848* (Columbia, SC: I. C. Morgan, 1848), 7.
3 Boyce, *Three Changes*, 35, 36.
4 Mims, *Orthodoxy,* 7.

same time had drawn thousands of members of Baptist churches away from some of the fundamental truths that Baptists profess to be biblical. Had he been in a theological seminary, the devastation could have been greater than it was. The recurrence of such a situation with no means of checking it and setting it right could "influence all our churches, and the fair fabric of our faith may be entirely demolished."[5]

Boyce added a footnote in the published version of his address. This footnote asserted that in those who teach the ministry, "No difference, however slight, no peculiar sentiment, however speculative, is here allowable." A teacher's "agreement with the standard should be exact. His declaration of it should be based upon no mental reservation, upon no private understanding with those who immediately invest him into office." Before signing a confession, he should be convinced that its position is "an exact summary of the truth" contained in the Bible. Under no circumstances should a principle be adopted that a professor may "sign any abstract of doctrine with which he does not agree, and in accordance with which he does not intend to teach." Nor is he "at liberty to modify the truth, which he has been placed there to inculcate." His opinions in doctrine as expressed in the confession "must be expressly affirmed to be upon every point in accordance with the truth we believe to be taught in the Scriptures."[6]

In this address, Boyce proposed the Charleston Baptist Association's confession, essentially the Second London Confession, as the most logical selection for such a confessional standard, because it "had almost universal prevalence in this State."[7] Again, Mims had ridiculed the idea that associational confessions had functioned as standards of orthodoxy at any time. In fact, the associations had used the confessions precisely in the way Mims implied they had not. Boyce knew this. The Charleston confession not only had been the confession of his childhood and youth; but it had, in its original Presbyterian form as the Westminster Confession of Faith, governed the theological education at Princeton and had already been implicitly functioning as a safeguard at Furman.

---

5 Boyce, *Three Changes*, 36.
6 Boyce, *Three Changes*, 35.
7 Boyce, 37, 38.

When Mims had appeared before the Board of Trustees in 1848 to answer for his theology of imputation, he protested against his accuser's method by proclaiming, "I shall now attempt to evince by unquestionable historical evidence, the truth of this proposition: that GOD'S WORD, AND NOT CONFESSIONS, HAS ALWAYS BEEN THE ACKNOWLEDGED STANDARD OF ORTHODOXY AMONG BAPTISTS."[8] Boyce knew that he must overcome Mims's historical argument against the regulative use of a confession. He made the claim, therefore, that such a confessional test had been common in Baptist life. Though he knew some would object, he pointed out that a theological institution, not being a scriptural institution, must only meet the criteria of not contradicting Scripture. It must conform to the most expedient rules that human wisdom can devise to "carry out the laudable designs of its founders." The confessional standard, therefore, guarantees that the doctrine taught will reflect the consensus of those that established the school in order to press forward the faith of their churches.[9]

Even in local churches, however, Boyce argued that Scripture abounds with exhortations about the faith that assume the church's commitment to a body of clearly enunciated doctrines and its obligation to preserve, propagate, and protect those doctrines. Baptists, so Boyce argued, had used confessions in a twofold way: (1) the declaration of faith, and (2) the "testing of its existence in others."[10] Boyce demonstrated that such a confession of truth operated during the ministry of Jesus. It was expanded and required as a test of faith under the apostles as they delivered the gospel in its fullness in establishing churches. Following the apostolic model, churches continued evaluating their teachers in light of the rule of faith for the next three centuries. Baptists of all ages have also used creeds in this twofold way.

Some have mistaken the Baptist commitment to liberty of conscience as a rejection of a creedal test in the church. Mims made this transfer. He applied the Baptist rejection of creeds as an instrument of civil repression as reason to reject their use as instruments of doctrinal purity in the church.[11] Virtually all denominations had

---

8 Mims, *Orthodoxy*, 11.
9 Boyce, *Three Changes*, 39.
10 Boyce, *Three Changes*, 40, 41.
11 Mims, *Orthodoxy*, 10.

done this; Baptists were excepted. Boyce agreed that Baptists have refused to use creeds to enforce civil punishment or disability. The spirituality of the church demanded this civil freedom; at the same time, the church's spirituality has "impressed upon us the necessity of excluding those who have violated the simplicity which is in Christ," and thus the necessity of a doctrinal standard.[12]

He closed his discussion of the third change with an intensified recommendation of the justness of such a provision. Boyce considered the adoption of a test of doctrine as perfectly consistent "with the position of Baptists, as well as of Bible Christians." Boyce saw this as "based upon principles and practices sanctioned by the authority of Scripture, and by the usage of our people." Requiring subscription, Boyce contended, "will infringe the rights of no man," and will secure the rights of those that expect a sound ministry to emerge from the educational experience. "It is no hardship to those who teach here," Boyce reasoned, "to be called upon to sign the declaration of their principles." He reminded his audience, "There are fields of usefulness open elsewhere to every man, and none need accept your call who cannot conscientiously sign your formulary." He reminded the trustees that a confession was no enemy of biblical truth but would help "to distinguish truth from error, and to embrace the former," and would enforce "the same precious truths of the Bible which were so dear to the hearts of its founders."[13]

Implementing the Idea

Through 1857 and 1858, plans were laid for beginning a seminary. Educational conventions, specially assigned committees, and designated tasks for faculty, location, endowment, confessions of faith, and bylaws proceeded for more than two years. In 1858, plans came to a virtual completion; but due to the hesitation of two of the appointed faculty members, another year's delay ensued. One afternoon in the meeting of 1858, Boyce presented the report on the "Plan of Organization, Plan of Instruction, Abstract of Principles." On May 4, 1858, the final adoption of the Abstract of Principles took place. Basil Manly Jr. wrote his reminiscences of that convention:

12 Boyce, *Three Changes*, 44.
13 Boyce, *Three Changes*, 44.

Those were memorable days to some at least of those who engaged in them. In the freedom of brotherly discussion, in the warmth occasioned by the contact and collision of the ideas of the younger and the older, the brethren from different sections of the country, and who had enjoyed different kinds of training and different associations, there was keen stimulus to thought. Every great topic in theology was handled earnestly, freely and yet reverently. The learning of the past was not ignored. The various forms of expression in which the faith had been declared in our own and other denominations of Christians were carefully compared and consulted; the safe-guards which had been thrown around other Seminaries, both as to doctrine and as to funds were thoughtfully considered; the different methods of instruction, by curriculum, by free election, by courses more or less flexible, were passed in review. The result was almost unanimously approved by the Convention after somewhat elaborate explanation and debate, and has remained practically without modification to the present day.[14]

The initial proposal in the report stated, "The name of the Common Seminary at Greenville, S.C., shall be *The Southern Baptist Theological Seminary.*" Article 9 of the report stated, "Every Professor of the Institution shall be a member of a regular Baptist Church; and all persons accepting Professorships in this Seminary, shall be considered, by such acceptance, as engaging to teach in accordance with, and not contrary to, the Abstract of Principles hereinafter laid down, a departure from which principles, on his part, shall be considered ground for his resignation or removal by the Trustees." [15]

The reporter for *The Southern Baptist*, J. P. Tustin, said that "the spirit and incidents of the meeting deserve special mention, but we can only say in a word, that the impression of the whole was so encouraging, that some of the oldest and most experienced ministers said that they had never before been so able to look hopefully into the future."

14 Basil Manly, Jr. "The Beginnings of the History of the Seminary, *The Seminary Magazine,* January 1892, 209.

15 William A. Mueller, *A History of Southern Baptist Theological Seminary* (Nashville: Broadman Press, 1959) 238.

Tustin also felt that an explanation of the adopted Abstract of Principles was in order. It was adopted as a "test for the Faculty," he explained, "and not as binding upon Baptist Churches." The statement would be a guarantee of the integrity of the endowment funds, protecting them against "future perversion from their original intent." He also explained the method used by the committee of five in forming the confession from a comparison of "the principal Ancient and Modern Symbols, both of our own and of other denominations," but particularly the family of confessions related to the Charleston Confession. It was condensed as far as seemed "practicable, without obscurity or weakness."[16]

The Confession

The initial paragraph introducing the abstract stated this important principle:

Every professor of the institution shall be a member of a regular Baptist Church; and all persons accepting professorships in this Seminary shall be considered, by such acceptance, as engaging to teach in accordance with, and not contrary to, the Abstract of Principles hereinafter laid down, a departure from which principles on his part shall be grounds for his resignation or removal by the Trustees.

The articles roughly follow the order of the Second London Confession (hereinafter *2LC*), with some alteration due to omissions of other articles and seeking to maintain the logical flow of the ideas. All referenced chapters and paragraphs are from the 2LC.

1. The Scriptures.

The Scriptures of the Old and New Testament were given by inspiration of God, and are the only sufficient, certain and authoritative rule of all saving knowledge, faith and obedience.

The 2LC's first article ("Of the Holy Scriptures") has ten paragraphs; the abstract has one sentence. That sentence is the first one of the 2LC substituting "authoritative" for "infallible" and adding "were given by inspiration of God."

---

16 J. P. Tustin, "Abstract of Principles," *The Southern Baptist*, May 11, 1858, 3.

2. God.

> There is but one God, the Maker, Preserver and Ruler of all things, having in and of himself, all perfections, and being infinite in them all; and to Him all creatures owe the highest love, reverence and obedience.

3. The Trinity.

> God is revealed to us as Father, Son and Holy Spirit each with distinct personal attributes, but without division of nature, essence or being.

These two articles come from a division of chapter 2 ("Of God and the Holy Trinity") of the 2LC. Some phrases are given new words for clarity for a Baptist audience and other ideas are summarized and conflated for the purpose of great economy. For example, in chapter 2, paragraph 1 of the 2LC, we have the words, "but one . . . infinite in being, and perfection." The *Abstract* says, "There is but one God . . . having in and of himself, all perfections, and being infinite in them all." The concepts of "Maker, Preserver, and Ruler," are conflated from other chapters and summarized in that series of words. The phrase "to Him all creatures owe the highest love, reverence and obedience" comes from the end of chapter 2, paragraph 2, "to him is due from Angels, and men, whatsoever worship, service, or obedience as Creatures they owe unto the Creator." In chapter 2, paragraph 3, we read, "In this divine and infinite Being there are three subsistences, the Father, the Word (or Son) and Holy Spirit, of one substance . . . but one God who is not to be divided in nature and Being." The "three subsistences" is captured in the phrase of the abstract, "each with distinct personal attributes."

4. Providence.

> God from eternity, decrees or permits all things that come to pass, and perpetually upholds, directs and governs all creatures and all events; yet so as not to destroy the free will and responsibility of intelligent creatures.

The wording of this article comes from selected phrases and clauses from chapter 5 ("Of Divine Providence") of the 2LC. The words "From eternity" condense several concepts such as "for the end for which they were created," (paragraph 1) and "his determinate counsel" (paragraph 4). "All things" arises from the assertion that he created "all things" for such disposition (paragraph 1). "Upholds, directs and governs" ("dispose" omitted) come immediately from chapter 5, paragraph 1. The final phrase summarizes the meaning of "he ordereth them to fall out, according to the nature of second causes, either necessarily, freely, or contingently" (paragraph 2), and "yet so, as the sinfulness of their acts proceedeth only from the Creatures" (paragraph 4).

5. Election.

> Election is God's eternal choice of some persons unto everlasting life—not because of foreseen merit in them, but of his mere mercy in Christ—in consequence of which choice they are called, justified and glorified.

This is taken from chapter 3 ("Of God's Decree") by collapsing into one sentence, phrases taken from paragraphs 3, 5, and 6. With some alterations for clarity, condensation, and continuity of thought, the phrases used are: "Some men and angels are predestinated, or foreordained to Eternal Life"; "Hath chosen in Christ ... out of his mere free grace and love; without any other thing is the creature as a condition or cause moving him thereunto"; "they who are elected . . . are effectually called ..., are justified ... and kept."

6. The Fall of Man.

> God originally created man in His own image, and free from sin; but, through the temptation of Satan, he transgressed the command of God, and fell from his original holiness and righteousness; whereby his posterity inherit a nature corrupt and wholly opposed to God and His law, are under condemnation, and as soon as they are capable of moral action, become actual transgressors.

This is taken from chapter 6 ("Of the Fall of Man, Of Sin, and Of the Punishment Thereof") and again reflects some exact wording, some condensations, some paraphrases, and some summaries. The first statement reflects words like "upright and perfect" (paragraph 1); the next phrase employs words and ideas in such statements as "did willfully transgress the Law of their creation and the command

given unto them" (paragraph 1), and "fell from their original righteousness and communion with God" (paragraph 2). The last phrase
pulls together vocabulary and concepts from this language. "The
guilt of sin was imputed" (paragraph 3, although due to sensitivity
to the controversy with Mims that word is not used), "and corrupt
nature conveyed, to all their posterity" (paragraph 3) "being now
conceived in Sin, and by nature children of wrath . . . the subjects of
death and all other miseries, spiritual, temporal and eternal" (paragraph 3); ... "From this original, corruption . . . do proceed all actual
transgressions" (paragraph 4).

7. The Mediator.

Jesus Christ, the only begotten Son of God, is the divinely
appointed mediator between God and man. Having taken
upon Himself human nature, yet without sin, He perfectly
fulfilled the Law, suffered and died upon the cross for the
salvation of sinners. He was buried, and rose again the third
day, and ascended to His Father, at whose hand He ever
liveth to make intercession for His people. He is the only
Mediator, the Prophet, Priest and King of the Church, and
Sovereign of the Universe.

This article is built on the words of chapter 8 ("Of Christ the
Mediator") of the 2LC and reflects individual phrases selected from
six of the ten paragraphs. The product is a simple, clear, and amazingly coherent affirmation, having synthesized small phrases and
individual words, but never a full sentence.

8. Regeneration.

Regeneration is a change of heart, wrought by the Holy
Spirit, who quickeneth the dead in trespasses and sins
enlightening their minds spiritually and savingly to understand the Word of God, and renewing their whole nature,
so that they love and practice holiness. It is a work of God's
free and special grace alone.

This article is taken from chapter 10 ("Of Effectual Calling"),
paragraphs 1 and 2. The phrase "change of heart" summarizes the
words "Taking away their heart of stone, and giving unto them an
heart of flesh" (paragraph 1). "Wrought by the Holy Spirit" combines

the idea "effectually to call by his word, and Spirit" (paragraph 1) with a phrase from paragraph 1 of chapter 14 ("Of Saving Faith") that says, "wrought by the Ministry of the Word." "[E]nlightening their minds spiritually and savingly to understand the Word of God," is taken directly from the 2LC (paragraph 1). "[R]enewing their whole nature, so that they love and practice holiness" conceptualizes the 2LC phrase "renewing their wills, and by his Almighty power determining them to that which is good" (paragraph 1). The last phrase directly reflects the first sentence of paragraph 2 except the word "It" replaces "This effectual call."

9. Repentance.

> Repentance is an evangelical grace, wherein a person being, by the Holy Spirit, made sensible of the manifold evil of his sin, humbleth himself for it, with godly sorrow, detestation of it, and self-abhorrence, with a purpose and endeavor to walk before God so as to please Him in all things.

It is significant that the articles on repentance and faith follow the article on regeneration, showing not only by the implication of the content of each of the articles but, by their order, that they saw regeneration as necessary before any sinner would have repentance unto life or saving faith. This order also reverses what one finds in the 2LC, which has the article on faith before the article on repentance. The article on repentance virtually duplicates paragraph 3 of chapter 15 ("Of Repentance unto Life and Salvation"). Two phrases omitted from the abstract present in the 2LC are: "praying for pardon, and strength of grace," and "by supplies of the Spirit."

10. Faith.

> Saving faith is the belief, on God's authority, of whatsoever is revealed in His Word concerning Christ; accepting and resting upon Him alone for justification and eternal life. It is wrought in the heart by the Holy Spirit, and is accompanied by all other saving graces, and leads to a life of holiness.

This article reflects several phrases in paragraphs 1 and 2 from chapter 14 of the 2LC ("Of Saving Faith"). The abstract uses the phrase "wrought in the heart by the Holy Spirit," whereas the 2LC says "wrought by the ministry of the Word." The New Hampshire

Confession employs the language "wrought in our souls by the regenerating Spirit of God." The words "accompanied with all other saving graces" are employed from paragraph 2 of chapter 11, the 2LC article on "justification."

11. Justification.

> Justification is God's gracious and full acquittal of sinners, who believe in Christ, from all sin, through the satisfaction that Christ has made; not for anything wrought in them or done by them; but on account of the obedience and satisfaction of Christ, they receiving and resting on Him and His righteousness by faith.

This article borrows words and summarizes ideas from chapter 11 ("Of Justification") of the 2LC. The words "gracious and full acquittal" and the words that follow render the words of 2LC (paragraph 3), "Christ by his obedience, and death, did fully discharge the debt of all those that are justified; and did by the sacrifice of himself, in the blood of his cross, undergoing in their stead the penalty due unto them, make a proper, real, and full satisfaction to God's justice in their behalf." Sentences from chapter 11, paragraph 1 ("not for anything wrought in them, or done by them") and paragraph 3 ("obedience and satisfaction") fill out the rest of the article.

12. Sanctification.

> Those who have been regenerated are also sanctified, by God's word and Spirit dwelling in them. This sanctification is progressive through the supply of Divine strength, which all saints seek to obtain, pressing after a heavenly life in cordial obedience to all Christ's commands.

This article distributes phrases from paragraphs 1 and 3 of chapter 13 ("Of Sanctification"). "By His Word and Spirit dwelling in them" is from paragraph 1. Some ideas, as usual, are condensed. "This sanctification is progressive" summarizes several phrases reflecting biblical ideas in paragraphs 1, 2, and 3. "Pressing after a heavenly life" is from paragraph 3 while the words "cordial obedience" are used for the words "evangelical obedience."

13. Perseverance of the Saints.

Those whom God hath accepted in the Beloved, and sanctified by His Spirit, will never totally nor finally fall away from
the state of grace, but shall certainly persevere to the end;
and though they may fall, through neglect and temptation,
into sin, whereby they grieve the Spirit, impair their graces
and comforts, bring reproach on the Church, and temporal
judgments on themselves, yet they shall be renewed again
unto repentance, and be kept by the power of God through
faith unto salvation.

This article duplicates in a fairly straightforward way sentences
from paragraphs 1 and 3 of chapter 17 ("Of Perseverance of the
Saints") of the 2LC. It finishes by employing Scripture language
used in paragraph 3.

14. The Church.

The Lord Jesus is the Head of the Church, which is composed
of all his true disciples, and in Him is invested supremely all
power for its government. According to his commandment,
Christians are to associate themselves into particular societies or churches; and to each of these churches he hath given
needful authority for administering that order, discipline
and worship which he hath appointed. The regular officers
of a Church are Bishops, or Elders, and Deacons.

Chapter 26 ("Of the Church") is the longest chapter of
the 2LC, containing 15 sizable paragraphs. The abstract article consists mainly of phrases from paragraphs 4, 5, and 7, and the names of
the officers from paragraph 8.

15. Baptism.

Baptism is an ordinance of the Lord Jesus, obligatory upon
every believer, wherein he is immersed in water in the name
of the Father, and of the Son, and of the Holy Spirit, as a sign
of his fellowship with the death and resurrection of Christ,
of remission of sins, and of his giving himself up to God, to
live and walk in newness of life. It is prerequisite to church
fellowship, and to participation in the Lord's Supper.

This imports a few phrases and ideas from paragraphs 3 and 4 but for the most part is a duplication of paragraph 1 of chapter 29 ("Of Baptism") of the 2LC. The last sentence is a paraphrase of a sentence in the New Hampshire Confession.

16. The Lord's Supper.

The Lord's Supper is an ordinance of Jesus Christ, to be administered with the elements of bread and wine, and to be observed by his churches till the end of the world. It is in no sense a sacrifice, but is designed to commemorate his death, to confirm the faith and other graces of Christians, and to be a bond, pledge and renewal of their communion with him, and of their church fellowship.

Out of the 8 paragraphs on this ordinance from chapter 30 ("Of the Lord's Supper") of the 2LC, this article employs sentences only from paragraphs 1 and 2. The exegetical and doctrinal polemic against the Mass is omitted as well as the concept of the body and blood of Christ being "spiritually present."

17. The Lord's Day.

The Lord's Day is a Christian institution for regular observance, and should be employed in exercises of worship and spiritual devotion, both public and private, resting from worldly employments and amusements, works of necessity and mercy only excepted.

Out of the 8 paragraphs from chapter 22 ("Of Religious Worship and the Sabbath Day"), the abstract employs words and ideas only from paragraphs 7 and 8. It condenses phrases from several sentences into this single sentence.

18. Liberty of Conscience.

God alone is Lord of the conscience; and He hath left it free from the doctrines and commandments of men, which are in anything contrary to His word, or not contained in it. Civil magistrates being ordained of God, subjection in all lawful things commanded by them ought to be yielded by us in the Lord, not only for wrath, but also for conscience sake.

This entire article is taken from paragraph 2 of chapter 21 ("Of Christian Liberty and Liberty of Conscience") and paragraph 3 of chapter 24 ("Of the Civil Magistrate") of the 2LC.

19. The Resurrection.

The bodies of men after death return to dust, but their spirits return immediately to God—the righteous to rest with Him; the wicked to be reserved under darkness to the judgment. At the last day, the bodies of all the dead, both just and unjust, will be raised.

The first sentence of this is taken, some verbatim and some condensed, from paragraph 1 of chapter 31 ("Of the State of Man after Death and of the Resurrection of the Dead"). The last sentence comes from a summary of paragraph 3.

20. The Judgment.

God hath appointed a day, wherein he will judge the world by Jesus Christ, when every one shall receive according to his deeds; the wicked shall go into everlasting punishment; the righteous, into everlasting life.

This article summarizes and condenses the language of paragraphs 1 and 2 of chapter 32 ("Of the Last Judgment") of the 2LC.

The Aftermath

In spite of such strong affirmations of the necessity of faithfulness to a confession, and the simplicity, clarity and latitude allowed in the confession, a decline inevitably set in.

William H. Whitsitt was elected president of The Southern Baptist Theological Seminary in 1895, after the death of John A. Broadus, the second president of the seminary. During Whitsitt's presidency, a shift began in the attitude of the faculty toward the vision cast by Boyce. This shift was most notable in William O. Carver, who began his professorial career in 1896 teaching New Testament and homiletics. He demonstrated little respect for Boyce or for his vision. Carver's critique of Boyce was learned from hearsay. About Boyce's teaching, Carver noted "His method was purely didactic"; "not creative or stimulating to original thought or research. He was training a ministry to pass on a theological tradition, not to independent experience and thought."[17] For Carver this was not a compliment but the notation of a fault.

Carver's intent in teaching demonstrated just as much starch as Boyce in seeking to mold students according to his perceptions of Christian ministry. His antipathy toward Calvinism matched Boyce's love for it. Election, in Carver's exposition, was instrumental and conditional. For example, Abraham was chosen, not for salvation, but for service—entirely conditioned on Abraham's willingness to respond. Cornell Goerner commented, "This was a new idea to many who brought with them to the seminary a rigid Calvinistic concept of Election." But Carver convinced them of his viewpoint through his approach to the Bible. "It may be that some rejected this modified Calvinism," Goerner speculated, "but I never heard a student who was able to debate it successfully with his professor."[18] One may be sure that Carver could overwhelm his students in debating the issue, but no amount of subtlety could put him in alignment with the institution's governing confession of faith, the Abstract of Principles. Dale Moody, the last graduate student to major under his supervision in Philosophy of Christianity, wrote, "As one deeply in debt, in both intellectual and personal ways, I wish to give thanks to God for the teacher who set the course of my theological pilgrimage more than any other."[19] This was a pilgrimage going the opposite direction from that inculcated by Boyce.

This clear confessional divergence on the part of Carver established a practice at The Southern Baptist Theological Seminary that teachers were allowed to sign the *Abstract* given as much interpretive latitude as they needed in order to fit within it. Frank Stagg, a professor of New Testament, said, "Through most of Southern Seminary's years, professors were permitted to sign the Abstract of Principles as they interpreted it, contrary to Boyce's demand."[20] This same

---

17 W. O. Carver, "Unpublished Notes," cited in William A. Mueller, *A History of Southern Baptist Theological Seminary* (Nashville, Broadman, 1959), 57.

18 Cornell Goerner, "The Greatest Teacher I Knew," in *God's Glory in Missions: In appreciation of William Owen Carver*, ed. John N. Jonsson (A private publication, 1985), 16.

19 Dale Moody, "Holding Fast that which is Good," in Jonsson, *God's Glory*, 94.

20 Frank Stagg, "As The Twig is Bent . . . Theological institutions and the J. P. Boyce legacy," *Baptist Record* (5 January 1995), 6.

principle was enunciated by Duke McCall in 1980 in his discussions with Dale Moody over his public disagreement with the abstract. He wrote to Moody, reminding him of "the freedom given to faculty members across the years in their interpretation of the document." He encouraged him to find a way to fit his understanding of the Bible into his understanding of the article on perseverance. Moody did not, and in an interview with Walter Draughon confided, "Well, I just simply think that Baptists need to shift away from confessionalism to biblical theology, and forget about their Calvinism."[21]

Frank Stagg felt keenly the difficulty posed by Boyce's confessional shadow cast across the faculty conscience. He argued that Boyce "built into Southern Seminary a major flaw which has plagued the seminary from its founding." He did this by establishing the school on a non-negotiable confessional basis. This requirement was "explicit" and "no mere formality." "No professor was to have his private interpretation of the abstract." Boyce erred in at least two ways, so Stagg contended. One was his belief that a confessional document could "insure the truth of the gospel." Boyce failed, according to Stagg, to reckon with his own finitude and fallibility and to realize that "an abstract can protect error as well as truth." Two, the specific strand of theology Boyce placed in the confession was Calvinism, long ago displaced by more critically and philosophically aware methods of searching for Christian truth. "If we now return to Boyce and the Abstract of Principles," Stagg warned, "it will be bondage to a mixture of truth and error, frustrating honest and competent search for truth."[22]

This lamentable decline in both fidelity and common honesty was soon to be called to account by the presidency of R. Albert Mohler Jr. He set the direction for the seminary straight to the past in his inaugural commencement address in 1993 entitled "Don't Just Do Something: Stand There!" He reminded the seminary audience that "the committee protected the integrity of the confession's witness to the doctrines of grace, and as Boyce indicated, spoke dubiously on no essential particular. Indeed, the *Abstract* remains a powerful

21 Dale Moody, "Dale Moody's Doctrine of the Atonement," appendix to Walter Draughon, *A Critical Evaluation of the Diminishing Influence of Calvinism on the Doctrine of Atonement in Representative Southern Baptist Theologians: James Petigru Boyce, Edgar Young Mullins, Walter Thomas Conner, and Dale Moody* (PhD Dissertation, Southwestern Baptist Theological Seminary, 1987), 272.
22 Stagg, "J. P. Boyce Legacy."

testimony to a Baptist theological heritage that is genuinely evangelical, Reformed, biblical, and orthodox."[23] Amazingly, Mohler's vision to recapture Boyce's vision has thus far been an exceptional success. Only with the leverage of the Abstract of Principles and the history surrounding it could such a thing even have been attempted.

23 R. Albert Mohler Jr., "Don't Just Do Something: Stand There!" (A transcript of the Convocation Address, August 31, 1993. Printed at The Southern Baptist Theological Seminary, Louisville), 6.

Part 3

Some Reflections on the Use of Confessions of Faith

8

The Use of Confessions among Southern Baptists[1]

Steve Weaver

A lthough the delegates who gathered in Macon, Georgia, in May of 1845 to form the Southern Baptist Convention did not officially adopt a confession of faith,[2] Baptists in America already had a long history of affirming and using confessions of faith in their churches and associations. Baptist historian Timothy George, founding dean of Beeson Divinity School at Samford University, argues that Baptists have used confessions of faith throughout their history: "The idea that voluntary, conscientious adherence to an explicit doctrinal standard is somehow foreign to the Baptist tradition is a peculiar notion not borne out by careful examination of our heritage."[3] Instead, an examination of Baptist history reveals that many Baptist leaders have promoted the use of confessions of faith for individual churches, associations, and institutions (seminaries and mission boards). These confessions have been used in at least

---

1 An earlier edition of this article was published as "The Use of Confessions of Faith Among Southern Baptists," *Criswell Theological Review* 18, 1 (Fall 2020), 105–120. It is used here with permission.

2 William B. Johnson, who convened the meeting and wrote the constitution, had an aversion to confessions and creeds that was the minority position among Baptists of his day.

3 Timothy George, introduction to *Baptist Confessions, Covenants, and Catechisms*, ed. Timothy and Denise George (Nashville: Broadman & Holman, 1996), 3.

three ways—to summarize essential Biblical beliefs, express unity, and protect from error. This chapter will explore how Baptists in the South utilized confessions in the nineteenth and early twentieth centuries, including a case study from the decade immediately preceding the formation of the Southern Baptist Convention. Before addressing how Southern Baptists have used confessions, it is important to understand the source of the confessions of faith commonly used by Baptists in America in the period under consideration.

From London to Nashville

When the Bryan Station Baptist Church (near Lexington, Kentucky) was constituted in March of 1786, they simply adopted the Philadelphia Confession of Faith "as the best human Composition of the Kind and Contains a summary of the articles of our Faith, particularly we Receive what is generally termed the Doctrine of Grace as they are therein contained."[4] In October of 1798, a committee made up of Ambrose Dudley, Leonard Young, Bartlett Collins, Henry Roach, and John Mason were appointed to revise their church covenant. The revised church covenant was summarily adopted by the church in December of 1798. Along with the rules for church government normally contained in a church covenant, this document also included six expansive points of doctrine which were seen as summaries of the doctrine contained in the Philadelphia Confession of Faith, concluding with the words "which doctrine is contained at large in the Philadelphia Baptist Confession of faith." The Philadelphia Confession of Faith was a direct descendent of the confession of faith popularly referenced by many today as the 1689 Confession, or the Second London Confession of Faith.

The Second London Confession of Faith had first appeared in 1677. In the minutes of the Petty France Church in London, an obscure reference is made in the entry from August 26, 1677, to the printing of a confession of faith.[5] This is commonly believed to be the same confession that was first published in 1677 but later adopted

---

4 Bryan's Station Church Book (unpublished mss), Entry from "Third Saturday of March One thousand seven and Eighty-six."

5 Petty France Church Minute Book, 6. The original confession was published as *A Confession of Faith Put Forth by the Elders and Brethren Of many Congregations of Christians (baptized upon Profession of their Faith) in London and the Country* (London: Benjamin Harris, 1677). Also available in William L. Lumpkin, *Baptist Confessions of Faith* (Valley Forge, PA: Judson, 1969), 241–95.

by the general assembly with messengers from over one hundred churches in 1689 and that would become known as the Second London Confession of Faith.[6] Therefore, it seems apparent that the Petty France co-pastors William Collins and Nehemiah Coxe were the chief architects of this historic document that thirty-seven pastors and ministers would affirm in 1689 in "the Name of and on behalf of the whole Assembly."[7] Further evidence of William Collins's hand in the original writing of the confession is that when the London General Assembly desired a catechism to be drawn up based on the confession, Collins was drafted for the role. The early English Baptist historian Joseph Ivimey stated that Collins's "eminence . . . as a scholar and theologian was very great"[8] and was therefore well suited to serve as one of the primary authors of the confession and to be asked to author the catechism since Coxe had died in 1688.

One may wonder what the Second London Confession of Faith has to do with Southern Baptists in America. After all, it is called the *London* Confession of Faith. To paraphrase Tertullian, "What hath London to do with Nashville?" There is a fascinating account passed down to us that helps explain how the Second London Confession became so influential in early American Baptist life. It was largely mediated through the ministry of Elias Keach (1665–1699).[9] Elias Keach was the son of Benjamin Keach, who was one of the men who had recommended the London Confession at the general assembly in 1689. Elias Keach would become the first minister of the historic Pennepack Baptist Church located in Philadelphia, Pennsylvania. However, when the son of the famous preacher first arrived in North America as a twenty-one-year-old, he was unconverted. Furthermore, he was a charlatan. He pretended to be a preacher in order to take monies from the unsuspecting colonists. Morgan

---

6 See Ivimey, *A History of the English Baptists* (London, 1823), 3:332. For an excellent analysis of the historical and theological context of the Second London Confession, see James M. Renihan, *Edification and Beauty: The Practical Ecclesiology of the English Particular Baptists, 1675–1705*, Studies in Baptist History and Thought (Milton Keynes, England: Paternoster, 2008), 17:17–29.

7 *A Confession of Faith, Put forth by the Elders and Brethren Of many Congregations Of Christians (Baptized upon Profession of their Faith) In London and the Countrey*, 3rd ed. (London: S. Bridge, 1699), front cover verso; Lumpkin, *Baptist Confessions of Faith*, 239.

8 Joseph Ivimey, *A History of the English Baptists* (London: 1814), 3:332.

9 A recent biographical sketch of Elias Keach is Wade Burleson, "Elias Keach (1665–1669)" in *A Noble Company: Essays on Notable Particular Regular Baptists in America*, (Springfield, MO: Particular Baptist Press, 2006), 1:267–281.

Edwards, an early chronicler of Baptist life in America, describes what happened on one occasion when Elias Keach tried to preach like his father.

> He was son of the famous Benj. Keach, of London. Arrived in this country a very wild spark about the year 1686. On his landing he dressed in black and wore a band in order to pass for a minister. The project succeeded to his wishes, and many people resorted to hear the young London divine. He performed well enough till he had advanced pretty far in the sermon. Then, stopping short, looked like a man astonished. The audience concluded he had been seized with a sudden disorder; but, on asking what the matter was, received from him a confession of the imposture with tears in his eyes and much trembling. Great was his distress though it ended happily; for from this time dated he his conversion. He heard there was a Baptist minister at Coldspring in Bucks county between Bristol and Trentown. To him did he repair to seek cousel [sic] and comfort; and by him was he baptized and ordained. The minister's name was Thomas Dungan. From Coldspring Mr. Keach came to Pennepek and settled a church there as before related; and thence travelled through Pennsylvania and the Jersies preaching the gospel in the wilderness with great success, in so much that he may be considered as the chief apostle of the Baptists in these parts of America. He and his family embarked for old England early in the spring of the year 1692, after having resigned the care of the church for a considerable time before to the Rev. John Watts.[10]

Elias Keach was converted by his own preaching. He would subsequently seek and receive baptism from Thomas Dungan of the Cold Spring Baptist Church and was thereafter ordained by him for true gospel ministry. Keach founded the Baptist church at Pennepack and became a means of starting many churches throughout "the wilderness" of Pennsylvania and "the Jersies" (during this period there was an East and West Jersey). So successful was his

---

10 Morgan Edwards, *Materials Towards a History of the Baptists in Pennsylvania Both British and German, Distinguished into Firstday Baptists Keithian Baptists Seventhday Baptists Tuncker Baptists Mennonist Baptist*s, (Philadelpha: Joseph Cruckshank and Isaac Collins, 1770), 1:9–11.

ministry that he became known "as the chief apostle of the Baptists in these parts of America." Clearly, he had an influential ministry in the Middle Colonies.

Keach would eventually return to London in 1692 and continued his pastoral ministry there. In 1697, he teamed up with his father, Benjamin, to produce *A Short Confession of Faith* which summarized the essence of the Second London Confession of Faith, but with some new articles, among which were: "Of Laying on of Hands" and "Of Singing Psalms, etc."[11] Meanwhile back in Pennsylvania, a group of churches that had been associated with Elias Keach, including the Pennepack Baptist Church, came together in 1707 to form the first Baptist association in America—the Philadelphia Baptist Association. In 1742, this association adopted as its confession of faith a revised version of the Second London Confession. The major changes were that two of the articles added by Benjamin and Elias Keach to their 1697 abridgement of the Second London were included, namely, the articles in chapter 31 on the laying of hands upon the baptized and chapter 23 on congregational singing of praises to God. These additions by American Baptists are best explained by recognizing the pervasive influence of Elias Keach upon the churches that became the Philadelphia Association of Baptists.

The Influence of the Philadelphia Confession of Faith

First published in 1743, the Philadelphia Confession went through several reprintings over the years. It was adopted by a variety of churches and associations. A list of these associations can be found in William L. Lumpkin's *Baptist Confessions of Faith*.[12] Lumpkin labeled the Philadelphia Confession as "perhaps the most influential of all confessions" in the South.[13] Even the Virginia Separate Baptists adopted the Philadelphia Confession. In their book *Baptists and the Bible*, Russ Bush and Tom Nettles state:

> In 1783, even the Separate General Association of Virginia agreed to adopt the *Philadelphia Confession*. Separate Baptists

---

11 *A Short Confession of Faith: Containing the Substance of all the Fundamental Articles of the Larger Confession Put Forth by the Elders of the Baptized Churches, Owning Personal Election and Final Perseverance* (London, 1697). There were other additions as well, but these two additions are of importance to demonstrate Elias Keach's influence upon American Baptists.

12 Lumpkin, *Baptist Confessions of Faith*, 352–53.

13 Lumpkin, 352.

had opposed written confessions, but they did accept this one along with an additional statement that such formal acceptance did not bind every Baptist to strict observance of every detail, nor should anyone ever think that the confession stood above or even equal to Scripture itself. They did say, however, that they agreed that this confession was "the best composition of the kind now extant" (Lumpkin, 353).[14]

This is a remarkable statement, given the Separate Baptists aversion to adopting confessions of faith. The fact that they adopted this confession demonstrates the pervasive influence of the theology of the Second London Confession mediated through the Philadelphia Confession as far south as Virginia by 1783. Interestingly, the same confession had already been adopted by the Regular Baptist Charleston Association in 1767 and nicknamed the Charleston Confession of Faith. Baptists in the South were clearly very familiar with this confession well before the formation of the Southern Baptist Convention in 1845.

Three Ways Baptists Utilized Confessions in the Nineteenth and Twentieth Centuries

Having seen how a historic Baptist confession of faith from London gained prominence in America, it remains to be seen how confessions were utilized by Baptists in the South in the nineteenth and early twentieth centuries. Baptist leaders in the nineteenth and early twentieth centuries promoted the use of confessions of faith as summaries of essential Biblical beliefs, expressions of unity, and protection from error. Confessions of faith summarized the essential teachings of Scripture in a topical manner. Confessions of faith expressed unity among those who were truly one in the truth. Confessions of faith protected churches and institutions from those who did not adhere to those doctrines commonly held by Baptists.

A Summary of Essential Biblical Beliefs

Baptists have never exalted a confession of faith above Scripture. Confessions of faith were used to summarize what Baptists believed

---

14 L. Russ Bush and Thomas J. Nettles, *Baptists and the Bible* (Nashville: Broadman & Holman, 1999), 344–45.

the Scriptures taught. Silas Mercer Noel, moderator of the Franklin Baptist Association in Kentucky, wrote a circular letter in 1826 that was sent to all the churches in his association. In this letter, Noel defended the historic Baptist use of confessions as a summary of Biblical teaching: "By a creed we mean an epitome, or summary exhibition of what the Scriptures teach."[15] Noel also notes that when one affirms a confession of faith "he simply declares by solemn act how he understands the Bible, in other words, what doctrines he considers it as containing."[16]

A little over twenty years later, in 1849, J. L. Reynolds wrote *Church Polity* in which he argued that a confession or creed "is a digest of the whole" of Scripture.[17] Reynolds continued by stating: "A creed is not intended to supersede the word of God, as the standard of faith and practice; for it derives its validity and authority solely from its agreement with that word. It is a standard or rule of faith only in a secondary sense, and only to those who adopt it as the exponent of their views. It does not create, it simply expresses the truth; and is to be viewed, not in the light of an authority but a testimony."[18]

Confessions were only seen as authoritative to the degree that they accurately reflected the teaching of Scripture. The ultimate allegiance of Baptists was to the Word of God, but they saw confessions as helpful summaries of biblical truth.

B. H. Carroll, founding president of Southwestern Baptist Theological Seminary, defended the use of creeds and confessions of faith in his treatise "Creeds and Confessions of Faith." There he argued that everyone has a creed because a creed merely summarizes what you believe: "There never was a man in the world without a creed. What is a creed? A creed is what you believe. What is a confession? It is a declaration of what you believe. That declaration may be oral or it may be committed to writing, but the creed is there either

---

15 S. M. Noel, "Circular Letter on Confessions of Faith," in *Treasures from the Baptist Heritage*, eds. Timothy and Denise George (Nashville: Broadman & Holman, 1996), 140.

16 Noel, "Circular Letter," 144.

17 J. L. Reynolds, "Church Polity or the Kingdom of Christ," in *Polity: Biblical Arguments on How to Conduct Church Life*, ed. Mark Dever (Washington, DC: Center for Church Reform, 2001), 337.

18 Reynolds, "Church Polity," 337.

expressed or implied."[19] Since confessions of faith are declarations of
what one believes, anyone who believes anything has one; the only
difference is whether someone has taken the care to write it down.

Another president of a Baptist seminary who defended the use of
confessions in Baptist life was E. Y. Mullins. Mullins served as the
fourth president of The Southern Baptist Theological Seminary at
the same time Carroll was serving as the president of Southwestern
at the beginning of the twentieth century.[20] Mullins, in his essay
"Baptists and Creeds" (probably written between 1920 and 1925),
defended confessions of faith as our attempt to summarize New
Testament teaching: "The New Testament, of course, is our final
standard and authority. Our confessions are simply our effort to
state what the New Testament teaches. They are all to be tested and
estimated according to the New Testament."[21]

An Expression of Unity

Baptists not only viewed their confessions as summaries of Scripture's teachings but they also used them in practical ways. One way
confessions of faith were used by Baptists was to show where true
unity existed. S. M. Noel, in his "Circular Letter," asked a series of
rhetorical questions to demonstrate the necessity of a confession of
faith to "preserve the unity":

> Are we to admit members into the church and into office,
> are we to license and ordain preachers without enquiring
> for their creed? Shall we ask them no question in regard to
> principles or doctrines? Shall we receive license and ordain
> candidates, upon a general profession of faith in Christ
> requiring of them this only, that they agree to take the Bible
> for their guide? Can we do this and still expect to preserve
> the unity, purity and peace of the church?[22]

The obvious answer to Noel's questions is no. Confessions of faith
are necessary to "preserve the unity, purity and peace of the church."

19 B. H. Carroll, "Creeds and Confessions of Faith," in *Baptists and their Doctrines*,
eds. Timothy and Denise George (Nashville: Broadman & Holman, 1995), 81.
20 Mullins served as the president for Southern from 1899 until his death in
1928. Carroll served a much shorter stint at Southwestern, serving as the president
from its formation in 1908 until his death in 1914.
21 E. Y. Mullins, "Baptists and Creeds," in *The Axioms of Religion*, eds. Timothy
and Denise George (Nashville: Broadman & Holman, 1997), 187.
22 Noel, "Circular Letter," 140.

J. L. Reynolds, in his *Church Polity*, also acknowledged that Christian unity requires a clear summary statement of Christian doctrine. Reynolds argues that it is appropriate to have a written confession of faith to show agreement about the nature of Christianity:

> The right of a Church to frame for itself a summary of Christian doctrine is evident from the nature of its organization. If "two cannot walk together except they be agreed," much less can professors of Christianity constitute a harmonious and efficient body, unless they concur in their views of what Christianity is. If it be proper for them to have correct views, it is proper to express them; and if it be proper to express them orally, it is equally so to express them in a written form. Again, each member of a church is bound to bear his testimony to the truth.[23]

Even more forceful are the following words of Reynolds concerning the nature of true Christian union: "Real uniformity can exist only among those who 'all speak the same thing, and are perfectly joined together in the same mind and in the same judgment.' 1 Cor. 1:10. A union of contradictions is an impossibility. Agreement in sentiment is the bond of Christian union."[24]

E. Y. Mullins described the limits of cooperation as the extent to which we agree doctrinally: "Practical cooperation is, after all, a fine test of doctrinal fellowship, and doctrinal fellowship is a fine test of the limits of practical cooperation."[25] Then, to be sure he was understood, Mullins adds the following example: "If a man holds consistently the Unitarian view of Christ's person, he cannot long cooperate with those who hold the deity of Christ."[26] Agreement upon the great doctrines of the faith is essential to unity, fellowship and cooperation. Confessions of faith provide the instrumentality to express this unity.

A Protection from False Teaching

Baptists used confessions of faith in another practical way. Confessions were not only used as a means of expressing unity but also

---

23 Reynolds, "Church Polity," 337.
24 Reynolds, 342.
25 Mullins, "Baptists and Creeds," 190.
26 Mullins, "Baptists and Creeds," 190–191.

to protect against error creeping into their churches or institutions. When James P. Boyce gave his inaugural address at Furman University, he called for "Three Changes in Theological Institutions." One of these changes involved confessional integrity, which required professors to sign a doctrinal statement to which they agreed to teach in accordance. In his address at Furman, Boyce stated the responsibility of that institution's trustees to preserve doctrinal truth by use of a confession of faith:

> It seems to me, gentlemen, that you owe this to yourselves, to your professors, and to the denomination at large; to yourselves, because your position as trustees makes you responsible for the doctrinal opinions of your professors, and the whole history of creeds has proved the difficulty without them of convicting errorists or perversion of the Word of God – to your professors, that their doctrinal sentiments may be known and approved by all, that no charges of heresy may be brought against them; that none shall whisper of peculiar notions which they hold, but that in refutation of all charges they may point to this formulary as one which they hold "ex amino," and teach in its true import – and to the denomination at large, that they may know in what truths the rising ministry are instructed, may exercise full sympathy with the necessities of the institution, and look with confidence and affection to the pastors who come forth from it.[27]

Boyce understood creeds to be necessary to fulfill the trustee's responsibility to their denomination in whose place they acted. Without a confession of faith, protection against false teaching would be impossible.

E. Y. Mullins, who followed Boyce as the fourth president of the seminary that he would help found, also saw the need of confessions of faith to protect the beliefs held by Baptists. Mullins argues that confessions do not violate an individual's rights—a common charge against those who utilize confessions—but rather preserve the right of the group:

> Baptists have always insisted upon their right to declare their beliefs in a definite, formal way, and to protect themselves

27 James P. Boyce, "Three Changes in Theological Institutions," in *Treasures from the Baptist Heritage*, ed. Timothy and Denise George (Nashville: Broadman & Holman, 1996), 129.

by refusing to support men in important places as teachers and preachers who do not agree with them. This group of self-protection is as sacred as any individual right. If a group of men known as Baptists consider themselves trustees of certain great truths, they have an inalienable right to conserve and propagate those truths unmolested by others inside the denomination who oppose those truths. The latter have an equal right to unite with another group agreeing with them. But they have no right to attempt to make of the Baptist denomination a freelance club.[28]

In other words, the individual has freedom but voluntarily surrenders that freedom when that individual unites with others based on shared convictions. The individual does not have the right to alter the doctrinal commitments of the group. Confessions of faith draw the boundary lines that prevent Baptists from merely being a freelance club.

Another interesting example of how the leaders of Southern Baptist entities utilized confessions of faith in their entities is James F. Love, who served as executive secretary of the Foreign Mission Board from 1914 to 1928. Like Boyce and Mullins, Love used a confessional statement to protect his entity from doctrinal deviation. Love wrote in the July 8, 1920, edition of *The Religious Herald* concerning the mission board's recently adopted statement of belief. This statement was adopted during the Board's annual meeting in June 1919.[29] Love described the reason for the adoption of this doctrinal statement as a stewardship to Southern Baptists:

> The Foreign Mission Board is . . . appointed to secure the proclamation of a Christian message. The men who compose it will not consent that young and immature people . . . shall revise the historic and generally accepted faith of Southern Baptists and set up for this message some bit of rationalism or irrationalism with which some teacher or school has inoculated them. The denomination chooses the Board and makes it responsible for these matters and it will not delegate its responsibility.[30]

---

28 Mullins, "Baptists and Creeds," 189–190.
29 J. F. Love, "The Statement of Belief by the Foreign Mission Board," *The Religious Herald* (July 8, 1920), 7.
30 Love, 15.

Southern Baptists used Confessions to ensure that they were not financially supporting teachers in their seminaries or missionaries in the field whom they could not also support theologically.

Baptist leaders in the nineteenth and early twentieth centuries promoted the use of confessions of faith as summaries of essential biblical beliefs, expressions of unity, and protection from error. One episode from Baptist history from the two decades preceding the formation of the Southern Baptist Convention serves to demonstrate the importance of confessions of faith for all three of these uses.

A Test Case in Baptist History: Silas Mercer Noel and the Campbellite Controversy

Silas Mercer Noel wrote his circular letters cited above in the contest of the Campbellite Controversy. This controversy centered around the teaching of Alexander Campbell (1788–1866). Campbell had his introduction to Kentucky in a debate with the Presbyterian minister W. L. McCalla held in Washington, Kentucky, in the Fall of 1823.[31] Campbell was an immediate hero to the pioneer-minded Baptists in Kentucky, due in large part to his raw biblicism and skill in dismantling the paedobaptist arguments. His teaching spread rapidly through his itinerant preaching ministry and his monthly periodicals—the *Christian Baptist* (1823–1830) and *Millennial Harbinger* (1830–1870).[32]

In the 1826 circular letter, written while the pastor of First Baptist Church of Frankfort, Kentucky, Noel argued for the use of confessions of faith against the Campbellite cry of "No creed but the Bible." Specifically, the purpose of the letter was to address the question "Is it lawful and expedient, to adhere to a Creed, in the admission of members into the fellowship of the Church, and particularly in the admission of candidates into office?" Noel answers this question in the affirmative. Of course, as a Baptist, Noel rejected creeds imposed

---

31   Alexander Campbell, *A Debate on Christian Baptism: Between the Rev. W. L. MacCalla, a Presbyterian Teacher, and Alexander Campbell, Held at Washington, Ky. Commencing on the 15th and Terminating on the 21st Oct. 1823, in the Presence of a Very Numerous and Respectable Congregation* (Buffaloe, VA: Campbell & Sala, 1824).

32   Of course, the *Millennial Harbinger* continued to be published four years after Campbell's death. These magazines had a wide circulation on the frontier and were inestimably influential.

on individuals by civil government. However, "those formed by voluntary Associations of Christians, enforced by no higher penalty, or sanction, than exclusion from membership in the society are not only lawful, but necessary, in the present state of the religious world." As noted above, Noel defined a creed as "an epitome, or summary exhibition of what the Scriptures teach." Noel argued that to fail to ask what a candidate for church membership or office believes is to invite division into the church. "Can we do this, and still expect to preserve the unity, purity and peace, of the Church?" Noel acknowledged that no creed is infallible. "Our confessions are human productions, they may all require revision, and be susceptible of amendment; but to erase them from our books, our memory and our practice, is to make a tremendous leap, a leap into chaos; into the awful vortex of Unitarianism." Noel further argued that a creed, contrary to the charge of some, does not supplant the authority of Scripture; it "does public homage to it." The one who affirms a creed is simply declaring "by a solemn act, how he understands the Bible, in other words, what doctrines he considers it as containing."[33] Noel was not afraid to use strong language to declare exactly what doctrines he believed the Scripture contains:

> While the Socinian professes to believe the Bible, and to understand it as teaching the mere humanity of Christ; while the Arian professes to receive the same Bible, and to find in it the Savior represented as the most exalted of all creatures, but still a creature; while the Pelagian and Semi-Pelagian, make similar profession of their general belief in the Scriptures, and interpret them as teaching a doctrine far more favorable to human nature, and far less honoring to the grace of God, than they appear to me really to teach. I beg the privilege of declaring FOR MYSELF, that while I believe with all my heart, that the Bible is the word of God, the only perfect rule of faith and manners, and the only ultimate test in all controversies; it plainly teaches as I read and believe, the deplorable and total depravity of human nature; the essential divinity of the Savior; a trinity of persons in

---

33   *Minutes of the Franklin Association of Baptists, Held at Buffaloe Lick, Shelby County, on the First Friday and Saturday in August, 1826* (Bloomfield, KY: W. H. Holmes, 1826), 6–12. Also published as S. M. Noel, "Circular Letter on Confessions of Faith," in *Treasures from the Baptist Heritage*, ed. Timothy and Denise George (Nashville: Broadman & Holman, 1996), 139–148.

the Godhead; justification by the imputed righteousness of Christ; and regeneration and sanctification by the Holy Spirit as indispensable to prepare the soul for heaven. These I believe to be the radical truths which God hath revealed in his word, and while they are denied by some, and frettered [*sic*] away, or perverted by others, who profess to believe that blessed word, I am verily persuaded, they are the fundamental principles, of the plan of Salvation.[34]

This letter was considered by many to be unanswerable from the Campbellite point of view. Of course, Alexander Campbell did respond in the pages of the August 6, 1827, issue of the *Christian Baptist*, contesting both Noel's methodology and definition of a creed.[35] Apparently the attacks on the letter brought such attention to it that it had gone through three printings by the time of the printing of the 1827 minutes and was still in high demand. No response to Campbell's response was given. "It carries within itself its own defence. It needs no other. Wherever it appears, the garbled extracts and base misrepresentations of its enemies are perfectly harmless."[36] The first blow against Campbellism had been delivered.

At the 1829 association meeting of the association held at the Forks of Elkhorn meetinghouse on September 19–21, Noel and the other messengers from the Frankfort church requested that the report of the Beaver Baptist Association from their August meeting be included in the minutes of the Franklin Association.[37] The letter is a strong indictment of the teachings of the Campbellites and its divisive and destructive work in the Mahoning Association. Frank Masters observed that "Alexander Campbell remained in complete control of the churches in the Mahoning Association until 1829."[38]

---

34 *Minutes of the Franklin Association of Baptists* (1826), 9.

35 *Christian Baptist* (August 6, 1827), 5.1. The review of Noel's circular letter is in two parts and there are other letters and responses in the issue responding to various arguments for creeds.

36 *Minutes of the Thirteenth Anniversary of the Franklin Association of Baptists, Held at Bethel Meeting House, Franklin County, Ken. on the First Saturday in August 1827* (Frankfort, KY: Amos Kendall and Company, 1827), verso of front cover.

37 The Beaver Baptist Association was made up of churches in both Ohio and Pennsylvania. For a history of the first fifty years of the association, see Abner G. Kirk, *History of the Churches of the Beaver Baptist Association, from 1809 to 1860* (Pittsburgh, PA: W. S. Haven, 1860).

38 Frank M. Masters, *A History of Baptists in Kentucky* (Louisville, KY: Kentucky Baptist Historical Society, 1953), 214.

The report asserts that those churches that had embraced the teaching of Alexander Campbell "now disbelieve and deny many of the doctrines of the Holy Scriptures, on which they were constituted." Specifically, these churches now believe the following:

> They contend that there is no promise of salvation without baptism—that it should be administered to all that say that they believe that Jesus Christ is the Son of God, without examination on any other point,—that there is no direct operation of the Holy Spirit on the mind prior to baptism— that baptism procures the remission of sins, and the gift of the Holy Ghost,—that the Scriptures are the only evidence of interest in Christ,—that obedience places it in God's power to elect to salvation,—that no creed is necessary for the church but the Scriptures as they stand,—and that all baptized persons have a right to administer that ordinance.[39]

The report concludes by declaring that its purpose was "to warn our brethren in other parts against them: believing that they have departed from the faith and order of the Gospel Church." The association took no further action in regard to those who had embraced Campbell's teaching in their own midst. That action would come the following year at a monumental meeting held in Frankfort.

In July of 1830, a special session of the Franklin Association was called to deal with the growing threat of Campbellism. J. H. Spencer called this meeting "probably the most important association ever held in Kentucky."[40] The goal of the meeting was "to define Campbellism," which had heretofore been difficult given "the ingenious ambiguity of Mr. Campbell's writings."[41] In the circular letter, written by Noel, the teaching of Alexander Campbell was systematically put together in thirty-nine articles of faith compiled from his own writings in the *Christian Baptist* and the *Millennial Harbinger*.[42]

---

39 *Minutes of the Franklin Baptist Association, Held at the Forks of Elkhorn Meeting-House. Franklin County, Kentucky. On the 19th, 20th, & 21st Days of September 1829* (Frankfort, KY: O'B. Pettit, 1829), 5.

40 J. H. Spencer, *A History of Kentucky Baptists. From 1769 to 1885* (For the Author, 1886), 1:624. Frank Masters concurred, "This was probably the most important called session of any association ever held in Kentucky." Masters, *A History of Baptists in Kentucky*, 217.

41 Spencer, *A History of Kentucky Baptists*, 1:624.

42 *Minutes of the Franklin Association of Baptists, Convened in Frankfort, Kentucky, on the Second Friday Saturday in July, 1830* (Frankfort, KY: A. G. Hodges, 1830), 5–15. Also published in abbreviated form as "Report and Warning about Campbel-

Noel ably demonstrates that, although Campbellites said they were being persecuted for not following a man-made confession of faith, it was "not so much their objection to this book, but rather *our* objections to *their* Confession of Faith, that makes the difference."[43] Noel helpfully provided citations for the quotations that he used from Campbell's publications, allowing interested readers to check out Campbell's teaching for themselves in their original context.

Alexander Campbell had indicated in a letter published in the *Christian Baptist* to a correspondent from Missouri that he "did intend to continue in connection with this people [Baptists] so long as they will permit me to say what I believe; to teach what I am assured of, and to censure what is amiss in their views or practices."[44] With the circulation of Noel's 1830 letter outlining the beliefs of Campbell, Baptists could no longer tolerate this teaching in their midst. When the Franklin Association met later in the year at their regular meeting on September 17–18 at the meetinghouse of the South Benson Church, they acted decisively by unanimously responding to a request from Noel's church "in regard to communing with those who have departed from original principles" by asserting,

> We wish it to be distinctly understood, that all persons aiming to prostrate our constitutions, and the union, by declaiming against creeds, or by sapping and mining the pillars of our constitutions, by innovations on our faith, customs and usages, ought to find no place in our pulpits, or at our communion tables. Our members should plainly understand, that by approaching any table set by those people to commune, they would thereby forfeit the fellowship of all regular or united Baptist churches.[45]

In addition to this general statement of separation, the association also took the action of specifically certifying that Jacob Creath Sr. (1777–1854) and Jacob Creath Jr. (1799–1886) had been "cut off

lism, 1830," in *Readings in Baptist History: Four Centuries of Selected Documents*, ed. Joseph Early Jr. (Nashville: B&H Academic, 2008), 95–99.

43   *Minutes of the Franklin Association of Baptists* (1830), 6.

44   Robert Richardson, *Memoirs of Alexander Campbell, Embracing A View of the Origin, Progress and Principles of the Religious Reformation Which He Advocated* (Cincinnati: R. & W. Carroll & Co., 1872), 2:135.

45   *Minutes of the Sixteenth Anniversary of the Franklin Association of Baptists, Held at the South Benson Meeting House, Franklin County, Ken. on the 17th and 18th Days of September, 1830* (Frankfort, KY: A. G. Hodges, 1830), 2–3.

from the General Union of Baptists by the competent tribunal"[46] and that Josephus Hewitt was suspended. Masters describes the effect of Noel's circular letter upon the wider Baptist fellowship in Kentucky: "The sending out of this wonderful document, adopted by the called session of the Franklin Association, stirred the churches and associations throughout Kentucky, and in less than six months almost a dozen associations took action, declaring their separation from all the Reformed forces."[47]

The year that this letter was published, Campbell began to pull away from the Baptists and unite his churches with Barton Stone's group of churches.[48] By defending Baptists' use of confessions of faith and then utilizing them, Noel helped the Baptists, not only of the Franklin Association, but all across Kentucky, to use their summaries of biblical teaching to express unity among those in true fellowship together and to reject the error introduced into Baptist life by Alexander Campbell.

Conclusion

Throughout the nineteenth and early twentieth centuries, Baptists in the South used confessions of faith to summarize the essential teachings of Scripture in a topical manner. Baptists used confessions of faith to express unity among those who were truly one in the truth. Baptists used confessions of faith to protect their churches and institutions from those who did not adhere to those doctrines commonly held by Baptists. Southern Baptists would go on in the twentieth century to adopt three iterations of a confession of faith known as the Baptist Faith and Message (1925, 1963, and 2000). The purpose of each was to summarize the teaching of Scripture, to express unity among their churches and institutions, and to protect against error. Just as Noel's assertion of Baptist confessionalism came at a time

46 *Minutes of the Sixteenth Anniversary of the Franklin Association of Baptists* (1830), 4. This uncle and nephew were both prominent Baptist preachers before embracing the Campbellite views. The uncle was distinguished from his nephew by the use of "senior" for the former and "junior" for the latter. For a biographical sketch of each, see P. Donan, *Memoir of Jacob Creath, Jr.: to which is Appended the Biography of Elder Jacob Creath, Sr.* (Cincinnati, OH: Chase & Hall, 1877).

47 Masters, *A History of Baptists in Kentucky*, 218.

48 Richard C. Traylor, *Born of Water & Spirit: The Baptist Impulse in Kentucky, 1776–1860* (Knoxville, TN: The University of Tennessee Press, 2015), 114. For a history of the Stone-Campbell movement, see William T. Moore, *A Comprehensive History of the Disciples of Christ* (Grand Rapids: Fleming H. Revell, 1909).

of doctrinal controversy, all three versions of the Baptist Faith and
Message were adopted in the face of doctrinal controversy. Baptists
responded to the threat of modernism in 1925, to the threat of higher
criticism in 1963, and to the threat of open theism, while also clos-
ing some loopholes on biblical inerrancy, in 2000. Southern Baptists continue to use their confession of faith as a summary of biblical
teaching, an expression of unity, and a protection against error. They
do this because of their commitment to the faithful proclamation of
the gospel to all peoples. To state it another way, the commitment
of Southern Baptists to the Great Commission demands their use of
confessions of faith to ensure the gospel message is preserved and
transmitted faithfully. As J. F. Love noted in his defense of the Foreign Mission Board's Statement of Belief in 1919,

> Southern Baptists have a message for a lost world, or they
> ought to abandon altogether this whole scheme of foreign
> missions. . . . The things contained in this **Statement** are
> the very things which we preach from Sabbath to Sabbath,
> which we use in calling sinners to repentance, which proba-
> bly every church in the South has adopted in its confession
> of faith, which every association of the nearly one thousand
> in the South requires of any church whose messengers apply
> for seats in the association, and which our two seminaries
> require, and much more besides, of every professor that
> holds a chair in them. This **Statement** is not, therefore,
> something new, but that which is new and revolutionary is
> criticism of such a statement of Baptist faith.[49]

49 Love, "The Statement of Belief," 15.

9

Confessional Subscription: Its Terms and Types

Robert Gonzales Jr.

W E NORMALLY ASSOCIATE THE TERM "subscription" with signing up to receive certain periodicals, journals, or magazines to which we have "subscribed." In ecclesiastical parlance, however, the term "subscription" or "subscribe" refers to one's affirmation of, agreement with, and commitment to a fixed body of doctrines or articles of faith that are officially representative of a local church's or denomination's beliefs. The issue of subscription is important for churches or ecclesiastical bodies that are self-consciously "confessional," especially as it relates to *the level of commitment* these institutions expect of their officers and teachers. In the space below, we will examine some of the key terminology associated with confessional subscription. Then we will attempt to provide a survey of the major types (or levels) of confessional subscription that have been used by churches and denominations.

The Main Terms Associated with Subscription

Before we survey the various types of subscription that have been or are currently practiced, we need to be conversant with terminology associated with confessional subscription.

Quia vs. Quatenus

These are two Latin terms. The first, *quia*, means "because"; the second, *quatenus*, means "insofar as." Thus, a *quia*-subscription entails subscribing to a confession *because* it is biblical, whereas a *quatenus*-subscription entails subscribing to a confession *insofar as* it is biblical. Traditionally, the first is associated with tighter views of subscription and the second with looser views. However, as we will note, there are some forms or shades of subscription that actually involve a combination of the two ideas.

Ex animo or "Good Faith"

The Latin phrase *ex animo* refers to the attitude and motive of the one subscribing to the creed. It basically denotes "from the heart" or the idea of "sincere." A similar Latin phrase, *bona fide*, translated, "good faith," is also employed to convey this idea. In other words, when a person subscribes to a creed or confession *ex animo* or in "good faith," he is affirming belief in and commitment to that particular statement of faith *sincerely* and *without any intention to deceive others*.

Scruples or Exceptions

Mental reservations about or objections to certain words, phrases, or doctrines in a given creed or confession are called "scruples" or, more commonly today, "exceptions." Some forms of subscription require the subscriber or candidate to identify his exceptions to words or statements in a confession. When a person takes exception to a term or a doctrine, he is not necessarily asserting that the terminology or doctrine is unbiblical. Exceptions can also mean that the word(s) or statement is a matter of opinion that should not be elevated to the level of a public confession. An exception simply implies that the statement is *not confessed*. It is not necessarily a "no vote." It may be viewed, rather, as an "abstention" on that particular statement.

Animus Imponentis

This Latin phrase means "the intention of the mind or heart." But in this case, the subscriber's attitude and motive are not in view. *Animus imponentis* has reference, rather, to the intention and expectations of the church or denomination. Applied to confessional subscription, it refers to *the imposing body's understanding of and intention behind its use of its confession*.[1] For example, in 1566 the Kirk (Church) of Scotland officially endorsed the Second Helvetic Confession, which had been drafted and published in Switzerland. However, the Scottish Kirk officially took exception to the Second Helvetic's allowance of certain Christian festivals.[2] Apparently, the Scots had a narrower understanding of the Regulative Principle of Worship. So they added a marginal note at the point where mention is made of these special Christian holy days.[3] In doing so, they were exercising the right to determine how they, as a national church, wanted to use that particular confession.

A modern example of *animus imponentis* can be seen in "A Position Paper Concerning the Regulative Principle of Worship" (RPW) of the Association of Reformed Baptist Churches of America (ARBCA).[4] One of the primary purposes of the paper is to clarify what the Second London Confession teaches on the topic of corporate worship. But the paper also serves to explain to the member churches how the association understands and intends to apply the confession's teaching with reference to issues like exclusive psalmody, musical instrumentation, and special music. In this case, ARBCA decides to take a slightly looser view of the RPW than that which their Puritan and Particular Baptist forefathers would have endorsed.[5]

---

1 For an exposition of the concept of animus imponentis as applied to confessional subscription, see Alan Strange's lecture "Animus Imponentis: Hits and Myths," which was delivered at the 2009 Animus Imponentis Conference of the Presbytery of Northern California and Nevada. The audio file, transcript, and lecture notes can be accessed here: http://www.pncnopc.org/audio/audio-presbytery/2009-animus-imponentis-conference (accessed August 31, 2020).

2 See *The Creeds of Christendom*, 6th ed, ed. Philip Schaff and David S. Schaff (1931; reprint, Grand Rapids: Baker Book House, 1990), 3:298.

3 J. Ligon Duncan III, "Owning the Confession: Subscription in the Scottish Presbyterian Tradition," *The Practice of Confessional Subscription* [hereafter, *PCS*], ed. David W. Hall (Oak Ridge, TN: Covenant Foundation, 1997), 79. See also Peter Lillback who notes that this is "the first instance of any Reformed Church taking an exception to a subscribed confession. "Confessional Subscription Among Sixteenth Century Reformers," *PCS*, 42.

4 A PDF of the position paper is available online here: https://www.csmedia1.com/arbca.com/regulative-principle.pdf (accessed August 31, 2020).

5 Many of the Puritans endorsed exclusive psalmody and viewed "uninspired" hymns as inappropriate for public worship. Moreover, nearly all the Puritans and Particular Baptists would have opposed the use of musical instruments in worship. Some Particular Baptists even went so far as to exclude congregational singing from

What Is a "Doctrine"?

In discussions and debates on confessional subscription, one frequently finds the term "doctrine" being used, particularly with respect to what *kind* of exceptions may or may not be allowed. Some types of subscription allow the minister or candidate to take exception to words or phrases but not to doctrines, whereas other types of subscription allow for doctrinal exceptions as well. Sometimes, parties fail to define precisely and clearly what is meant by a "doctrine." This can cloud the discussion and hinder the debate. Thankfully, Morton Smith and William Barker agreed in a 2005 public debate on the following definition: "Every declaratory statement states something true or false. And every declaratory statement in the [Westminster] Standards is either one doctrine or several doctrines."[6]

The reader should note that the definition above does not limit a "doctrine" to the overall doctrinal theme of a given chapter, article, section, or paragraph within the confession. Rather, a doctrine, more generally defined, is a declaration or proposition that affirms something as true or false. Hence, we can say, for example, the doctrine of the trinity in the Westminster Confession (2.3) consists of several doctrinal declarations or propositions. This definition of a "doctrine" is important since a proponent of full subscription (Smith), which disallows doctrinal exceptions, and an advocate of

---

worship. Joel Beeke argues that exclusive psalmody was the prevalent view among the Puritans. "Psalm Singing in Calvin and the Puritans," *Sing a New Song: Recovering Psalm Singing for the Twenty-First Century* (Grand Rapids: Reformation Heritage Books, 2010), 16–40. R. Scott Clark makes a similar case pointing to the Westminster Assembly's "Directory for Public Worship," which asserts, "It is the duty of Christians to praise God publicly, by singing of psalms together in the congregation, and also privately in the family." *Recovering the Reformed Confession: Our Theology, Piety, and Practice* (Phillipsburg: Presbyterian and Reformed, 2008), 249–51. For a survey on the Puritans' view of musical instruments in public worship, see John Price, *Old Light on New Worship: Musical Instruments and the Worship of God, a Theological, Historical, and Psychological Study* (Avinger, TX: Simpson, 2005). James Renihan documents the debate among Particular Baptists over the lawfulness of congregational singing in his dissertation "The Practical Ecclesiology of the English Particular Baptists, 1675–1705" (PhD diss.; Trinity Evangelical Divinity School, 1997), 298–310.

6   This definition was actually proposed by someone in the audience seeking clarification of Smith's position. It occurs toward the end of the "Confessional Subscription Debate," about 29 minutes into part two. The two-part audio debate can be accessed here: https://www.sermonaudio.com/sermoninfo.asp?sid=12505102413 (accessed August 31, 2020).

system subscription (Barker), which allows for limited doctrinal exceptions, mutually endorsed it. It is the definition we will employ when making distinctions between the major types of confessional subscription below.

The Basic Types (or Levels) of Subscription

Most churches and denominations require a higher level of commitment to their doctrinal standards from their leaders and teachers than they expect from their members.[7] Historically, there have also been different degrees or levels of subscription expected of church officers, teachers, or candidates for the ministry. On the one hand, some advocate modes of subscription that allow for a looser or more flexible commitment to the local church's or denomination's official creedal statements. On the other hand, others advocate a mode of subscription that requires complete or nearly complete agreement with the doctrinal standards in view. Those who support looser forms of subscription often express a concern to protect the subscriber's liberty of conscience and the primacy of Scripture's authority. Those who support tighter forms of subscription are concerned to protect the church from too much doctrinal latitude that could open the door to serious theological error.

Before I attempt to distinguish the types of subscription, I need to preface my taxonomy with some qualifications and a disclaimer. First, a title or description assigned to a particular position may originate from those who oppose it, not from those who endorse it. Therefore, some common titles for this or that kind of subscription might seem pejorative. Second, some titles have a kind of "official status" (i.e., a church or denomination has officially adopted the nomenclature). But other titles for this or that kind of subscription are not necessarily official titles. They are, rather, non-official attempts to describe the kind of subscription in view. Third, advocates or the opponents of

---

7 Some, like R. Scott Clark, believe that the same level of commitment to the church's confessional standards should be expected of the clergy and the laity. "It is not obvious," Clark observes, "that establishing two levels of subscription, one for laity and another for ordained officers, is either biblical or consistent with the Reformation. . . . If the Reformed confession defines what it is to be Reformed, then establishing two distinct relations to the same constitutional document would seem to be a recipe for confusion and effectively two churches within one." *Recovering the Reformed Confession*, 179. I will provide a critique of Clark's position in the next chapter.

a given type of subscription may define it differently and at times seem to equivocate (i.e., give a definition of it in one place that is narrower or broader than they give in another place). Thus, by way of disclaimer, my distinctions below will entail generalizations to some degree.

With the clarifications and disclaimer aside, let us survey the primary types of confessional subscription. I will begin with the tighter forms of subscription first and move toward the looser forms since this is generally the direction creedal subscription has moved historically.

Absolute Subscription

Absolute subscription requires the individual to subscribe to the entire creed or confession *ex animo* and without any exceptions to wording, phrases, or doctrines. Lutherans, Dutch Reformed, and Scottish Presbyterians adopted and practiced this form of subscription in the sixteenth and seventeenth centuries. Accordingly, one might legitimately refer to it as the classical Protestant view of subscription.[8] For example, the Dutch Reformed Classis of Alkmaar adopted the following subscription formula in 1608:

---

8 Summarizing confessional subscription of the sixteenth century, Peter Lillbeck remarks, "First, all confessional churches insisted that Holy Scripture was over confession. Second, all confessional churches believed that the Scriptures themselves compelled them to confess their faith in the pure truths of Holy Scripture. Third, without obvious exception, the intent of subscription to the confession was to be complete, because the confession was deemed to be the very teaching of Scripture. Thus, a *quia*-subscription rather than a *quatenus*-subscription was expected. . . . Fourth, nevertheless, such a high view of subscription was not possible in a universal sense.... Fifth, the sixteenth century solution to this problem of reaching confessional agreement by subscription in the face of disagreements included writing a more precise confession or catechism, and then demanding a *quia*-subscription that was enforced by ecclesiastical discipline. But even those who had subscribed to the same Confessional Consensus, found that they could not always perfectly agree as brothers as in the case of Calvin's confession on predestination in relationship with the Zurichers, or the Scots disagreement with the Swiss over holy days.... Although the sixteenth century Reformers did not conclude their struggles over confessional subscription in terms of the American Presbyterian solution, they created the historical context and need for the practical and biblical wisdom of the Presbyterian Church of America's second ordination vow and its theological brother found in the Westminster Confession of Faith, 20:2: . . . Precisely because the Scriptures are the *norma normans*, the confession must be the *norma normata*. Because only fallen people have composed confessions, we may not dare give more than a quatenus-subscription." "Confessional Subscription Among the Sixteenth Century Reformers," 59–62.

We the undersigned preachers, under the jurisdiction of the Classis of Alkmaar, declare and witness that the teaching which is in that catechism adopted unanimously by the Reformed [the Heidelberg Catechism] and which is comprehended in the 37 articles of the Dutch Reformed Churches [the Belgic Confession] agrees in everything with the Holy Word of God, and consequently with the foundation of the teaching of salvation. We promise to maintain this same teaching, through God's grace; and openly to reject teachings that are brought against or oppose it; and with all diligence and faithfulness according to our ability to stand against them, as we affirm the same with our signatures.[9]

According to Robert Godfrey, "This earliest form of subscription expresses a characteristic of the Dutch Reformed tradition, namely that all of the doctrines of the confessional standards are accepted as part of one's subscription. No exceptions are permitted."[10] It should also be noted that it was usually national churches that adopted this form of subscription—at least in the sixteenth and seventeenth centuries—and it was compulsory for all ministers.

Historical Subscription

In a paper entitled "Confessional Subscription," James Renihan introduces the category of "historical subscription" and likens it to the view of "strict constitutionalism" that is used in American constitutional parlance. According to Renihan, this view focuses on the original intent of the framers of the creed or confession in view and requires the subscriber to agree and affirm that intent. One might argue that this approach is simply "absolute subscription" applied in a later historical context. By way of illustration, Renihan uses an anecdotal reference to the late John Gerstner. Gerstner, a Reformed classical apologist, allegedly suggested that a Reformed presuppositional apologist like Cornelius Van Til could not hold to a strict historical view of the Westminster Confession since, in Gerstner's view, the seventeenth century Puritans affirmed the classical view of apologetics.[11] Apparently, then, the historical view requires one

---

9 Cited by Robert Godfrey in "Subscription in the Dutch Reformed Tradition," PCS, 68–69.

10 Godfrey, "Subscription in the Dutch Reformed Tradition," 69.

11 "Confessional Subscription," included as Appendix VII in Tom Chantry and David Dykstra, *Holding Communion Together* (Vestavia Hills, AL: Solid Ground Books, 2014), 278.

to agree not merely with the basic sense of the words, propositions, and doctrines in a confession, but also with all the metaphysical and epistemological viewpoints of the confession's authors or signatories.

Full (or Strict) Subscription

Advocates of this kind of subscription include Reformed and Presbyterian scholars R. Scott Clark,[12] Morton Smith,[13] and George Knight III,[14] as well as the Reformed Baptist scholar James Renihan.[15] Like absolute subscription, full or strict subscription requires the person to subscribe to *the entire* creed or confession *because (quia)* it is biblical. Unlike absolute subscription, however, full subscription allows the subscriber to take exception to words or phrases, but not to any doctrines. Smith, for example, identifies "full subscription" with *quia*-subscription[16] and argues, "In professing the Confession and Catechisms of this Church [Presbyterian Church in America] as his confession, [the ordinand, minister, or teacher] is subscribing to all of the doctrines in the Confession and Catechisms; they are all part of the system of doctrine."[17]

More specifically, for Smith and Knight, "The Confession and Catechisms assert nothing more or less than *the very doctrines of the Word of God.*"[18] This perspective seems consistent with Clark's

---

12   See *Recovering the Reformed Confession*, 177–91.

13   See Morton H. Smith, "The Case for Full Subscription," in *PCS*, 185–205.

14   See George W. Knight III, "Subscription to the Westminster Confession of Faith and Catechisms," in *PCS*, 119–148.

15   "Confessional Subscription," *Holding Communion Together,* 275–94. See also "What Is Full Subscription?" in appendix 1 in ARBCA's Constitution (revised April 25, 2017), which is available online here: http://www.arbca.com/arbca-constitution (accessed November 2, 2020).

16   *Holding Fast to the Faith: A Brief History of Subscription to Creeds and Confessions with Particular Reference to Presbyterian Churches* (Self-Published, 2003), 15.

17   "The Case for Full Subscription," in *PCS*, 185.

18   Emphasis added. This language, which Smith cites approvingly, is taken from a study paper submitted to the 10th General Assembly of the PCA. The paper is available online at https://www.pcahistory.org/documents/subscription/1982paper.html (accessed Nov. 16, 2011). In the audio debate on subscription between William Barker and Morton Smith, Barker cites this phrase as representative of Smith's position. The audio debate can be accessed here: https://www.sermonaudio.com/sermoninfo.asp?sid=12505102413 (accessed August 31, 2020). The summary of the debate, which is available on the Orthodox Presbyterian Church website (https://opc.org/OS/html/V9/2d.html), also employs this clause to describe Smith's position. Knight also refers to the study paper and affirms the "doctrines of the Confession are to be regarded as 'the very doctrines of the Word.' " "Subscription to the Westminster Confession of Faith and Catechisms," in *PCS*, 129.

view of confessional subscription, which requires the ordinand and the church to view the teaching of the confession as equivalent to that of Scripture. Writes Clark, "It is not that the authority of the confessions is 'very nearly tantamount to that of Scripture,' but it *is* tantamount to that of Scripture, assuming that a given confession is biblical and intended to be subscribed *because* (quia) it is biblical."[19]

Full subscription acknowledges that not all doctrines in the confession are of equal importance, just as all teachings in Scripture are not of equal importance.[20] Moreover, while strict subscription requires agreement with *every doctrine*, it does not require full agreement with *every word* or *phrase* in the confession. At least this is true of the version advocated by Smith and Knight. Smith clarifies, "Full subscription does not require the adoption of every word of the Confession and Catechisms, but positively believes that we are adopting every doctrine or teaching of the Confession and Catechisms."[21]

This raises certain questions. To begin with, what constitutes a "doctrine" or "teaching"? As noted above, Morton Smith agreed to the following definition or description in his debate with William Barker: "Every declaratory statement states something true or false. And every declaratory statement in the Standards is either one doctrine or several doctrines."[22] But since the meaning of a "declaratory statement" is determined by the words and phrases that constitute the statement, how can one disagree with a word or a phrase without in some sense *modifying* the doctrine or teaching?

When pressed for examples, Smith offered two examples where one might take issue with phrases that employ archaic language. For instance, the Westminster Confession uses the term "vulgar language" to mean the *vernacular* (1.8).[23] Smith also alluded to the Larger Catechism's prohibition of "keeping of stews" (WLC Q139).[24] In these cases, we may suppose that Dr. Smith would

---

19 Emphasis his. Clark, *Recovering the Reformed Confession*, 178.

20 "The Case for Full Subscription," in *PCS*, 185.

21 "The Case for Full Subscription," 186.

22 This definition was actually proposed by someone in the audience seeking clarification of Smith's position. It occurs toward the end of the debate about 29 minutes into part 2: https://www.sermonaudio.com/sermoninfo.asp?sid=12505102455 (accessed August 31, 2020).

23 Today, "vulgar language" normally denotes crude, coarse, or obscene language.

24 The reference to "stews" in the Larger Catechism is slang. At one time "stews" referred to public bathhouses. Since these bathhouses were often associated

recommend we substitute these terms with *synonymous expressions* that would be intelligible to a modern audience.

Smith gave two more examples that seem to allow for actual differences at a semantic level. He acknowledged, for instance, that there is a difference of opinion as to whether the term "testament" is the best term to portray the biblical concept of covenant (cf. WCF 7.4). Apparently, one could disagree with the term "testament" as an appropriate gloss for the underlying Hebrew and Greek terms yet still affirm the doctrine that term conveys. Smith also alluded to the practice of Dutch churches requiring full subscription to the Three Forms of Unity but allowing the subscriber to question whether Paul really wrote the epistle to the Hebrews, as the Belgic Confession suggests when it refers to the "fourteen Epistles of the Apostle Paul," which includes "one to the Hebrews." Preferring the ordinal "thirteen" instead of "fourteen" would not constitute, in Smith's view, a disagreement with a doctrine but simply with *the wording* of a doctrine.[25]

What about scruples or exceptions? For R. Scott Clark, the answer appears quite simple: "If a confession is not biblical, it should be revised so that it is biblical, or it should be discarded in favor of a confession that is biblical."[26] Apparently, Clark does not believe a subscriber should be allowed to have scruples or take exceptions to his church's confession. In his words, "Why should a church adopt a confession that some or even most of the church believe to be at least partially unbiblical? Why should a church not draft and adopt a confession she believes to be wholly biblical? . . . Wherever there are exceptions, then it is no longer clear which document is being subscribed. Every time an exception is taken, the document being subscribed functionally changes at least for that subscriber and arguably . . . for the body permitting the exception."[27] "One could hold," writes Smith, "that no exceptions to doctrines taught in the Confession and Catechisms should be allowed." He continues,

---

with prostitution or illicit sex, the catechism is apparently using the term by way of association.

25 I gleaned these examples from the audio debate between Barker and Smith.

26 Clark, *Recovering the Reformed Confession*, 178.

27 Clark, 180. These remarks would seem to place Clark in the category of absolute or historical subscription. However, elsewhere Clark argues that we shouldn't be expected to take phrases like the WCF's depiction of God's work of creation "in the space of six days" as they may have been originally understood by some of the Assembly divines. See *Recovering the Reformed Confession*, 47–61.

"This is the position that the full subscriptionist prefers."[28] On the other hand, Smith suggests, "One could hold that exceptions may be allowed so long as those who take the exceptions are not permitted to teach views contrary to the Standards."[29] In his debate with William Barker, Smith made clear that in allowing an exception the presbytery was in effect labeling the exception as "error" but deeming that the error did not strike at the heart of the gospel.[30]

System Subscription

System subscription is the product of early American Presbyterianism. Advocates of this view include "Old School Presbyterians" Samuel Miller,[31] Charles Hodge,[32] B. B. Warfield,[33] J. Gresham Machen,[34] and John Murray.[35] More recent proponents include William Barker,[36] James Urish,[37] David Calhoun,[38] and John Fesko.[39]

---

28 *Holding Fast to the Faith*, 60.

29 *Holding Fast to the Faith*, 60.

30 This was stated at about 49 minutes into the debate.

31 See his *The Utility and Importance of Creeds and Confessions* (1824; reprint, Dallas: Presbyterian Heritage Publications, 1989), 61–62, 100–04.

32 Hodge expresses his views in a number of writings including *The Constitutional History of the Presbyterian Church in the United States of America*, 2 vols. (1851; reprint, Wrightstown, NJ: American Presbyterian Press, 1984), 1:145–66, 170–72, 185–86, the sections of which are included in *PCS*, 105–18; *Discussions in Church Polity* (New York: Scribner's, 1878); "Remarks on Dr. Cox's Communication," *Biblical Repertory and Theological Review* 3:4 (Oct 1831): 520–25; "Adoption of the Confession of Faith," *Princeton Review* (Oct 1858): 672–92; "Presbyterian Reunion," *Princeton Review* (Jan 1866): 53–83; "The General Assembly," *Princeton Review* (July 1867): 440–522.

33 See his "Presbyterian Churches and the Westminster Confession," *Presbyterian Review* 10:40 (Oct 1889): 646–57.

34 For Machen's thoughts on creeds and subscription, see *What is Christianity?* (Grand Rapids: Eerdmans, 1951), 229–33; *Christianity and Liberalism* (Grand Rapids: Eerdmans, 1981), 163–64; "The Creeds and Doctrinal Advance," *Scripture and Confession*, ed. John H. Skilton (Nutley, NJ: Presbyterian and Reformed, 1973), 149–57.

35 "Creed Subscription in the Presbyterian Church in the U.S.A.," *PCS*, 247–62; "The Theology of the Westminster Confession of Faith," *Scripture and Confession*, 125–48.

36 "System Subscription," *Westminster Theological Journal* 63 (2001): 1–14. See also his "The Samuel Hemphill Heresy Case (1735) and the Historic Method of Subscribing to the Westminster Standards," *PCS*, 149–69.

37 "A Peaceable Plea About Subscription: Toward Avoiding Future Divisions," *PCS*, 207–36.

38 " 'Honest Subscription': Old Princeton Seminary and Subscription to the Westminster Standards," *PCS*, 237–45.

39 "The Legacy of Old School Confession Subscription in the OPC," *The Journal of the Evangelical Theological Society* 46:4 (Dec 2003): 678–96.

System subscription is the official position of the Orthodox Presbyterian Church and the Presbyterian Church in America.[40]

Ironically, system subscription is probably the most discussed and yet most often misunderstood and mischaracterized type of confessional subscription. For example, in Morton Smith's mind, "loose or system subscription maintains that we subscribe to a system of doctrine, which is not specifically defined, but which is contained in the Confession and Catechisms of the Church."[41] This is not exactly correct. As we note below, system subscription requires the adoption of the confessional standards *as a whole*. But it allows for non-essential doctrinal exceptions. Similarly, James Renihan appears to confuse system subscription with a much looser "substance subscription" (see below) that only requires an affirmation of "the essential truths of the gospel."[42]

Part of the difficulty is the fact that articulations and defenses of this view are often based on (1) interpretations of the Adopting Act of 1729 and (2) the meaning of the ministerial vow taken by the candidate in which he promises to adopt the confessional standards "as containing the system of doctrine taught in the Holy Scripture."[43] The Adopting Act of 1729 required ministers of the Presbyterian Church to subscribe to the Westminster Standards as a whole.[44] But

---

40 See John Muether, "Confidence in Our Brethren: Creedal Subscription in the Orthodox Presbyterian Church," *PCS*, 301–10. Taking up cultural influences first was a refreshing and unexpected way into the topic. Every believer faces these imperceptible forces, and it appears that they have encouraged opposition to the use of confessions.

41 Smith, *The Subscription Debate: Studies in Presbyterian Polity* (Greenville, SC: Greenville Presbyterian Theological Seminary, n.d.), 6.

42 "Confessional Subscription," in *Holding Communion Together*, 279–81.

43 This is the wording from the second vow for officers of the Orthodox Presbyterian Church and the Presbyterian Church in America. The vow required of the professors of old Princeton is similar: "In the presence of God and of the Directors of this Seminary, I do solemnly and *ex animo* adopt, receive, and subscribe the Confession of Faith, and the Catechisms of the Presbyterian Church in the United States of America, as the confession of my faith; or as a summary and just exhibition of that system of doctrine and religious belief which is contained in the Holy Scripture, and therein revealed by God to man for his salvation;..." Cited by Calhoun, " 'Honest Subscription': Old Princeton Seminary and Subscription to the Westminster Standards," *PCS*, 237.

44 "All the ministers of this Synod now present ... after proposing all of the scruples that any of them had to make against any articles and expressions in the Confession of Faith, and Larger and Shorter Catechisms of the Assembly of Divines at Westminster, have unanimously agreed in the solution of those scruples, and in declaring the said Confession and Catechisms to be the confession of their faith, excepting only some clauses in the twentieth and twenty-third chapters, concerning

the "Preliminary Act," which was drafted on the same day and served as a kind of preface to the Adopting Act, makes repeated reference to the "essential and necessary articles" of the Standards as the basis on which a candidate's subscription is to be assessed.[45] Hence, most scholars and historians believe the Adopting Act requires ministers and candidates to adopt the Standards *as a whole*, but it also allows for exceptions to articles in the Standards that the Presbyteries deem non-essential or unnecessary.[46]

This seems to be consistent with Charles Hodge's interpretation of the Act. On the one hand, Hodge can assert, "There can be no doubt, therefore, that the adopting act, as understood and intended by its authors, bound every new member to receive the Confession of Faith and Catechisms, *in all their parts*, except certain specified clauses in chapters twentieth and twenty-third."[47] Thus, in Hodge's view, the Adopting Act called for subscription to the confession *as a whole*, excluding those articles the Synod officially excepted.[48]

which clauses the Synod do unanimously declare, that they do not receive those articles in any such sense as to suppose the civil magistrate hath a controlling power over Synods with respect to the exercise of their ministerial authority; or power to persecute any for their religion, or in any sense contrary to the Protestant succession to the throne of Great Britain." Cited in Barker, "System Subscription," 4.

45   For example, "[A]ll the Presbyteries . . . shall always take care not to admit any candidate of the ministry . . . but what declares his agreement in opinion with all the essential and necessary articles of said Confession"; "[I]n case any minister . . . or candidate for the ministry, shall have any scruple with respect to any article or articles of said Confession or Catechisms, he shall at the time of his making said declaration declare his sentiments to the Presbytery or Synod, who shall, notwith-standing, admit him to the exercise of the ministry, . . . if the Synod or Presbytery shall judge his scruple or mistake to be only about articles not essential and nec-essary in doctrine, worship, or government"; "And the Synod do solemnly agree, that none of us will traduce or use any opprobrious terms of those that differ from us in these extra-essential and not necessary points of doctrine." Cited in Barker, "System Subscription," 3–4.

46   See Luder G. Whitlock, "The Context of the Adopting Act," *PCS*, 98–100; Barker, "The Samuel Hemphill Heresy Case (1735) and the Historic Method of Subscribing to the Westminster Standards," 160–64; "System Subscription," 3–6; Lillbeck, "Confessional Subscription Among the Sixteenth Century Reformers," 36; James Urish, "A Peaceable Plea About Subscription," 208–14; Calhoun, " 'Honest Subscription': Old Princeton Seminary and Subscription to the Westmin-ster Standards," 243–44. For dissenting opinions, see Morton Smith, "The Case for Full Subscription," *PCS*, 191–94, and George W. Knight III, "Subscription to the Westminster Confession of Faith and Catechisms," *PCS*, 120–26.

47   Emphasis added; "The Constitutional History of the Presbyterian Church in the United States of America," *PCS*, 111.

48   Namely, those touching on the civil magistrate's role in religion. Note here an-other example of *animus imponentis*. The ecclesiastical body using the Confession reserves the right to define how it will be understood and used.

"System of doctrine" for Hodge was not simply "the general substance" of the doctrines of the confession but those doctrines of the confession in their "integrity."[49] Hence, he remarks, "Ever since the solemn enactment under consideration, every new member or candidate for ministry has been required to give his assent to this confession, as containing the system of doctrines taught in the Word of God. He assents not merely to absolutely essential and necessary articles of the gospel, but to the whole concatenated [i.e., integrated] statement of doctrines contained in the Confession."[50]

On the other hand, Hodge can refer to the Adopting Act as "a compromise," with the common ground being "the essential and necessary articles of that Confession."[51] Thus, Hodge seems to concede that there might be non-essential elements in the confession that do not impinge on the integrity of its teaching as a whole. This reading of Hodge is confirmed later when he writes, "We do not expect that our ministers should adopt every proposition contained in our standards. This they are not required to do. But they are required to adopt the system; and that system consists of certain doctrines, no one of which can be omitted without destroying its identity."[52] Elsewhere Hodge laments the extremes of overly lax and overly strict views of subscription:

> On the one hand, there are some, who seem inclined to give the phrase in question [system of doctrine], such latitude as that any one, who holds the great fundamental doctrines of the Gospel, as they are recognized by all evangelical denominations, might adopt it [the Confession]; while on the other, some are disposed to interpret it so strictly as to make it not only involve the adoption of all doctrines contained in the

49 "Adoption of the Confession of Faith," *Princeton Review* (1858): 672, 678, cited in Calhoun, 241.

50 Hodge, *Constitutional History*, 1:183, as cited in Barker, "System Subscription," 9.

51 "The Constitutional History of the Presbyterian Church," 109.

52 "The General Assembly," *Princeton Review* (1867): 509, cited in Calhoun, 243. Hodge elaborates on what he considers to be essential to the Confession's system of doctrine: "In professing to adopt the Confession of Faith as containing the system of doctrines taught in the sacred Scriptures, a man professes to believe the whole series of doctrines constituting that system, in opposition to every other. That is, he professes to believe the whole series of doctrines which go to make up the Calvinistic system in opposition to the Socinian, Pelagian, Semi-Pelagian, Arminian, or any opposite and inconsistent view of Christianity." "Remarks on Dr. Cox's Communication," 522, cited in Barker, "System Subscription," 8.

Confession, but to preclude all diversity in the manner of conceiving and explaining them.[53]

Thus, system subscription, like full subscription, rejects the "all-or-nothing" approach of absolute subscription. Both take the entire confessional standard as their starting point.[54] Moreover, both approaches allow for exceptions deemed by the church non-essential to the system of doctrine contained in the confession. The difference, it would appear, is that full subscription limits exceptions to mere words and phrases, whereas system subscription allows the subscriber to take exception to non-essential propositions or doctrines.[55] For adherents to a Reformed creed, such include any doctrinal propositions in the confession that do not undermine the Augustinian, Protestant, Reformed, and Calvinistic system of doctrine as opposed

---

53   "Remarks on Dr. Cox's Communication," *Biblical Repertory and Theological Review* (1831): 520, cited by Calhoun, 239. For those who would require the adoption of every doctrinal proposition of the Confession, Hodge had strong words: "There doubtless have been, and there still may be, men who would do all this, and in the mingled spirit of the Pharisee and Dominican, rejoice in the desolation they had wrought, and shout, 'The temple of the Lord, the temple of the Lord are we.' God forbid that such spirit should ever gain the ascendancy in our church. Let us keep our hands off of God's ark, and not assume to be more zealous for his truth, or more solicitous for the purity of his church, than he is himself." "Adoption of the Confession of Faith," *Princeton Review* (1858): 685, cited in Calhoun, 241–42.

54   John Fesko, a church historian and theologian of the OPC, has stressed this point in a recent lecture entitled "System Subscription," which he delivered at the 2009 Animus Imponentis Conference. The audio file, transcription, and lecture notes are available for download here: http://www.pncnopc.org/audio/audio-presbytery/2009-animus-imponentis-conference (accessed November 2, 2020).

55   This approach is not only seen in Hodge but also in his successors. For example, B. B. Warfield remarks, "The most we can expect and the most we have the right to ask is, that each one may be able to recognize [the Confession] as an expression of the system of truth which he believes." He continues, "To go beyond this and seek to make each of a large body of signers accept the Confession in all its propositions as the profession of his personal belief, cannot fail to result in serious evils—not least among which are the twin evils that, on the one hand, too strict a subscription overreaches itself and becomes little better than no subscription; and, on the other hand, that it begets a spirit of petty, carping criticism which raises objections to forms of a statement that in other circumstances would not appear objectionable." From his "Presbyterian Churches and the Westminster Confession," as cited by George W. Knight III in "Subscription to the Westminster Confession of Faith and Catechisms," 135. Similarly, John Murray writes, "It seems to the present writer that to demand acceptance of every proposition in so extensive a series of documents would be incompatible with the avowal made in answer to the first question in the formula of subscription and comes dangerously close to the error of placing human documents on par with Holy Scripture." "Creed Subscription in the Presbyterian Church in the U.S.A." quoted in Morton H. Smith, *The Subscription Debate* (Greenville, SC: Greenville Presbyterian Theological Seminary, n.d.), 79.

to the Pelagian, Semi-Pelagian, Socinian, and Arminian systems.[56] This distinction is further supported by well-documented examples of real doctrinal exceptions either allowed for or taken by Old School Presbyterians like Hodge, Thornwell, Warfield, Machen, and Murray.[57]

Nevertheless, as suggested earlier, the distinction between wording and doctrines is not always clear. For instance, both Hodge (system) and Renihan (full) allow that one might take exception to the confession's identification of the pope of Rome as "that Antichrist" (WCF 25.4; 2LCF 26.4). For Hodge, this is an exception to a propositional declaration or doctrine.[58] But Renihan portrays this as merely an exception to the wording of the confession. "Reluctance to identify the pope with *the* man of sin," he avers, "is vastly different from signing *Evangelical and Catholics Together*."[59] I would agree. But it seems to me (*pace* Renihan) that this is *not* simply a case of quibbling over words. Rather, this is a disagreement over a teaching or doctrine in the confession—albeit, a non-substantial doctrine.[60]

In summary, system subscription seeks to steer a middle course (*via media*) between absolute or full subscription, on the one hand, and the versions of "substance subscription" that we highlight below. David Calhoun aptly captures this Old School Presbyterian view when he writes, "In the view of the Princetonians, there were three positions on subscription: one was too strict, one was too lax, and one (like the porridge of the smallest bear in the story of Goldilocks) was 'just right.' The Princeton men held consistently to their middle

---

56 See Charles Hodge, *Church Polity*, 336–37, cited in Fesko, "The Legacy of Old School Confession Subscription in the OPC," 678, 679; Robert Lewis Dabney, "The Doctrinal Content of the Confession," *PCS*, 173; A. A. Hodge, *The Life of Charles Hodge*, 407–08, referenced in Calhoun, 245; Barker, "System Subscription," 8–10; Urich, "A Peaceable Plea About Subscription," 217–18.

57 See, for example, Barker, "System Subscription," 11–12; Fesko, "The Legacy of Old School Confession Subscription in the OPC," 679–96.

58 "There are many propositions contained in the Westminster Confession which do not belong to the integrity of the Augustinian, or Reformed System. A man may be a true Augustinian or Calvinist, and not believe that the Pope of Rome is the Antichrist predicted by St. Paul; or that the 18th chapter of Leviticus is still binding." *Church Polity*, 336, cited in Fesko, "The Legacy of Old School Confession Subscription in the OPC," 679.

59 "Confessional Subscription," in *Holding Communion Together*, 279.

60 This conclusion is supported by the fact that the article in question has been removed in the official versions of the WCF used by the OPC and PCA.

position and, when necessary, criticized those who were, in their view, too strict or too lax."[61]

This leads us to consider two looser types of confessional subscription.

Substance (of the Evangelical Faith) Subscription

"Substance subscription" is the nomenclature assigned to those approaches of confessional subscription that require adherence to a set of core doctrines within the confession. So long as the minister or candidate affirms belief in and commitment to the core doctrines of the confession, whatever they may be, his subscription is deemed sufficient. Moreover, substance subscription normally does not require the subscriber to identify his exceptions to the confession.

As noted above, system subscription is sometimes confused with substance subscription because it allows for a distinction between doctrines that are essential and necessary to the system of doctrine contained in the confession and doctrines non-essential to that system. In the case of the Westminster Standards, that system would be Reformed theology. However, system subscription takes the whole confession as its starting point and requires the subscriber to identify any propositions in that standard to which he may take exception. Thus, system and substance are not the same.

The early American Presbyterian Jonathan Dickinson may be categorized as an advocate of a kind of "substance subscription" that requires affirmation of and adherence to the essential doctrines of the evangelical faith within a confession. In Dickinson's mind, "we may not so much as shut out of Communion, any such Dissenters, as we can charitably hope Christ won't shut out of Heaven: But should open *the Doors of the Church* as wide as Christ opens *the Gates of Heaven*; and *receive one another*, as Christ also received us, to the Glory of God."[62]

Charles Hodge confirms that Dickinson intended this subscriptional latitude to apply to ministers as well as to laypeople when he

---

61   "'Honest Subscription': Old Princeton Seminary and Subscription to the Westminster Standards," 237.

62   Emphasis his; In Maurice Armstrong, Lefferts Loetscher, and Charles Anderson, eds. *The Presbyterian Enterprise* (Philadelphia: Presbyterian Historical Society, 1956), 26-27, cited in Urish, 209.

discusses Dickinson's involvement in the Adopting Act of 1729. "It is very evident," says Hodge,

> that the Adopting Act was a compromise. Both parties were very desirous to avoid a schism.... Mr. Dickinson had avowed his wish to establish the 'essential and necessary doctrines of Christianity' as the condition of ministerial communion. Mr. Thomson wished the explicit adoption of the Westminster Confession, to be that condition. The common ground on which they met was the essential and necessary articles of that Confession.[63]

Dickinson did not get his way and, instead, acquiesced to the system subscription position. Nevertheless, his personal preference serves as a paradigm for an evangelical version of substance subscription.

James Renihan provides an apt example of this form of subscription among early American Baptists. In 1787 John Leland facilitated a merger between the Regular Baptists and Separate Baptists of Virginia. With respect to confessional subscription, the "Plan of Union" concludes:

> After a long debate about the utility of adopting a Confession of faith, agreed to receive the Regular Baptists [i.e., the Philadelphia Confession]. But to prevent its usurping a tyrannical power over the consciences of any, we do not mean that every person is to be bound to the strict observance of everything therein contained: yet that it holds forth the essential truths of the gospel, and that the doctrine of salvation by Christ, and free unmerited grace alone, ought to be believed by every Christian, and maintained by every minister of the gospel.[64]

Renihan believes this loosening of confessional subscription was probably an overreaction of the Baptists to the political attempt of the Anglican state church in Virginia to impose its creed on ministers. The resultant watering down of confessional commitment, notes Renihan, "contributed to decline in Baptist theology."[65]

---

63 *Constitutional History*, 1:152, cited in Urish, 210.

64 From A. D. Gillette, ed. *Minutes of the Philadelphia Baptist Association, from A.D. 1707 to A.D. 1807* (Atlas, MI: Baptist Book Trust, n.d. facsimile reprint), 233, as cited in Renihan, "Confessional Subscription," 280.

65 "Confessional Subscription," 280. Unfortunately, Renihan lumps this form of "loose" subscription together with "system" subscription.

Substance (of the Christian Religion) Subscription

As is often the case, the well-meant intentions of some (i.e., broad-minded evangelicals) can open the door to the bad intentions of others (i.e., theological liberals). The step of subscribing to a confession as containing the substance of *the evangelical faith* may lead to the further step of reducing the "essentials" to broader fundamentals or tenets of *the Christian religion*. This very loose form of substance subscription is where many of the mainline denominations landed in the twentieth century.

A case in point was the action of the general assembly of the Presbyterian Church in the United States of America (PCUSA) in 1910. In response to complaints about ministers questioning fundamental doctrines, such as the virgin birth of Christ, the Assembly produced a doctrinal statement that identifies five articles it deems essential and necessary to the Christian faith. The articles themselves are orthodox and explicitly oppose modernist views.[66] But this seeming victory for conservative evangelicals in the PCUSA was only temporary. In 1924 the Auburn Affirmation was published and signed by 150 pastors and elders within the church. In essence it called for greater liberty of conscience and doctrinal latitude. Three years later the general assembly of 1927 gave the right to each Presbytery to decide what it considered "essential and necessary." Eventually, liberalism and neo-orthodoxy became the dominant doctrinal currents in the PCUSA, resulting in a rather general and under-defined commitment to "lead a life in obedience to Scripture and conformity to the historical standards of the church."[67]

Conclusion

This concludes our survey of the terms and types of confessional subscription. In the following chapter, we will consider some biblical principles for choosing and using a creed or confession of faith. Additionally, we will offer a critical assessment of the types of subscription we have surveyed above and suggest some recommendations for

---

66   The five articles are available online here: http://www.pcahistory.org/documents/deliverance.html (accessed October 23, 2014).

67   See the PCUSA's Book of Confessions: http://oga.pcusa.org/section/mid-council-ministries/constitutional-services/constitution (accessed August 31, 2020).

developing a balanced and, we believe, biblically informed view of confessional subscription.[68]

---

68 Of course, this assumes that writing and using creeds and confessions are legitimate for churches and religious institutions. For a defense of the validity and value
of confessions, see chapter 2.

10

Choosing and Using a Confession

Some Biblical and Theological Guidelines

Robert Gonzales Jr.

———————— ·✦· ————————

O NCE WE GRANT THE LEGITIMACY AND usefulness of a confession of faith, we face two practical questions. First, what
particular confession of faith should a local church or collective body of churches adopt? Second, what type or level of subscription to the confession should such a church or body of churches
require of its officers and members?[1] Below I would like to suggest
a few biblical and theological guidelines to assist in answering these
questions.

The Bible does not provide explicit instructions on how a
Christian church must use a particular confession of faith. Nowhere
do Jesus and the apostles directly address the issue of confessional
subscription. And obviously, the biblical writers do not explicitly
identify what creed we should use, since the creeds and confessions
framed throughout the history of the church did not yet exist. So we
cannot answer the questions above with a simple proof text or two.
Nevertheless, I would suggest that the Bible provides us with some
biblical and theological parameters not only for choosing a good
confession but also for deciding how we should use and subscribe to

---

1 See the previous chapter for the discussion on levels of subscription.

that confession. These parameters are not so narrow as to restrict us to only one possible confession or even to one specific form of subscription. But they are relatively narrow enough to exclude certain confessions and kinds of subscription as either wrong or unwise.

The Main Purpose of a Confession

The Bible calls us to confess our faith publicly (Matt. 10:32–33; Rom. 10:9–10) and to explain precisely what we mean by what we confess (Neh. 8:5–8; Acts 17:1–4; Eph. 4:11–14).[2] In other words, the very aim and goal of publicly confessing our faith is to provide others an accurate summary of what we believe the Bible teaches. This conviction should influence which confession we choose as a church, as well as the type or kind of subscription we require. If our beliefs and practice correspond most closely with, say, the Reformed and the Baptist traditions, why would we choose a confession of faith that is not Reformed and that is not Baptist?

For instance, if I believe in the doctrine of election and God's absolute sovereignty, why would I choose a creed or confession that denies the truths of election and limits God's sovereignty? I suppose I could take an Arminian statement of faith like, say, "A Treatise on the Faith of the Free Will Baptists" and find a "substance" of core truths within that confession I could agree with.[3] But an Arminian confession as a whole would not convey to others what I really believe about God's sovereignty and the grace of the gospel. In this case, I would be using a confession that substantially misrepresents some of my core beliefs.

Let us use another example that is closer to home. What about the Westminster Confession of Faith (WCF)? Could I, as a church leader, or could my local church adopt and subscribe to the WCF as its official confession? After all, the WCF does affirm election and God's absolute sovereignty, as well as many of the core beliefs my

---

2 See my article "The Validity and Value of Confessions of Faith" in chapter 2.

3 Historically, Baptist churches that deny the doctrine of particular election have been called General or Arminian Baptist churches. In 1827 an association of such churches agreed to formulate a statement of faith articulating its views and distinguishing them (in places) from Particular Baptist churches that affirmed the doctrine of election. The confession or "treatise" (as it was called) was first published and adopted in 1834. Later, the association of Free Will Baptists revised and adopted the confession in 1948. See William Lumpkin, *Baptist Confessions of Faith*, rev. ed. (Valley Forge: Judson, 1969), 367–76.

church and I share. Certainly, I would share much more in common with the WCF than I would with the Arminian statement of faith referenced above. I suppose I could adopt and subscribe to the WCF provided that I could take exception to some aspects of its covenant theology, its view of baptism, and its form of church government. However, why would I, as a Reformed Baptist, choose the WCF as the confession for my church when I have at my disposal the Second London Confession of Faith (2LCF)—a Baptist revision and adaptation of the WCF?

My point is that a church should choose a confession of faith that accurately and substantially represents its beliefs about the teachings of the Bible.

The Virtue of Clear and Honest Communication

The general principle underlying the ninth commandment requires us to speak the truth to our neighbor clearly and honestly. Conversely, the ninth commandment prohibits any kind of communication or behavior that is sinfully deceptive (Ex. 20:16). As the psalmist David declares to the Lord, "Behold, you delight in truth in the inward being" (Ps. 51:6). And the New Testament writers also commend this virtue of truthfulness and honesty. The apostle Paul exhorts the members of the church in Ephesus, "Therefore, having put away falsehood, let each one of you speak the truth with his neighbor, for we are members one of another" (Eph. 4:25).

Now the fact that the Bible tells us to communicate to our neighbor in a truthful and sincere way has a bearing on the confession we choose and the type of subscription we use. Obviously, we want to avoid confessions that advocate clear and serious falsehoods. We want a confession that accurately, though not infallibly, summarizes the Word of God. Moreover, we want to employ a form of confessional subscription that requires transparency and honesty. Modes of subscription that allow *undisclosed* mental reservations about this or that doctrine are, I think, imprudent. Whatever form of subscription we require should be one that disallows the proverbial "crossing of the fingers behind the back." If the subscriber or ministerial candidate has a conscientious scruple about this phrase or that doctrinal proposition, he needs to make it known to the elders and, if necessary, to the entire church.

At this point, I have basically ruled out confessions that are substantially erroneous or inaccurate. I have also ruled out types of "substance subscription" that require only a commitment to a set of ambiguous and undefined "core" teachings of the confession but that do not require one to openly and honestly identify those parts of the confession to which he takes exception.

The Doctrine of Progressive Sanctification

Sanctification is a lifelong process according to Scripture. Not all of God's people are at the same place in their journey. Some are babes in Christ and need the simple "milk of the Word" (Heb. 5:12–13; 1 Peter 2:2). That is, their understanding of Christian doctrine is fairly basic and rudimentary. Conversely, other believers have had time to grow in the grace and knowledge of the Lord. They are no longer babes in Christ who need milk, but they are more mature disciples who are ready for doctrinal meat (Rom. 15:14; Gal. 6:1; Heb. 5:14). This principle of progressive sanctification applies not only to individual Christians but also to local churches. Some churches have been well taught and are firmly grounded in the faith. Other churches, because they are new or immature or just at the beginning of doctrinal reformation, are still in the process of searching the Scriptures in order to see if this or that doctrine is so. See, for example, Christ's description of the seven churches of Asia Minor in chapters 2 and 3 of Revelation.

The reality of progressive sanctification (individual and corporate) has a bearing on the questions of what confession a church should use and what form of subscription it should require of its members and officers. I believe church officers and teachers of the Word should be held to a stricter standard than the average layperson (James 3:1). Moreover, some members in our churches have not arrived at the level of spiritual and doctrinal maturity to understand and receive some of the deeper doctrines in a more comprehensive confession of faith like, say, the 2LCF.

To accommodate for this reality, a church might adopt two different confessions: one that is more comprehensive and detailed like the 2LCF for its officers and another that is more simple and concise for its members (e.g., the Abstract of Principles or New Hampshire

Confession of Faith).[4] On the other hand, a church might adopt a single confession (e.g., 2LCF) but allow for two types or levels of subscription, that is, a tighter form for the church officers and a looser form for the church members. We might differ on which of those two approaches is better. But I hope we agree on the need to take into account the doctrine of progressive sanctification when we are trying to choose and use a confession of faith.

Excursus: Different levels of commitment for church members and officers?

Is it biblical to make a distinction in the level of commitment to a church confession one requires of a member as opposed to the level of commitment one requires of a pastor or church officer? Some, like Reformed scholar R. Scott Clark, believe the same level of commitment to the church's confessional standards should be expected of the clergy and the laity. In his book *Recovering the Reformed Confession*, Clark remarks, "It is not obvious that establishing two levels of subscription, one laity and another for ordained officers, is either biblical or consistent with the Reformation. . . . If the Reformed confession defines what it is to be Reformed, then establishing two distinct relations to the same constitutional document would seem to be a recipe for confusion and effectively two churches within one."[5]

I am not convinced that Clark's position is biblical or wise. First, in the New Testament, baptism and church membership usually *precede* a thorough grounding in Christian doctrine (Matt. 28:19–20; Acts 2:41–42; Eph. 4:11–14). Thus, while a fuller affirmation of the church's confession may be the goal for membership, it should not be a prerequisite for membership. This seems to place the cart before the horse.

---

4 See Bethlehem Baptist Church's distinction between their "Elders' Affirmation" and "Members' Affirmation." Bethlehem Baptist Church, where John Piper once served as a pastor, has a fuller and more comprehensive "Elders' Affirmation" for the church officers and a small, more concise "Members' Affirmation" for the church members. These are available on a page of Bethlehem Baptist Church's website here: https://bethlehem.church/new-here/about-us/#our-beliefs (accessed January 27, 2021).

5 *Recovering the Reformed Confession: Our Theology, Piety, and Practice* (Phillipsburg: Presbyterian and Reformed, 2008), 179.

Second, the approach Clark advocates is not consistent with the Second London Confession's standard for church membership. According to 26.2 ("Of the church"), "All persons throughout the world, professing the faith of the gospel and obedience unto God by Christ according unto it, not destroying their own profession by any errors everting the foundation, or unholiness of conversation, are any may be called visible saints; and of such ought all particular congregations to be constituted."

Thus, the prerequisite for church membership is, simply, *a credible profession of faith* that is not contradicted by serious doctrinal error or ungodly behavior. Mastery of the confession as a requirement for membership is conspicuously absent from the confession itself.

In the third place, creeds and confessions are designed to protect the church from false teachers, not from new or immature believers. The eighteenth-century Reformed Baptist scholar Andrew Fuller underscores this point well:

> If a religious community agrees to specify some leading principles which they consider as derived from the Word of God, and judge the belief of them to be necessary in order to any person's becoming or continuing a member with them, it does not follow that those principles should be equally understood, or that all their brethren must have the same degree of knowledge, nor yet that they should understand and believe nothing else. The powers and capacities of different persons are various; one may comprehend more of the same truth than another, and have his views more enlarged by an exceedingly great variety of kindred ideas; and yet the substance of their belief may still be the same. *The object of articles [of faith] is to keep at a distance, not those who are weak in the faith, but such as are its avowed enemies.*[6]

Finally, a creed or confession is an extension of ecclesiastical authority. Many church constitutions require members to be teachable and submissive to the church's constitution, confession, and covenant. God's requirement that we submit to such authority does not necessitate that we fully agree with the authority, especially on matters that are non-essentials.

---

6 Andrew Fuller, *The Complete Works of Andrew Fuller*, 3 volumes, ed. Joseph Belcher (1832; reprint, Harrisonburg: Sprinkle, 1988), 3:450; emphasis mine.

For these reasons, I do not believe we should require full subscription to a larger confession like the 2LCF of our members. An affirmation of and commitment to the essential truths of the gospel is the minimum requirement. As a matter of prudence, we should make them aware of our distinctives (Calvinist, Reformed, Baptist, etc.). Moreover, we should make sure they are teachable and willing to be submissive to pastoral leadership.[7] Otherwise, allowing for different levels of commitment for church members and officers seems consistent with biblical principles and with a healthy confessionalism.

The Holy Spirit's Ongoing Work of Illumination

We cannot understand God's word properly and truly apart from the Holy Spirit's work of illumination (1 Cor. 2:12–14). This applies not only to the individual believer, but also to the church has a whole (Eph. 1:18–23). And I think it is fair to assume that the Holy Spirit has been illuminating Christians and the church as a whole *throughout* church history. We might even say that the Spirit's work of illumination is like the Spirit's work of sanctification: it is progressive.

In light of the Spirit's ongoing work of illumination throughout the history of the church, we should not despise church tradition. Much of church tradition—if it is good—reflects the Spirit's work of bringing the church to a better understanding of God's word. Thus, a deep reverence for the authority of Scripture is not incompatible with a profound respect for the church's historical understanding of God's word. Indeed, the Protestant Reformers, who championed *sola Scriptura*, read the Bible in conversation with earlier church tradition because they believed such tradition reflected the Holy Spirit's activity.[8] To despise all older church tradition is not only an act of "chronological snobbery," as C. S. Lewis would put it, but it may also be an instance of despising the Spirit's work of illumination in earlier times.[9]

---

7 For a further development of this position, see Carl Trueman, *The Creedal Imperative* (Wheaton: Crossway, 2012), 171–75.

8 For this reason, I agree with Clark when he asserts, "If you're not reading the Scriptures with the church and in communion of the saints, you're not following sola Scriptura and the confessional Protestants." "The Difference Between Sola Scriptura and Biblicism," *The Heidelblog*, April 19, 2015, accessed January 27, 2021, https://heidelblog.net/2015/04/the-difference-between-sola-scriptura-and-biblicism.

9 See his autobiography, *Surprised by Joy: The Shape of My Early Life* (New York:

Nevertheless, the Spirit's work of progressive illumination is a two-edged sword and, therefore, chronological snobbery can manifest itself in disdain for anything modern.[10] Not only must we resist despising all historical doctrine; we must also be open to the Spirit's present work of illumination, which enables the church to further reform and refine aspects of its doctrinal beliefs. This is the doctrine of *semper reformanda*.[11] And it is this doctrine that constrained the Particular Baptists to disagree respectfully with prevailing tradition and to make revisions to the otherwise excellent Westminster Confession.[12] Later, when American Presbyterians developed a more biblical (and Baptist!) understanding of the roles of church and state, they made significant revisions to chapter 23 "Of the Civil Magistrate."[13] In principle, then, we should be open to the possibility that the Holy Spirit can prompt and enable the church to make further refinements or additions to its confession of faith.[14] Furthermore, and to the point of this essay, we should avoid forms of confessional subscription that require us to equate *unqualifiedly* the doctrine of the confession with the teaching of Scripture. If the two are one-and-the-same, then potential revisions are necessarily ruled out before they can even be considered. John Fesko agrees

---

Harcourt, Brace, Jovanovich, 1955), 207–08.

10 I agree with Lewis's censure of the mindset that's biased for the present and prejudiced against the past. However, some who entertain a nostalgic love for the past can manifest a similar disdain for the present. This too is a form of chronological snobbery.

11 This comes from the Latin phrase *ecclesia reformata, semper reformanda*, which means something like "the church reformed, always reforming." Some argue that this principle only applies to practice and not to doctrine. Whether that was the original application of the phraseology is, in a sense, a moot point. Biblically, the church should be growing in knowledge and practice. Accordingly, it is not inappropriate to apply the principle to doctrine.

12 I am referring to the Second London Confession, which is a Baptist adaptation of the Westminster Confession. See Haykin, chapter 4 of this volume.

13 For a comparison and analysis of the relevant texts, see Lee Irons, "The 1788 American Revision of the Westminster Standards," 2007, accessed January 27, 2021, http://www.upper-register.com/papers/1788_revision.pdf.

14 I have been asked whether I am aware of any modern examples. In my opinion, the contributions of Cornelius Van Til in the areas of epistemology and apologetic methodology represent an example of the Holy Spirit's ongoing illumination in the twentieth century. Van Til was a professor at Westminster Theological Seminary from 1927 to 1972, and he labored to develop an epistemology and apologetic methodology that is informed by the Bible itself and not by autonomous reason. His approach became known as "presuppositional apologetics" and is exemplified in such works as his *The Defense of the Faith,* 4th ed. (1955; repr., Phillipsburg: Presbyterian and Reformed, 2008).

and writes, "If we posses [*sic*] the very doctrines of Scripture in the Standards, then how is one supposed to disagree or revise 'the very doctrines of Scripture'?"[15]

The Doctrine of Scripture

Our doctrine of Scripture has an important bearing on the question of what confession we use and what form of subscription we employ. In fact, the Westminster Confession and Second London Confession highlight several attributes of Scripture that should guide us in our choice of a confession and our manner of subscription.

The Qualified Clarity of Scripture

While the message of Scripture is clear and intelligible (Deut. 30:11–13; Ps. 19:7–8; 1 John 5:11–13), not every teaching in Scripture is equally clear or intelligible (2 Peter 3:15–16). In the words of the confession, "All things in Scripture are not alike plain in themselves" (WCF/2LCF 1.7). Now one purpose of a good confession is to clarify ambiguities in Scripture. For example, the New Testament does not explicitly refer to the Lord's Day as a "Christian Sabbath." Nevertheless, one may infer a (carefully defined) sabbath character for the Lord's Day from a holistic consideration of the biblical data.[16]

However, one must beware of "adding" to Scripture what is not there in an effort to "clarify" the Bible's teaching (Deut. 4:2). The

---

15 "The Legacy of Old School Confession Subscription in the OPC," *Journal of the Evangelical Theological Society* 46:4 (Dec 2003): 695. One would have to *renounce his vow* before he could ever entertain the thought that something he is reading in the Bible does not seem to mesh with something taught in his Confession. As John Frame points out, "[Confessions] could never be amended; anyone who advocated change would automatically be a vow-breaker and subject to discipline." *The Doctrine of the Knowledge of God* (Phillipsburg: Presbyterian and Reformed, 1987), 308. Similarly, James E. Urish remarks, "Of course, if one took the 'strict' full subscriptionist position, one could not teach anything contrary to any articles in the Confession or Catechism. One wonders how the Church could ever perfect these standards with this kind of constraint. It does seem that from the full subscriptionist position there is an implicit assumption that the Westminster Standards fully or satisfactorily summarize the teaching of the Bible and ought not to be amended." "A Peaceable Plea About Subscription: Toward Avoiding Future Divisions," in *The Practice of Confessional Subscription*, ed. David W. Hall (Oakridge, TN: The Covenant Foundation, 1997), 223.

16 See my essay, "Commemorating Christ's Coronation: How to Justify a First-Day Sabbath," *In Service to the Church: Essays in Honor of Dr. Robert Paul Martin*, ed. Brian Borgman (Conway, AR: Free Grace Press, 2020), 101–11.

Pharisees were prone to this mistake (Matt. 15:1–9). In light of this danger, we should avoid adopting a confession that attempts to offer a level of epistemic certainty that exceeds that which Scripture itself warrants. Moreover, we may allow for exceptions to a teaching in a given creed or confession that is not *clearly* taught in Scripture.

For example, the WCF and 2LCF assert, "Elect infants dying in infancy are regenerated and saved by Christ through the Spirit" (10.2). If an infant dying in infancy is numbered among "the elect," he or she will certainly go to heaven. What is more, there are certainly lines of biblical teaching that one may use to provide comfort to grieving parents. But some Bible scholars question whether the passages and doctrines used to support either the notion that all infants go to heaven or the idea that infants of believers are elect teach that doctrine clearly and unambiguously. It may be that God in his wisdom has chosen to remain silent on this issue.[17] If that is true, we should allow subscribers to abstain from affirming the confession unreservedly at this point, though we may sympathize with the pastoral concern underlying the confession's assertion.[18]

The Infallibility and Inerrancy of Scripture

A good confession may not always express every doctrine in the best possible way, but a good confession should be accurate as a whole. Nevertheless, even accurate confessions are not infallible, that is, *incapable of error*. That attribute belongs to Scripture alone.

But may we refer to a confession as "inerrant" if he believes that confession contains no error? I do not believe that such a practice would be wise. Theologians today usually reserve the term

---

17 I can think of reasons why. If the Bible taught that all who die in infancy automatically go to heaven, we may be tempted to refrain from our efforts to stop abortion. Indeed, we might begin to view abortion as a form of evangelism or missions. Now I realize that such a conclusion would be unwarranted. But the sinful human heart is quite good at finding ways to justify unholy means in light of an assumedly positive end.

18 Sam Waldron's analysis is helpful. He does not believe the Bible addresses the destiny of those who die in infancy directly or clearly. Accordingly, he remarks, "It seems to me that in some respects it would have been better for the Confession to say nothing at this point." Nevertheless, given the high mortality rates for infants when the Confession was written, Waldron sympathizes with the pastoral concern of the Confession and believes the Bible does provide some biblical perspectives that can provide some help to the bereaved Christian parent. See his full analysis in *A Modern Exposition of the 1689 Baptist Confession of Faith*, 5th ed. (Darlington, Co. Durham, England: Evangelical Press, 2016), 175–78.

"inerrant" for the Bible. Indeed, the 1689 Baptist Confession refers to the Holy Scripture as "the only . . . certain . . . rule of all saving knowledge, faith, and obedience" (2LCF 1.1). If the modifier "certain" is the seventeenth-century equivalent of "inerrant," as some scholars argue,[19] then referring to or even treating the confession as inerrant is unconfessional since the confession reserves that attribute for Scripture alone.[20]

The Ultimate Authority of Scripture

Although confessions are wonderful guides and summaries of biblical teaching, we must beware of elevating them to the level of Scripture. The Protestant doctrine of *sola Scriptura*[21] insists that the Bible is the ultimate authority for all questions of faith and practice. Confessions like the WCF and 2LCF express this doctrine magnificently:

> The supreme judge, by which all controversies of religion are to be determined, and all decrees of councils, opinions of ancient writers, doctrines of men, and private spirits, are to be examined, and in whose sentence we are to rest, can be no other but the Holy Scripture delivered by the Spirit, into which Scripture so delivered, our faith is finally resolved (WCF/2LCF 1.1).

> All synods or councils, since the Apostles' times, whether general or particular, may err; and many have erred. Therefore, they are not to be made the rule of faith, or practice; but to be used as a help in both (WCF 31.3).

Reflecting on this strand of the Westminster Confession's teaching, Chad Van Dixhoorn draws an appropriate conclusion:

> Are there "controversies of religion" that need to be settled? Then there is only one standard that is necessary for us to use, one court to which every Christian and church must appeal. Are there "decrees of councils" that need to be evaluated? Then there is only one canon by which these councils

---

19   See L. Russ Bush and Tom J. Nettles, *Baptists and the Bible*, revised and expanded (Nashville: Broadman & Holman, 1999), 49.

20   This scenario is not purely hypothetical. I have heard some who subscribe to a confession without exception refer to that confession as "inerrant." This often can result in a theological pride that refuses any criticism from others outside one's own confessional tradition.

21   The doctrine that the Bible alone is the ultimate authority for all truth claims.

and their decrees—*including the decisions of the Westminster assembly and this confession of faith*—can be authoritatively considered right or wrong.... And that "can be no other but the Holy Spirit speaking in the Scripture."[22]

Placing a confession of faith on the same level as Scripture may never be an issue among Protestants at a *theoretical* or *doctrinal* level. It can, however, be a problem at a *practical* level. Churches and individuals have sometimes treated the confession as if it were the "last word" in any doctrinal dispute. They judge another church or Christian as "unorthodox" simply on the basis of the confession itself. Such a practice is not only unbiblical; it is profoundly unconfessional![23]

Conclusion

We have already ruled out confessions that do not substantially express what we believe. We have also ruled out forms of subscription that do not demand complete transparency and honesty from the one subscribing the confession.[24] We should likewise avoid adopting a confession (or a teaching in a confession) that tries to be more precise than Scripture warrants and that, therefore, adds to Scripture.[25] Moreover, forms of "absolute," "historical," and an *unqual-*

---

22 Emphasis added; *Confessing the Faith: A Reader's Guide to the Westminster Confession of Faith* (Edinburgh: Banner of Truth, 2014), 27–28.

23 Of course, a church and its leaders may fall back on its Confession at some point. For example, if they are dealing with someone in the congregation who questions or even denies, say, the deity of Christ, they should first seek to present the relevant biblical support for that doctrine. Should their exegesis and exposition of Scripture not convince the erring individual, they are warranted to fall back on the teaching of the Confession as expressing their understanding of Scripture. But appealing immediately or solely to the Confession should not be the church's default response to error.

24 For a description of these types of subscription, see the previous chapter "Confessional Subscription: Its Terms and Types."

25 Clark refers to this as "The Quest for Illegitimate Religious Certainty" in *Recovering the Reformed Confession*, 39–69. He refers to instances in which some in the Reformed tradition, motivated by a desire for greater religious certainty, want to add more to the confession or attempt to read into the confession more than the Scriptures warrant. One may not agree entirely with every one of the specific examples he offers, but his concern is valid. I also believe his concern should caution us against a mode of subscription that allows for no exceptions—something Clark himself rejects. He believes a confession should be corrected or rejected if it is not entirely in line with Scripture (178–80). Such an approach is, I believe, unrealistic this side of glory.

ified "strict" or "full" subscription can undermine the Spirit's on-going work of illumination and the doctrine of *semper reformanda*. In principle, we should be able to amend our confessions. Thus, forms of subscription that require a Christian or a church to affirm the confession's teaching as "the very doctrines of Scripture" and the confession's authority as "tantamount to Scripture" can, if not carefully qualified, undermine the very doctrine of Scripture they are seeking to protect.

Where does that leave me? Personally, I believe the 2LCF best represents what I believe the Bible teaches. It intersects with the contours of the Bible's teaching more consistently than other confessions I have seen. Nevertheless, I do not think the 2LCF is inerrant. Also, my commitment to the supremacy of Scripture leads me to favor a form of subscription that allows for minor, non-substantial doctrinal exceptions, provided that those exceptions are communicated openly and honestly. This places me somewhere between "system subscription" and an unqualified "full (or strict) subscription." Elsewhere, I advocate "substantial subscription," which I define as a form of full subscription that allows for minor exceptions or as a conservative version of system subscription.[26] The precise nomenclature one prefers is of secondary importance. What's most important is that we allow Scripture's own teaching and theology to guide us in our choice and use of a confession of faith. I hope this essay proves helpful to this end.

---

26 For a fuller defense of my position, see my "How Shall We Confess the Faith? Strict vs Substantial Subscription," *It is Written*, February 20, 2021, https://bob-gonzal.es/index.php/2021/02/20/how-shall-we-confess-the-faith-strict-vs-substantial-subscription.

Part 4

Important Theological Contributions of the Second London Confession of Faith

11

The Covenant Theology of the Second London Confession

Jeffrey D. Johnson

HISTORICALLY, REFORMED BAPTISTS are covenantal. Though they differ from their Presbyterian brothers on a few key issues, according to the 1689 London Baptist Confession of Faith, Baptists were equally committed to a robust covenantal framework of the history of redemption. In fact, every chapter of the confession is built on a covenantal matrix. Though chapter 7 is devoted entirely to the covenants, the chapters on creation, providence, the fall of man, Christ, justification, repentance, the gospel, good works, and perseverance are explained from a covenantal perspective.

For our Baptist forefathers, an alteration of the doctrine of the covenants is an alteration of the gospel of Jesus Christ. The gospel, in its broader context, includes the fulfilling of the covenant of works by the Second Adam, Jesus the Christ, that was broken by the first Adam; the Second Adam endured its curses and established its blessings for all those who are chosen by God to be represented by the Second Adam in the covenant of grace.

With this in mind, chapter 7 of the confession stresses three essential truths relating to its covenantal framework. Paragraph 1 confesses a prelapsarian covenant of works. Paragraph 2 confesses a postlapsarian covenant of grace. Paragraph 3 confesses an eternal covenant of redemption.

The Covenant of Works

Paragraph 1 confesses a prelapsarian covenant of works. Though
the phrase "covenant of works" is located in 7.1 of the Westminster Confession but is missing in 7.1 of the 1689, it is not because
the 1689 denies that God's pre-fall arrangement with Adam was a
covenant of works. This is made clear in 20.1, where the 1689 calls
it "*the covenant of works*." Moreover, in 19.1, the 1689 explains that
this prelapsarian covenant was based on works:

> God gave to Adam a law of universal obedience written in
> his heart, and a particular precept of not eating the fruit of the
> tree of knowledge of good and evil; by which he bound him
> and all his posterity to personal, entire, exact, and perpetual
> obedience; promised life upon the fulfilling, and threatened
> death upon the breach of it.

Adam, in his state of innocence (7.3), was to merit eternal life
through obedience to God's moral law. Anything short of perfect
obedience would result in death. And, as Nehemiah Coxe reminded
us, this covenant did not include "the least iota of pardoning mercy."[1]

The Necessity of the Covenant of Works

Moreover, the 1689 states that the covenant of works was necessary
for *eternal life* to be promised to man. As 7.1 says: "Although reasonable creatures do owe obedience to him as their creator, yet they
could never have attained the reward of life but by some voluntary
condescension on God's part, which he hath been pleased to express
by way of covenant."

This implies that the quality of life that God promised to man was
of a greater value than what man possessed in his innocence and of a
greater value than that which God was obligated to reward man for
his obedience. Without this covenant, according to the confession,
eternal life couldn't have been offered to man.

The Perpetuity of the Covenant of Works

Of course, the confession states that the covenant of works was
broken (20.1). A broken covenant, however, does not mean an

---

1   Nehemiah Coxe and John Owen, *Covenant Theology: From Adam to
Christ* (Palmdale, CA: Reformed Baptist Academic Press, 2005), 49.

abrogated covenant. Though the covenant of works was broken by Adam, the 1689 teaches that it remains binding on all of Adam's posterity. That is, the same covenant of works that was established with Adam before the fall continues to be enforced on all of Adam's unredeemed posterity after the fall.

First, the covenant of works continues after the fall because its curses continue to plague the human race after the fall. The confession teaches that the first Adam was the federal head of the human race and that he brought universal condemnation and death to all his descendants by his failure to keep the covenant of works (6.1, 2, 3). Because universal condemnation and original sin continue, the covenant of works continues.

Second, the covenant of works continues after the fall because its legal demands continue to bind the human race after the fall. The terms of the covenant of works consisted of more than just refraining from eating from the forbidden tree; it required complete obedience to God's moral law that was written on Adam's conscience (19.1). And though it is impossible for Adam's descendants to eat of the forbidden tree, they are able to violate God's moral law that is equally written in their consciences. As the confession states: "The same law that was first written in the heart of man continued to be a perfect rule of righteousness after the fall" (19.2).

Third, the covenant of works continues after the fall because man's moral inability does not nullify man's moral *culpability*. Though the confession clearly teaches that fallen man is unable to keep the demands of the covenant of works,[2] it states that the terms and promises and threats of the covenant of works continue to all of Adam's children. For instance, according to the confession, Israel was reminded of the terms of the prelapsarian covenant of works in the postlapsarian covenant that was established with them at Mount Sinai. The "same law" that was written on Adam's heart, according to the confession, was "delivered by God upon Mount Sinai" (19.2). So even though fallen man cannot obey, they are still required by God to obey.

Fourth, the covenant of works continues after the fall, as 19.6 strongly implies, because the only way to be free from the demands

---

2 For example, "The covenant of works being broken by sin, and made unprofitable unto life" (20.1).

of the law "as a covenant of works" is to be justified by Christ and brought into the covenant of grace by faith. Unlike our Presbyterian friends, Baptists do not believe in any dual covenantal membership. According to the 1689, Adam's descendants are either under the covenant of works or they are under the covenant of grace. It is one or the other: for it is impossible for those represented by the first Adam (i.e., the natural seed of believers) to be members of the covenant of grace. Moreover, just as it is impossible for those represented by the first Adam to keep the covenant of works, it is impossible for those represented by the second Adam to break the covenant of grace. This is a major Baptist distinctive that is confirmed by the 1689.

In summary, the covenant of works consisted of God's promising Adam and his children eternal life for perfect obedience and threatening eternal death for a single act of disobedience. Though Adam broke the covenant of works and brought death and condemnation on all his seed, the demands and curses of the covenant of works continue to be enforced on all of Adam's seed who are outside of faith in Jesus Christ.

The Covenant of Works and the Mosaic Covenant

The conditional terms of the prelapsarian covenant of works, which consisted of the moral law, were the same conditional terms in the postlapsarian covenant established with the Israelites at the base of Mount Sinai (19.2). According to the 1689, along with the moral law (which, as we have seen, cannot be altered or change or abrogated) were added various positive laws (which can be altered, changed, and abrogated). The positive laws, which included the ceremonial and judicial laws, according to the confession, were to be enforced only until "the time of reformation" when Christ brought an end to them at his death (8.2, 3).

The moral law, because it demanded perfect obedience, was added to the Mosaic covenant not to encourage Israel to seek to obtain life through works, but to show the Israelites that they were already condemned by the law and in need of a savior. Nehemiah Coxe stated it this way:

> This must also not be forgotten: that as Moses' law in some way included the covenant of creation and served for a memorial of it (on which account all mankind was involved

in its curse), it had not only the sanction of a curse awfully denounced against the disobedient, but also a promise of the reward of life to the obedient. Now as the law of Moses was the same in moral precept with the law of creation, so the reward in this respect proposed was not a new reward, but the same that by compact had been due to Adam, in the case of his perfect obedience.[3]

Though it promised life for perfect obedience, it could not give life to those who have already fallen short in Adam. As Philip Cary, another seventeenth-century Baptist, claimed: "For although in its self it requires a perfect righteousness, and gives a promise of life thereon, he that doth these things, shall live in them. Yet, it could give neither righteousness nor life to any in a state of sin."[4]

The Covenant of Grace

Because the covenant of works leaves sinners hopeless, sinners need the gospel. Because of this, paragraph 2 introduces the gospel by introducing the covenant of grace: "Moreover, man having brought himself under the curse of the law by his fall, it pleased the Lord to make a covenant of grace, wherein he freely offereth unto sinners life and salvation by Jesus Christ" (7.2). The union between the covenant of grace and the gospel is reaffirmed in chapter 20: "The covenant of works being broken by sin, and made unprofitable unto life, God was pleased to give forth the promise of Christ, the seed of the woman, as the means of calling the elect, and begetting in them faith and repentance: in this promise of the gospel" (20.1).

The Covenant of Grace Is the Only Means of Salvation

Though the confession teaches the perpetuity of the covenant of works throughout the Old and New Testament dispensations, it strongly affirms that salvation in both dispensations is by grace and grace alone. The continuation of the covenant of works was not to drive sinners to the law, but to drive them to their knees. Because the law is unable to bestow eternal life to covenant breakers, God revealed the gospel immediately after the fall (20.1). Adam and all his fallen offspring were given hope of eternal life through the

---

3 Coxe and Owen, *Covenant Theology*, 46.
4 *A Solemn Call* (London: John Harris, 1690), 132.

proclamation of the gospel, and through the proclamation of the gospel alone.

What is interesting about paragraph 2 is the absence of the main distinctive of Presbyterian covenant theology: that the old and new covenants are two different administrations of the same covenant of grace. The Westminster Confession states, "There are not therefore two covenants of grace, differing in substance, but one and the same, under various dispensations" (7.6). This allows for Presbyterians to incorporate unbelieving children into the covenant of grace. This phrase was removed from the 1689, and for good reason. The 1689 does not claim that the Mosaic covenant was an administration of the covenant of grace. Rather, it simply says that the covenant of grace was innately revealed in the *protoevangelium* (Gen. 3:15), and then with greater clarity it was revealed throughout the progression of the Old Testament dispensation until it came to its fullest manifestation in the New Testament: "This covenant is revealed [not established] in the gospel; first of all to Adam in the promise of salvation by the seed of the woman, and afterwards by further steps, until the full discovery thereof was completed in the New Testament" (7.3).

More explicitly, the 1689 says that the covenant of grace, which was established by the blood of Jesus, was retroactive during the Old Testament dispensation: "Although the price of redemption was not actually paid by Christ until after His incarnation, yet the virtue, efficacy, and benefit thereof were communicated to the elect in all ages" (8.6). This is in agreement with Benjamin Keach, who said, "All believers, who lived under the Old Testament, were saved by the covenant of grace, which Christ was to establish."[5]

This implies that the covenant of grace is identical to the new covenant. So rather than the covenant of grace being established through various administrations of the different covenants of the Old Testament (Abrahamic, Mosaic, and Davidic), it was established by Christ in the new covenant. As the confession says, the Old Testament saints were saved by the blood of the new covenant: "Although the price of redemption was not actually paid by Christ until after His incarnation, yet the virtue, efficacy, and benefit thereof were communicated to the elect in all ages, successively from the beginning of the world, in and by those promises, types,

5 Benjamin Keach, *The Display of Glorious Grace: The Covenant of Peace Opened in Fourteen Sermons* (London: S. Bridge, 1698), 115.

and sacrifices wherein He was revealed, and signified to be the seed which should bruise the serpent's head" (8.6).

Therefore, Old Testament believers were saved by faith in Christ, in the same way New Testament believers are saved by faith in Christ. As chapter 11.6 states: "The justification of believers under the Old Testament was . . . one and the same with the justification of believers under the New Testament." Or as paragraph 3 of chapter 7 states: "It is alone by the grace of this covenant that all the posterity of fallen Adam that ever were saved did obtain life and blessed immortality."

And, if membership in the covenant of grace is by faith in Christ alone, then only believers alone, and not their unbelieving children, are in the covenant of grace. In fact, this is one of the main distinctives of Baptist covenant theology: only believers, in any dispensation, are members of the covenant of grace. This formation of covenant theology makes the 1689 distinct from the covenant theology of the Westminster Confession of Faith.

The Covenant of Grace Is the Fulfillment of the Covenant of Works

Moreover, according to the 1689, Christ established the covenant of grace by fulfilling the legal demands of the covenant of works: as the 1689 says, "[the Lord] was made under the law, and did perfectly fulfil it" (8.4). Not only did he obey the same demands of the covenant of works that we were obligated to obey, he "underwent the punishment due to us, which we should have borne and suffered, being made sin and a curse for us" (8.4). For instance, Philip Cary claimed, "It is evident that Christ submitted to it as a covenant of works. And if it was so to Christ, it was so to us, and would have been so, and the curse thereof had accordingly lighted on us, had not Christ interposed for our relief. But, (says the Apostle) when the fullness of time was come, God sent forth his son made of a woman, made under the law, to redeem them that were under the law." Cary went on to say,

> The law was therefore no other than a covenant of works, from which Christ hath now redeemed us, by his blood and sufferings for us. The law indeed shows us our sin and misery

without Christ, but relieves us not. Which the covenant of faith doth, Rom. 10:6–9. Nay the law, instead of relieving or curing us, it brings us under the curse, which the covenant of faith delivers us from, Gal. 3:8, 9, 10. But though we are delivered from the law as a covenant of life, do this, and live.[6]

This is why we are saved by works, but the works that save us are the imputed works of Christ that come by faith alone and grace alone. The covenant of grace is the fulfillment of the covenant of works, or it could be said that the new covenant is a covenant of works for Christ, but a covenant of grace for believers. As Benjamin Keach stated, "As it refers to Christ ... it was a conditional covenant. Christ receives all for us, wholly upon the account of His own merits. But whatsoever we receive by virtue of this covenant, it is wholly in a way of free grace and favor, through His merits, or through that redemption we have by His blood."[7]

In this covenantal framework we see the unity of the Scriptures and a single plan of redemption throughout the Old and New Testaments. Adam's children are either condemned by the first Adam, or they are justified by the second Adam. They are either under the covenant of works or under the covenant of grace—and this depending on who is their federal head. Again, this separates Baptists from Presbyterians, as it does not allow for either unbelieving children or covenant breakers to be members of the covenant of grace.

The Covenant of Redemption

The last paragraph of chapter 7 explains why the history of redemption does not depict God as adjusting his plans on the fly. The covenant of grace was established by Christ enduring the penalty of the covenant of works in His death and by His meriting the reward of the covenant of works in His resurrection. Yet, all this was in accordance with God's eternal plan that was established between the Father and Son before the foundation of the world (7.1). Or, as chapter 8 explains it, "it pleased God, in His eternal purpose, to choose and ordain the Lord Jesus, his only begotten Son, according to the covenant made between them both, to be the mediator between God and

---

6 *A Solemn Call*, 137.
7 Keach, "The Display of Glorious Grace," 157.

man" (8.1). Thus, the history of redemption, including the prelapsarian covenant of works and the postlapsarian covenant of grace, is the outworking of the eternal covenant of redemption.

Conclusion

The covenant theology of the 1689 is brilliantly laid out. It clearly states the main distinctives of Baptist covenant theology. There is (1) a prelapsarian covenant of works that was broken by the first Adam and condemns *all* unbelievers, (2) but that was fulfilled by the second Adam who established the postlapsarian covenant of grace for *only* believers, (3) and this was in accordance with the eternal covenant of redemption.

With a clear distinction between the covenant of works and the covenant of grace, and with a clear distinction between unbelievers and believers, the 1689 presents a distinct covenant theology that is thoroughly Baptistic.

12

The Gospel and the Extent of Its Grace in the Second London Confession of Faith

Thomas K. Ascol

CHAPTER 20 OF THE SECOND LONDON Baptist Confession of Faith is drawn exclusively from its Congregational ancestor, the Savoy Declaration, which was published in 1658. The Westminster does not contain a separate chapter on the gospel. In the preface to their declaration, the Congregationalists state the reason for including a new chapter (entitled "Of the gospel and the extent of the grace thereof") after chapter 19, which is on the law of God: "After the 19th *cap*. Of the Law, we have added a *cap*. Of the Gospel, it being a Title that may not well be omitted in a Confession of Faith: In which Chapter, what is dispersed, and by intimation in the Assemblies' Confession, with some little addition, is here brought together, and more fully, under one head."[1] A few paragraphs before that explanation the authors of the Savoy write, "A few things we have added for obviating some erroneous Opinions, that have been more broadly and boldly here of late maintained by the Asserters,

---

1 Philip Schaff, *The Creeds of Christendom*, (1931; repr., Grand Rapids: Baker Book House, 1983), 3:715.

than in former times; and made some other additions and alterations in *method*, here and there, and some clearer Explanations, as we found occasion."[2]

So, the rationale for adding a new chapter is the sensed need to have a separate statement on the gospel itself, especially following a separate chapter on the law of God. Further, it could well be that this addition was made, as Sam Waldron suggests, in light of the growing influence of certain erroneous opinions surrounding the saving nature of the gospel and the limitations of natural revelation. Waldron surmises that perhaps the tendency that would result in full-blown Deism later in the century was already being engaged and that this chapter was designed, in part, to stand against it.[3] Whether that is precisely the case or not, it is certainly true that Deism did come to full bloom in the latter seventeenth century and eighteenth century (John Toland [1670–1722], Anthony Collins [1676–1729], Voltaire [1694–1778]). However, the matter that chapter 20 addresses is of perennial interest to Christians because of questions that the exclusivity of the gospel inevitably provoke.

From the early centuries after the New Testament down to the present, believers have been confronted with challenges about the extent of God's grace. Common questions that Christians regularly face include:

+ Will everyone ultimately be saved?

+ How were people saved before the coming of Christ?

+ Can people be saved apart from the gospel of Christ?

+ What about those who have never heard the gospel?

+ How can God hold men accountable if they never had the opportunity to believe the gospel?

+ Doesn't everyone deserve a chance to hear the gospel?

+ What about sincere followers of other religions?

As a young seminary student, I once discussed this issue over breakfast with Anglican Bishop of Woolwich, John A. T. Robinson (d. 1983), whose 1963 book, *Honest to God*, helped popularize liberal theology's displacement of orthodox Christianity. Deep into the

---

2 Schaff, *Creeds of Christendom*, 3:714.

3 Samuel E. Waldron, *A Modern Exposition of the 1689 Baptist Confession of Faith*, 5th ed. (Darlington, Co. Durham, England: Evangelical Press, 2016), 290–91.

conversation I asked him pointedly whether his views inevitably lead to the idea that everyone everywhere would finally be saved. His answer, though void of biblical fidelity, was refreshingly candid as he responded, "I take great pleasure in thinking so."

Chapter 20 of the Second London Confession stands in complete contradiction of Bishop Robinson's pleasurable fantasy. It asserts the exclusivity of Christ as the only Mediator between God and mankind as well as the necessity of the Holy Spirit in sovereignly regenerating those who hear the gospel message, thereby granting them spiritual life. Apart from the redemptive revelation of God given to us in the Holy Scriptures, there is no salvation for sinners.

The truths set forth in this chapter are as relevant for us today as they were in the seventeenth century when they were written into the confession. In North America, the Unitarian Universalist Church has steadily grown in the twenty-first century. From 2000–2010 its membership grew by 15.8 percent according to the Association of Statisticians of American Religious Bodies.[4] This group believes that any and every kind of belief will get you to heaven. It does not matter, because everyone will ultimately be saved. It is, as their name declares, universalism.

Even more alarming is the increase in the number of evangelicals over the last 30 years who have begun to suggest that perhaps there is more than one way to salvation. They are not universalists, but rather "inclusivists," who believe that the salvation that is found in Christ is available in other religions as well. The late Clark Pinnock is perhaps the best known of these modern advocates. His book, *A Wideness in God's Mercy*, signaled his departure from the orthodox confession that salvation is found exclusively through faith in Jesus Christ. Sadly, he has attracted a significant following.

Over against universalism and all forms of inclusivism, the Second London Confession's chapter 20 plainly affirms the uniqueness and finality of the gospel of Jesus Christ as the only way of salvation. This gospel is revealed exclusively in the written Word of God.

---

4   Bob Smietana, "Unitarian faith growing nationwide," *USA Today*, October 2, 2012, https://www.usatoday.com/story/news/nation/2012/10/01/unitarian-faith-growing-stronger-nationwide/1607243.

The Gospel and Salvation

As the first paragraph states, the gospel—the good news of God's gracious provision of salvation in Jesus Christ, is first revealed in the Bible in Genesis 3:15. As Adam stands in the ashes of his own moral and spiritual ruins ("The covenant of works being broken by sin, and made unprofitable unto life") God promised to send Christ, "the seed of the woman," to destroy the devil and save his elect people.

This promise must have landed on the ears of Adam and Eve as sheer grace. They had clearly violated God's command not to eat of the tree of the knowledge of good and evil and knew that they had earned the penalty of death (Gen. 2:16–17). Yet, even before God pronounces his just judgment against their sin, he includes these words of grace and mercy in the midst of his curse against the serpent: "I will put enmity between you and the woman, and between your offspring and her offspring; he shall bruise your head, and you shall bruise his heel." This is an undeserved promise of blessing—the blessing of a coming Savior. Adam and Eve believed this promise (which is the only way to receive the gospel) and were provided a sign of God's salvation through it when the Lord sacrificed animals in order to provide clothing for them (Gen. 3:21).

This point eliminates Deism, inclusivism, and all other views that would allow for a way of salvation for sinners other than through faith in Jesus Christ (including classic Dispensationalism). What is being asserted is that there has always been only one way of salvation for sinners—only one way that sinners can attain eternal life, and that is through faith in God's promised Redeemer.

Granted, what Adam and Eve could know of the coming Redeemer is far less than what we know today. The knowledge of the coming Christ was progressively revealed across the Old Testament until it was fully and finally revealed in the New Testament. But what was revealed in Genesis 3:15 is neither different from nor other than what is more fully and finally revealed in the rest of Scripture. As the confession puts it, "in this promise the gospel, as to the substance of it, was revealed." It is like the relationship of a bud to a flower, or like the breaking of dawn to the noonday sun.

The only way that sinners have ever been or ever can be saved is through the gospel of Jesus Christ. Old Testament saints were not made right with God by keeping His commandments. Rather, as the confession states, they were saved by believing the gospel—the promise of God's provision of salvation through a Redeemer. This is why we teach our children in Question 54 of the Children's Catechism, "How were godly persons saved before the coming of Christ? By believing in the Savior to come."[5]

The Gospel and the Word

The gospel has only been made known by special revelation. Because of sin, it had to be this way. As paragraph 2 of chapter 20 says, "This promise of Christ, and salvation by him, is revealed only by the Word of God; neither do the works of creation or providence, with the light of nature, make discovery of Christ, or of grace by him."

God does reveal himself in nature but not in a way that sinful people can come to know him savingly. Psalm 19 is perhaps the classic passage in Scripture that shows the distinction between general revelation in nature and saving revelation in Scripture. Verses 1–6 describe the heavens, the sky, day, night, and the sun as declaring the glory of God to all people everywhere. There is objective, truthful revelation from God to be found in creation and providence.

However, none of that revelation—as God-glorifying as it is—can do what Scripture does in revealing Christ, as verses 7–11 make plain. God's Word revives the soul and make the simple wise (v. 7). It rejoices the heart and enlightens the eyes (v. 8). God's written words are more desirable than gold, sweeter than honey (v. 10), warn his servants and reward those who keep them (v. 11). In other words, the way of salvation and the blessings of God's grace are revealed only in Scripture.

The confession goes on to say that "men destitute of the revelation of Him by the promise or gospel" cannot be "enabled thereby to attain saving faith or repentance." We can learn some things about God from the light of nature, but we cannot learn the gospel of his grace from that source. Paul explains it like this in Romans 1:18–20, "For the wrath of God is revealed from heaven against all ungodliness and unrighteousness of men, who by their unrighteousness suppress the truth. For what can be known about God is plain to them, because God has shown it to them. For his invisible attributes,

5 Thomas K. Ascol, ed., *Truth & Grace Memory Book 1* (Cape Coral: Founders, 2017), 32.

namely, his eternal power and divine nature, have been clearly perceived, ever since the creation of the world, in the things that have been made. So they are without excuse."

People who never hear the gospel are accountable to God for their sin because God has revealed himself to everyone in creation. Nature sheds enough light about the character, power, and nature of God so that people are without excuse before him. But nature does not reveal the gospel of Christ, whereby sinners can be saved. It is only the message of the person and work of Jesus that brings salvation.

This is why Christian churches must be zealous in their efforts to proclaim the gospel throughout the whole world. The message of Christ is the only message that God uses to save sinners. As Paul writes in Romans 10:14, "How then will they call on him in whom they have not believed? And how are they to believe in him of whom they have never heard? And how are they to hear without someone preaching?"

That verse is printed on the title page of William Carey's 1792 treatise, *An Enquiry into the Obligations of Christians to Use Means for the Conversion of the Heathens.* He, along with his fellow Particular Baptist pastor friends of the Northampton Association in England (whose confession of faith was the Second London Confession), were fully convinced that only through the divinely revealed gospel of Jesus can sinners be saved. This conviction led to the formation of the Particular Baptist Society for the Propagation of the Gospel Amongst the Heathen and fueled what became known as the modern missionary movement.

Because the gospel is the only saving message that God has revealed, we who have been entrusted with it must be faithful stewards of it by making it widely known.

The Gospel and Providence

The exclusivity and necessity of the gospel for salvation raises the question of why this saving message has been made known to some people and not others. Paragraph two addresses this question by attributing the access to and spread of the gospel to the providence of God: "The revelation of the gospel unto sinners, made in divers times and by sundry parts, with the addition of promises and precepts for the obedience required therein, as to the nations and persons to whom it is granted, is merely of the sovereign will and good pleasure of God."

Here the confession safeguards the sovereignty of God's grace in salvation by underscoring that not only the provision of salvation but also the spread of its message is "according to the counsel of the will of God," as paragraph 3 goes on to explain. God is neither contingent nor reactionary in his dealings with his creatures. In other words, he does not help those who help themselves. He does not send the gospel to those who, by virtue of the light of nature, do all that they can to reach him. He does not wait for people to take the first step toward him before he goes to meet them.

Rather, out of sheer grace, according to his inscrutable providence (see chapter 5 of the confession), he causes the gospel to spread to people and nations. It must be this way because of the ravages of sin on fallen humanity. At this point, chapter 20 is underscoring what has already been taught in chapter 9: "Man, by his fall into a state of sin, hath wholly lost all ability of will to any spiritual good accompanying salvation; so as a natural man, being altogether averse from that good, and dead in sin, is not able by his own strength to convert himself, or to prepare himself thereunto" (paragraph 3).

The doctrine of total depravity recognizes that sinners are enslaved to sin such that they are by nature spiritually dead (Eph. 2:1–3) and without spiritual ability to improve their standing before God (Rom. 8:7–8). Salvation is by God's grace from beginning to end, including how, when, and to whom the saving message spreads.

Some see the confession's teaching at this point as destroying the missionary mandate. But the truth is the exact opposite. To whom much is given, much is required, and no person or people could ever be given more than the gospel. And what does faithful stewardship of the gospel of Christ entail? It entails obeying the commission that Christ gave to the people whom he saves when he said, "Go therefore and make disciples of all nations, baptizing them in the name of the Father and of the Son and of the Holy Spirit, teaching them to observe all that I have commanded you. And behold, I am with you always, to the end of the age" (Matthew 28:19–20).

This understanding of God's sovereignty in salvation was one of the chief principles that undergirded William Carey's incredible missionary work in India. On October 7, 1805, he and his fellow missionaries met in Serampore and entered into a "Form of Agreement" outlining the principles on which their mission work would operate. The first of those principles answers the question, "Why are we here?"

> The Redeemer, in planting us in the heathen nation, rather than in any other, has imposed upon us the cultivation of peculiar qualifications. We are firmly persuaded that Paul might plant and Apollos water, in vain, in any part of the world, did not God give the increase. We are sure that only those ordained to eternal life will believe, and that God alone can add to the church such as shall be saved. Nevertheless, we cannot but observe with admiration that Paul, the great champion for the glorious doctrine of free and sovereign grace, was the most conspicuous for his personal zeal in the word of persuading men to be reconciled to God. In this respect he is a noble example for our imitation. Our Lord intimated to those of His apostles who were fishermen, that he would make them fishers of men, intimating that in all weathers, and amidst every disappointment they were to aim at drawing men to the shores of eternal life. Solomon says: "He that winneth souls is wise," implying, no doubt, that the work of gaining over men to the side of God, was to be done by winning methods, and that it required the greatest wisdom to do it with success. Upon these points, we think it right to fix our serious and abiding attention.[6]

This statement, along with the other principles of the compact, were read aloud three times each year at their stated workers' meetings in order, as they said, "to keep these ideas alive in our minds." The weight of stewardship that comes with being entrusted with the gospel caused Paul to say, "Necessity is laid upon me. Woe to me if I do not preach the gospel!" (1 Cor. 9:16; cf. 9:17). May that same sense of stewardship be kindled among all those today who recognize the sovereignty of God's grace in salvation!

---

6 William Carey, Joshua Marshman, William Ward, John Chamberlain, Richard Mardon, John Biss, William Moore, Joshua Rowe & Felix Carey (1947) "The Serampore Form of Agreement," *Baptist Quarterly*, 12:5: 129–130.

The Gospel and the Spirit

The last paragraph of chapter 20 reaffirms that the gospel is "the only outward means of revealing Christ and saving grace, and is, as such, abundantly sufficient thereunto." But it adds that in order for "men who are dead in trespasses" to be "born again, quickened, or regenerated, there is moreover necessary an effectual insuperable work of the Holy Spirit upon the whole soul, for the producing in them a new spiritual life." In other words, for anyone to be saved not only must the Word of God (the gospel message) come to him outwardly but also the Spirit of God must work in Him inwardly. This is what happened to Lydia in Philippi. Luke records that as Paul taught the word, "the Lord opened her heart to pay attention to what was said" (Acts 16:14). It is what happened at Pentecost when Peter preached the gospel in the power of the Spirit. Those who heard the only outward means of revealing Christ from the apostle's lips were "cut to the heart," resulting in their repentance and faith.

Just as Christians are stewards of the gospel so we are also dependent on God's Spirit to make our proclamation of the gospel effectual in those who hear our message (as the confession teaches in chapter 10, paragraph 1). So, we must not only preach, we must also pray. The gospel is the only message that saves. And that message only saves when it is powerfully owned by the sovereign Spirit to grant new life to those who hear.

Conclusion

Chapter 20 is an appropriate addition to the Second London Baptist Confession as an explanation of and safeguard to the exclusivity and necessity of the saving message of Christ. If sinners are to be saved, it will only be through the gospel. The evangelistic and missionary implications of this are clear even if they are not fully articulated in the four paragraphs of this chapter.[7] Men will be lost if they never hear the gospel. If they do not hear, then they will never even have the opportunity to be saved. No one deserves to hear the gospel by virtue of his own merit or effort. Salvation is all of grace, both in its provision as well as in its accessibility. No one deserves to be saved. Those who are saved are indebted to God's grace in both redemption

---

7 See Tom J. Nettles, "A Suggested Addition to the Second London Confession," *Founders Journal*, no. 61 (Summer 2005): 22–26.

and providence. Left to themselves, and to the light of nature, none will be saved. There is enough revelation of God in nature to leave people without excuse, but not enough to save them. Therefore, all people need the gospel of Jesus Christ proclaimed to them (Rom. 10:13–15). And those who hear the gospel need the Holy Spirit to open their hearts and minds to turn from sin and believe it. Those who savingly believe the gospel must take it to those who have not believed it. Because it is the only message that saves, the commission of our Lord to make disciples is an urgent matter of stewardship. To whom much is given, much will be required.

13

The Civil Magistrate and the Second London Confession of Faith

Samuel E. Waldron

D OES IT SURPRISE YOU THAT THE confession contains a chapter on the subject "Of the Civil Magistrate"? Are you inclined to ask, "What does politics have to do with Christ?"

If that is something of your response, may I suggest that you are a victim of a religious background that has retreated from its social responsibilities under a wrong view of the separation of church and state? Such an attitude has virtually denied the sovereignty of God over all areas of life. To restrict Christianity to the "spiritual" realm is, ultimately, to destroy it.

The Divine Ordination of the Office of Civil Magistrate

Paragraph 1: God, the supreme Lord and King of all the world, hath ordained civil magistrates to be under him, over the people, for his own glory and the public good and to this end hath armed them with the power of the sword, for defense and encouragement of them that do good and for the punishment of evil doers.

The first and central point asserted in this paragraph is that civil magistrates are divinely appointed. They derive their authority from God. This strikes at the root of a fundamental modern error. A. A. Hodge properly remarks,

> Some have supposed that the right or legitimate authority of human government has its foundation ultimately in "the consent of the governed," "the will of the majority," or in some imaginary "social compact" entered into by the forefathers of the race at the origin of social life. It is self-evident, however, that the divine will is the source of all government and the obligation to obey that will, resting upon all moral agents, the ultimate ground of all obligation to obey human governments.[1]

As Hodge makes clear, we obey because God wills it, not because we have voluntarily committed ourselves to certain men to whom we have given authority. The Bible does not teach the social contract theory of government that many of us were taught in school. According to Romans 13:1–2, the Roman emperors were divinely ordained rulers even though they did not derive their authority from "the consent of the governed." The theory that says we obey our rulers because they ultimately obey us is neither true, nor biblical.

This paragraph makes three specific points about the divine ordination of the Civil Magistrate.

His Ordained Position

This is described as being "under him [God] and over the people." In Romans 13:2, 4, and 6, this position of authority is described variously as "the ordinance of God," "the minister of God," and "the servant of God." These descriptions epitomize the statement of the confession. The civil authority is bound to obey God in how it rules, just as we are bound to obey it. God has given them all the authority they possess. "To whom much is given of them much will be required" (Luke 12:48).

His Ordained Purpose

This is described by the confession in the following words: "for his own glory and the public good." This purpose is also mentioned in

---

1   A. A. Hodge, *The Confession of Faith* (Edinburgh: Banner of Truth, 1869), 293.

the phrase "for defense and encouragement of them that do good and for the punishment of evil doers." Note also the statement of paragraph 2, "to maintain justice and peace." What does the Bible teach as to the specific function or task of civil rulers? The following passages address this subject: Gen. 6:11–13 with 9:5–6, Pss. 58:2; 72:14; 82:1–4; Prov. 21:15; 24:11, 12; 29:14, 26; 31:5; Ezek. 7:23; 45:9; Dan. 4:27; Matt. 22:21; Rom. 13:3, 4; 1 Tim. 2:2; 1 Peter 2:14. The teaching of such passages is that the task of civil government is to maintain social and civil justice and peace by suppressing violence and social injustice and praising (defending and promoting) those who socially and civilly do what is good.

His Ordained Power

The confession states with reference to the power of the civil magistrate, "And to this end [God] hath armed them with the power of the sword." This statement confirms that the sphere of action of the civil magistrate is the civil sphere. Swords are not used to train children or to discipline unrepentant professing Christians. They are suitable to suppress violent criminals and public injustice.

The Bible teaches that God has armed this office with the sword (Gen. 9:6; Prov. 16:14; 19:12; 20:2; 21:15; Acts 25:11; Rom. 13:4; 1 Peter 2:14). G. I. Williamson pointedly remarks,

> In our own nation today, there is a growing trend in the direction of abolishing capital punishment. And many liberal Protestant groups have sanctioned this change on the grounds that it does not benefit society, reform the criminal, or reflect the humane teachings of the New Testament. In other words, for various reasons, it is widely advocated today that the civil government be denied the power of the sword to punish evil. Such a view of civil authority is, to say the least, highly unbiblical. We do not think that it can be proved that capital punishment does not benefit society. We believe that it does, if for no other reason because the Scripture says that the faithful exercise of justice is a terror to evil works and an encouragement to good. Opponents of capital punishment deny this, but they deny it in vain. It may be true that capital punishment fails to reform the criminal. But we completely doubt that the absence of terror against

evil reforms the criminal either. Furthermore, we doubt not that it encourages evil. But above all, we deny that civil power and authority is supposed to reflect the modernist notions of the "humane" teachings of the New Testament. Justice is not any more "humane" in the New than in the Old Testament. And the ordinance of civil government is not meant by God to teach the New Testament; it is to punish crime and to protect those who do good. However, we doubt that the scheme of the liberals who advocate abolishing capital punishment is "humane." We believe that much modern crime is due to the fact that there is too much unbiblical concern for the wicked and too little biblical concern for the upright.[2]

The Christian's Involvement in the
Office of Civil Magistrate

Paragraph 2: It is lawful for Christians to accept and execute the office of a magistrate when called there unto; in the management whereof, as they ought especially to maintain justice and peace, according to the wholesome laws of each kingdom and commonwealth, so for that end they may lawfully now, under the New Testament wage war upon just and necessary occasions.

The main point of this paragraph is clearly that it is not unlawful for a Christian to be a civil magistrate and to fulfil the full range of that office's duties up to and including waging war. The biblical support for this assertion is varied. In Luke 3:14 soldiers who repented at the preaching of John the Baptist and who desired to live a Christian life were not told to forsake their soldiering, even though the very essence of their function as a soldier would be to make war. In Romans 13:2, 4, and 6 call this position of authority "the ordinance of God," "the minister of God," and "the servant of God." These lofty descriptions clearly assume the lawfulness of the office. Furthermore, they assume this lawfulness in direct relation to the power of the sword. The use of the sword in Romans 13:4

---

2   G. I. Williamson, *The Westminster Confession of Faith: For Study Classes* (Philadelphia, PA: Presbyterian and Reformed, 1964), 242.

has direct reference to military actions to put down rebellion. Note especially the words used in verse 2. Thus, it is used as a form of war. Capital punishment, while assumed, is not the original use of the sword contemplated here. The examples of Nehemiah, Daniel, his three friends, and all the just judges in Israel also support the assertion of the confession. Finally, the legitimacy of this office for Christians is assumed by frequent assertions of the book of Proverbs (14:35; 16:10, 12; 20:26, 28; 25:2; 28:15–16; 29:4, 14; 31:4–5).

Christian pacifists of every kind ask, "How can this be?" "What about the sixth commandment and the teaching of Jesus in Matthew 5:38–48?" The scriptural response to such objections consists in a crucial biblical distinction. The Bible distinguishes between the personal vocation and duties of individuals and the public vocation and duties of magistrates. While the personal duty of individuals is not to take vengeance into their hands, the solemn and public duty of magistrates is to exercise God's vengeance on civil evildoers. Note this distinction implied in a comparison of Romans 12:17–21, especially verse 19, with Romans 13:3–4. It is wrong for a private person to take revenge. It is right for a public magistrate. Matthew 5:37–48 is referring to the duty of private persons, not public officials. It is only with this distinction in mind that the Mosaic law, especially the Sixth Commandment, is relieved of an insoluble problem. If it is wrong to kill, how can Yahweh, through his servant Moses, in the very chapter succeeding the one where this commandment is given, tell judges to take the life of, that is, to kill certain criminals? Only the orthodox distinction between the public and private spheres makes any sense of this.

Two important lessons are suggested by all of this. The first is ethical, the second historical.

First, one's duty before God greatly depends on one's vocation or calling. It might be, in some cases it would be, wrong for you to do what others may do. Why? Their calling in life is different. For instance, it is certainly right for a parent on certain occasions to spank his child. It would not be right for someone else to discipline that parent's child without his consent. Why? The other person has no divine calling to be "the parent" of someone else's child. The child's own parents are "called" to parent the child. The concept of vocation is a key part of biblical ethics rediscovered and re-emphasized by the Reformation.

Second, our Baptist forefathers were not Anabaptists. It was Anabaptists who taught that Christians could not occupy the office of the civil magistrate without sin. It was they who taught that this office was "of the devil." Clearly, our Baptist forefathers completely rejected such a view of government and the resultant pacifism it implied. They publicly distanced themselves from it in their Confession of faith. It is appropriate to note here that the mainstream of Baptists in America are descended from Puritans who came to Baptist convictions, not Anabaptists. Most modern Baptists are historically Calvinist and Puritan in their origin, not Anabaptist and Arminian.

The Believer's Subjection to the Office of Civil Magistrate

> Paragraph 3: God hath decreed in himself, from all eternity, by the most wise and holy counsel of His own will, freely and unchangeably, all things, whatsoever comes to pass; yet so as thereby is God neither the author of sin nor hath fellowship with any therein; nor is violence offered to the will of the creature, nor yet is the liberty or contingency of second causes taken away, but rather established; in which appears His wisdom in disposing all things, and power and faithfulness in accomplishing His decree.

Though this statement is taken verbatim from the First London Confession, the teaching of this paragraph is firmly rooted in the preceding paragraphs. Note the opening words. The confession asserts that since the civil magistrate is ordained by God to maintain justice and peace, two clear duties follow.

The Duty of Obedience

Besides Romans 13:1–7, the following passages clearly teach the duty of submitting to, honoring, and, consequently, obeying the civil authorities: Prov. 16:14–15; 19:12; 20:2; 24:21–22; 25:15; 28:2; Titus 3:1; 1 Peter 2:13–14. This duty of submission is, of course, not unrestricted. The confession states a clear qualification: "Subjection, in all lawful things commanded by them, ought to be yielded by us." See the following passages: Dan. 1:8; 3:4–6, 16–18; 6:5–10, 22; Matt. 22:21; Acts 4:19, 20; 5:29.

Obedience to rulers is only appropriate "in all lawful things." The great question is, however, "What defines what is lawful?" The answer must be the Word of God alone, not our opinions, our feelings, our traditions, or our convenience. The Word of God written is the sole authority for what is lawful.

Note that there is no precedent for a Christian displaying a belligerent, rebellious attitude toward civil authority in the Bible. Peter's response in Acts 4:19 is remarkably tame, when it is compared with the belligerence of certain segments of professing Christianity in our day. There is an instructive example of such belligerence. It is that of Paul in Acts 23:1–5. There, however, Paul quickly apologizes, even though he was provoked to it by a miscarriage of justice! Neither belligerent attitudes nor deliberately provocative behavior are appropriate, even when a Christian must decline obedience.

The Duty of Prayer for Civil Magistrates

The key text here is 1 Timothy 2:1–4. The clear goal of our prayers for our civil authorities is our tranquility of life to the end of the gospel's prosperity. Thus, the character of these prayers is that they are to be "entreaties, prayers, petitions, and thanksgivings" to God "on behalf of kings and all who are in authority." We are to pray for the welfare of all men and especially for the welfare of our rulers in order that, firstly, they might be saved and secondly, that their rule might prosper and prevail so that they can protect us from those who would disturb our tranquility. This, of course, does not mean that imprecatory prayers are never appropriate. It does mean that our basic attitude toward our rulers as expressed in our prayers is to be supportive.

The Biblical Doctrine of Human Authority

In this exposition of the biblical doctrine of human authority it is my conviction that everything I will say is completely consistent with the 1689 Baptist Confession. I believe, however, that in light of the contemporary importance of this doctrine it is necessary to go into detail about some matters about which the confession is silent.

Acts 5 records that early in the history of the fledgling church at Jerusalem, in an effort to stop the spread of the gospel, the Sanhedrin (the supreme court of the Jewish nation) forbade the Apostles to preach any longer in the name of Jesus Christ. The response of the apostle Peter is universally recognized as the classic statement of Scripture on the subject of conscientious disobedience. In response to a court order from the highest court of the nation, Peter affirmed, "We must obey God rather than men" (Acts 5:29). By way of introduction to the subject of conscientious disobedience, observe two things from Peter's words.

First, notice that the duty to obey God rather than men is rooted in the reality that God's authority has priority over human authority. Peter said, "We must obey God rather than *men.*" We cannot have proper views on the subject of conscientious disobedience unless we understand clearly that the authority which we must disobey as a matter of conscience before God is human authority which requires of us something contrary to God's will.

Second, notice that Peter's response to the Sanhedrin is stated in terms of a general principle. Peter does not say "we must obey God rather than the Sanhedrin" but "we must obey God rather than men." This principle must not be restricted to the Christian's relation to civil authority. The Sanhedrin, in fact, was a religious (or ecclesiastical) authority as well as a civil authority. Thus, the axiom "we must obey God rather than men" applies to the Christian's relation to every kind of human authority, not just to civil authority.

The importance of this observation is to be seen in the fact that conscientious disobedience is often thought of almost exclusively in terms of civil disobedience. Civil disobedience, however, is only part of the larger biblical doctrine of conscientious disobedience to human authority. The Bible's teaching on conscientious disobedience applies also to our relation to every kind of human authority, including that of husbands, parents, pastors, and employers.

There is profound confusion on this subject today. Women are confused about their duty to their husbands. Reacting against feminism, some have gone to terrible extremes trying to obey ungodly husbands. Pastoral authority certainly is abused in some cases; but in other cases, the legitimate exercise of pastoral authority is berated as tyrannical, overbearing, or even cultic. There is much to be learned from a study of human authority and conscientious disobedience, not only because of the debate over social action, but because of the light it sheds on our duty to human authority in general.

As observed above, Acts 5:29 teaches that the biblical doctrine of conscientious disobedience is intimately connected with the nature of human authority. The key, therefore, to understanding the biblical view of civil disobedience (and, indeed, of all conscientious disobedience) is to understand the nature of human authority. This being so, the place to start when addressing the subject of conscientious disobedience is to examine the nature of human authority.

The nature of human authority may be summarized in one sentence. All human authority is delegated, divine authority. No one has stated this truth more eloquently than John Calvin when he said,

> For to those, to whom he gives any preeminence, he communicates his own authority, as far as is necessary for the preservation of that preeminence. The titles of Father, God, and Lord, are so eminently applicable to him, that, whenever we hear either of them mentioned, our minds cannot but be strongly affected with a sense of his majesty. Those, therefore, on whom he bestows these titles, he illuminates with a ray of divine splendour, to render them all honourable in their respective stations. Thus in a father we recognize something Divine; for it is not without reason that he bears one of the titles of the Deity. Our prince, or our lord, enjoys an honour somewhat similar to that which is given to God.'[3]

The Bible's use of the term "gods" *(Elohim)* to refer to civil authorities clearly illustrates Calvin's point. In Psalm 82:1, 6 and perhaps other texts[4] this word is the same word used countless times in the Old Testament to refer to the Creator.

In what follows we will consider four truths implied by the fact that all human authority is delegated, divine authority. From each of these truths, we will derive a rule crucial to our understanding of conscientious disobedience.

Human Authority Is Divine in Its Origin

All human authority comes ultimately from God, not from man. Human authority, therefore, is divine in its origin. As Calvin said, it is

---

3 John Calvin, *The Institutes of the Christian Religion,* ed. John Allen, (Philadelphia: Presbyterian Board of Christian Education, n.d.), 2:432, 433 [2.8.35].
4 See Ex. 21:6; 22:8, 28.

"a ray of divine splendour."[5] No portion of Scripture more pointedly underscores this truth than Romans 13:1–7.

> Let every soul be in subjection to the governing authorities. For there is no authority except from God, and those which exist are established by God. Therefore, he who resists authority has opposed the ordinance of God; and they who have opposed will receive condemnation upon themselves. For rulers are not a cause of fear for good behavior, but for evil. Do you want to have no fear of authority? Do what is good, and you will have praise from the same; for it is a minister of God to you for good. But if you do what is evil, be afraid; for it does not bear the sword for nothing; for it is a minister of God, an avenger who brings wrath upon the one who practices evil. Wherefore it is necessary to be in subjection, not only because of wrath, but also for conscience's sake. For because of this you also pay taxes, for rulers are servants of God, devoting themselves to this very thing. Render to all what is due them: tax to whom tax is due; custom to whom custom; fear to whom fear; honor to whom honor.

Here, in the most emphatic language, the apostle Paul teaches that "there is no authority except from God, and those which exist are established by God" (v. 1). Paul underscores this truth throughout the remainder of the passage by using such language as "the ordinance of God" (v. 2), "the minister of God" (v. 4), and "the servant of God" (v. 6).

The practical reason for Paul's emphasis on the divine origin of civil authority was the Apostle's fear that a revolutionary political philosophy would influence the church at Rome. Many of the Roman brethren were Jewish Christians with very conservative and typically Jewish scruples.[6] In less than a decade, a violent, revolutionary, Jewish nationalism would produce the Jewish rebellion of AD 66–70. Paul perhaps feared that those influenced by typically Jewish scruples might be vulnerable to typically Jewish politics.[7]

Thus, he emphasizes the divine authority of the Roman government. A logical inference from Paul's teaching is that what God has

---

5 *Institutes*, 2.8.35.
6 See Rom. 14:1–6.
7 John Murray, *The Epistle to the Romans,* (Grand Rapids: Eerdmans: 1968), 2:146.

given only God can take away. Paul warned, "He who resists the authority has opposed the ordinance of God" (v. 2). For us to tear the crown from the head of the one on whom the supreme Sovereign has set it is arrogant defiance of God. Those (including evangelicals) who manifest belligerence, contempt, and rebellion toward the civil authorities are in direct contradiction of the call for subordination found in Romans 13:1–7. The divine origin of such authority must be reverenced.[8] Long ago Calvin caught the essence of Paul's teaching.

The crucial issue is not our duty to submit to "a magistrate who truly answers to his title, who is a father to his country," but our duty to wicked magistrates in whom their subjects "discover no appearance of the image of God."[9] Calvin asserts that "if we direct our attention to the word of God, it will carry us much further; even to submit to the government, not only of those princes who discharge their duty to us with becoming integrity and fidelity, but of all who possess the sovereignty, even though they perform none of the duties of their function."[10]

What rule concerning conscientious disobedience may we deduce legitimately from the divine origin of human authority? Our answer is, *The right to disobey must not be made the pretext for violent revolt.* There are clear limits as to how far even justifiable disobedience may go. Even if respectful disobedience is sometimes proper, we must not deduce from this the right to dishonor divinely originated authority by contempt, belligerence, or revolt. In the history of the church, time and again even good men have failed to recognize this crucial distinction. For example, Francis Schaeffer, in his *Christian Manifesto*, deduces from the right of disobedience the liberty to use violence against "the powers that be."[11] This betrays a failure to

---

8 In Samuel Waldron, *Political Revolution in the Reformed Tradition: A Historical and Biblical Critique* (Conway, AR: Free Grace Press, 2021), the massive biblical support for the interpretation of Rom. 13:1–7 suggested in these sentences is surveyed.

9 *Institutes*, 4.20.24.

10 *Institutes*, 4.20.25. I quote Calvin here not only because he is correct in the deduction he draws from the divine origin of civil authority, but for another reason. The Reformed tradition is often identified with the theory of just revolution. To some degree this association cannot be denied. But Calvin frequently is cited—actually misquoted—as if he originated the revolutionary tradition of Reformed theology. Those who will read Book 4, Chapter 20 of the Institutes with an unprejudiced mind can easily see that Calvin did not believe in the theory of just revolution. It is indefensible to quote Calvin as if he agreed with later Reformed revolutionaries. There is a Reformed tradition that is not revolutionary in its politics.

11 Francis Schaeffer, *A Christian Manifesto* (Westchester: Crossway, 1981),

appreciate the biblical limits of disobedience. Conscientious disobedience is one thing, violence and revolt are something completely
different.

Human Authority Is Delegated in Its Character

Under this second point an implication of the first must be explored.
Human authority, since it is derived from God, is delegated to men
from God. It must, therefore, be used for God. It is a special form of
bearing the image of God. 1 Corinthians 11:7, for instance, makes
this clear when it asserts that the man in his headship over the woman "is the image and glory of God; but the woman is the glory of
the man." As delegated authority, that authority is limited. It must
not be used to contradict the laws of the God who gave it. It must
not transgress the boundaries of the purpose for which God gave it.
Calvin draws the necessary, practical application:

> We are commanded to obey them "in the Lord;" and this
> is evident from the foundation before laid; for they preside
> in that station to which the Lord has exalted them by com-
> municating to them a portion of his honour. . . . Therefore,
> if they instigate us to any transgression of the law we may
> justly consider them not as parents, but as strangers, who
> attempt to seduce us from obedience to our real Father. The
> same observation is applicable to princes, lords, superiors
> of every description. For it is infamous and absurd, that
> their eminence should avail to depreciate the preeminence
> of God, upon which it depends, and to which it ought to
> conduct us.[12]

The rule regarding conscientious disobedience which this truth
teaches us is obvious. *When human authority requires the violation
of God's law, then it must be disobeyed.* This is the manifest meaning
of Peter's statements in Acts 4:19, 20 and 5:29. We must be careful
to assure ourselves from the Scriptures that a divine precept is at

---

89–102.

12 Such statements from Calvin are often cited in favor of the idea of just revolution. This is patently a misuse of Calvin's words. Calvin is speaking in the first place
of parental authority. He cannot mean that if a father once attempts to instigate us
to a transgression of the law of God, he loses his position of authority entirely and
perpetually. Calvin is simply saying—and saying very clearly—that with reference
to the specific matter in which they are attempting to command us to sin, we must
disregard their authority.

stake. Too many in our day mistake their own feelings, impulses, and opinions for the law of God. Where, however, a biblical command will be violated, disobedience is demanded.

Some believe that the rule we have just stated composes the only ground upon which we may disobey human authority. It would, indeed, be much simpler if the exposition could simply stop here and say that this is the only ground for disobeying human authority. "Unfortunately," the teaching of the Bible is not that simple. We must proceed to a third truth and another rule which justifies disobedience to human authority.

Human Authority Is Diverse in Its Form

Even a superficial reading of the Bible teaches us that God has appointed a diversity of human authorities, each with a defined and limited sphere of jurisdiction. There is not just one universal sphere of human authority. God alone has universal authority over every sphere of human life. The civil authority, while impressive in its power, is not the only human authority, nor is its authority unlimited. It does not grant to husbands authority over their wives or to parents authority over their children or to elders authority in the church. The civil government does not give the family the right to be family or the church the right to be church; nor may it speak for God, telling families and churches what to do. It must not claim authority which God has denied it. It may not deny to those in authority in the family and in the church the right to perform their God-given tasks in their divinely delegated spheres of authority.

This brings us to a third rule regarding conscientious disobedience. When human authority exceeds the limits of its jurisdiction, it *may* be disobeyed. Notice that I used the word "may," not "must." Human authority may on occasion command us to do things that are not unlawful even when exceeding its jurisdiction. We may, out of self-interest, prudence, or some other motivation, choose to conform to requirements that do not require us to sin, even though we have no obligation to do so. We may obey, or we may disobey.

This is implied in Jesus's affirmation, "Render to Caesar the things that are Caesar's and to God the things that are God's."[13] Some things

---

13 See Luke 20:25.

do not come within the sphere of Caesar's jurisdiction. This truth is echoed in Romans 13:7, "Render to all *what is due* them." Various duties are owed to the various authorities, and we must render to all what is due *them*. This clearly means that no human authority may claim for itself what we owe to another human authority.

This is pointedly illustrated where two authorities conflict. Suppose that a pastor commands a Christian teenager to attend a Christian high school and offers her a scholarship to do so, but the teen's parents oppose this plan and want her to attend another high school. Further suppose that attending either high school would not violate Scripture. Whom shall she obey? Clearly one of those in authority over her must be disobeyed. In this case I believe she must obey her parents and disobey her pastor. The pastor clearly has gone beyond the boundary of his sphere of authority and has usurped the authority of the parents. God gave the task of educating children to parents, not to pastors. The young lady *may* choose to disobey her pastor. Indeed, in this case she must disobey him because her parents have a claim on her obedience in such a matter.

Let me illustrate this in another way. Suppose that a pastor commanded a young lady to marry a certain young man and that she would be violating no command of the Bible if she did so. Is she sinning to disregard pastoral command in this instance? No! The pastor has exceeded his jurisdiction. She *may* disobey him.

Suppose that the civil authorities have prohibited all midweek church meetings. Can we prove from the Bible that it is sin for a church not to meet during the week? Personally, I would not like to have the burden of proving it. Are we obligated, then, to obey the civil authorities in this case? No. The civil authority's jurisdiction does not include the right to make laws which dictate when churches meet. That authority is the province of the elders of the church. Thus, such civil laws are a usurpation of the rights and functions of another God-ordained authority. The church *may* disobey.

Suppose an unconverted husband forbids his Christian wife to attend church. Is she sinning if she disobeys her husband in this matter? My conviction is that she is not. This conviction is based on Jesus' statement, "If anyone comes to me, and does not hate his own father and mother and wife and children and brothers and sisters, yes, and even his own life, he cannot be my disciple."[14] In spiritual matters—and the selection and attendance of a church is a spiritual matter—the Christian wife owes supreme allegiance to Christ. A husband has exceeded his jurisdiction by usurping Jesus' right as the Lord of his disciples' consciences. She may disobey. Furthermore, in this case, since obedience would involve sin, she must disobey.

Suppose that the state prohibits parents from educating their own children and requires that they be sent to a school with certified teachers. It is impossible to prove on the basis of the Word of God that parents are sinning if they choose to send their children to a certified Christian school. Thus, the state, arguably at least, is not specifically requiring the Christian to sin. The question is, would a Christian parent be sinning if he chose to disobey such a law? My conviction is that he would not be. God has never given the task of educating children to the civil authorities. God has given this task to parents.[14] Therefore, by a law which practically forbids parents to educate their own children, the state is exceeding the boundaries of its own jurisdiction and is usurping the rights of another divinely constituted human authority. In this case, the state may be disobeyed without sin.

Human Authority Is Discriminate in Its Bestowal

God does not give the same authority to everyone. God has not given civil authority to everyone indiscriminately. The same is true of parental authority, husbandly authority, and pastoral authority. God only bestows authority in these cases on those who actually occupy the office in view, i.e., civil ruler, parent, husband, or pastor. The significance of this observation is that until God bestows authority on us in a given sphere, we may not claim it or exercise it. The authority which we have over others corresponds to the office to which God has called us. To claim the authority of an office to which God has not called us, to exercise power that God has not given us, is rebellion against the providence of God.

This brings us to a fourth principle regarding conscientious disobedience. The right of conscientious disobedience must never be made the pretext for usurping the vocation, privileges, and functions of an authority which God has not given us. To seize such functions

---

14 See Luke 14:26.

is blatant sin. As we have seen in our study of Romans 13:1–7, the civil authorities have privileges and rights which for others to exercise would be clearly sinful. We observed that the Bible commands the civil authorities to take vengeance on evildoers (13:4), while forbidding Christians in their private capacity to do so (12:17–19). We saw that the Bible arms the civil authorities with the sword (13:4), while telling individual Christians that all those who take up the sword shall perish by the sword (Matt. 26:52).

There are many right and good things which ought to be done, but which it is not my place to do. I may be aware of a murderer that should be put to death. If the civil authority puts the man to death, it is justice. If I do it, it is murder. I may know women who need the love of a godly husband. If their husbands give them such love, it pleases God. If I do it, God calls it adultery. It is not my place, my privilege, or my vocation to do these and many other good things. My duty is conditioned by the providential vocation God has given me.

Excursus: A Recent Rejection of the Confession

Brandon Adams has become known in Reformed Baptist circles as a defender of 1689 Federalism. It is a little surprising, then, given his confessionalism in other respects, that he has seen fit in recent days to take exception to the teaching of the 1689 in chapter 24 and paragraph 1. It has been a little difficult for me to grasp his reasoning. I have, therefore, corresponded with him to assure myself that I am following his reasoning and correctly representing him in this excursus. I take no delight in publicly criticizing his views on this matter. Indeed, I have only reluctantly concluded that it is necessary to do so in this article—after being advised to do so. After prayerful consideration, it seems necessary so to do.

Let me, however, provide just a little more background to this interaction. Adams has interacted in his writing with my unpublished ThM thesis entitled "Political Revolution in the Reformed Tradition: An Historical and Biblical Critique."[15] I think he has treated my work respectfully even though he has come to disagree with certain of my conclusions. I congratulate him particularly on

---

15 See the forthcoming Samuel Waldron, *Political Revolution in the Reformed Tradition: A Historical and Biblical Critique (Conway, AR: Free Grace Press, 2021).*

his recognition that the Reformed revolutionary tradition did not originate with Calvin, and, in fact, Calvin would have emphatically disagreed with it. Let me be clear. Adams disagrees with Calvin and me. He supports the Reformed revolutionary tradition, but he recognizes as accurate my assessment of Calvin as anti-revolutionary.

Let me add that I do not regard my anti-revolutionary views of this matter as explicit in the 1689. Even though I think they are consistent with the 1689, I would not claim that they are explicit there. But that brings us back to the point of this excursus. Adams has come to a view which forces him to take exception to the 1689 in 24.1.[16]

What, then, is the view adopted by Adams which has led him to take exception to the 1689 at 24.1? The key point seems to be how the ordination of the "powers that be" in Romans 13 is to be understood. In light of the two possible connotations of ordain (depending on whether you take it as a reference to God's preceptive will or God's decretive will), Adams identifies three possibilities. First, the ordination is preceptive. Second, the ordination is both preceptive and decretive. Third, the ordination is decretive. While he favors Rutherford's pro-revolutionary view which takes ordination here as preceptive, he disagrees with Rutherford's exegesis and opts instead for the view that the ordination is decretive. Here is his summary:

If Romans 13 refers to God's providential ordaining of powerful rulers (mighty men) whether they be good or evil, then it does not refer to God's preceptive ordaining of an office. Conversely, if Romans 13 refers to the institution of civil government, then the command to be subject is limited to rulers who properly fulfill their duty of punishing evildoers. If they punish those who do good, they do not have to be submitted to: rebellion is permissible. That is the logically necessary conclusion as Rutherford ably showed. Calvin, following Theodoret and Aquinas, attempted to avoid this necessary

---

16 Brandon Adams's work on this subject is mainly unpublished and may be found on his website (https://www.1689federalism.com/). In an email, Adams identified the places in his work that articulate his position. He says: "Here are some relevant ones that collectively articulate my understanding: (1) *Nebuchadnezzar and Romans 13: Person (Decretive) or Office (Preceptive)?* (2) *Romans 13: Person (Decretive), Office (Preceptive), or Both?* (3) *Is John MacArthur Right About Revolution? (Intended as an example to show the contradictory nature of that interpretation of Rom. 13)* (4) *Romans 13 Forbids Revolution, not Disobedience (and where Calvin erred)* (5) *Romans 13:6 "For this reason, pay your tribute"* (6) *The Avenger of Blood (I need to revise this as it is a bit too bombastic at places, but it explains why I disagree with 2LBCF 24.1 and is relevant to my understanding of Romans 13).*"

conclusion by conflating the two concepts. We owe obedience to the office because it has been instituted by God, but when a person in that office oversteps his office, he must still be submitted to because God is providentially using him for His purpose. But Calvin cannot have his cake and eat it too. He must pick one or the other. The majority of his followers saw the contradiction and chose the ordination of office interpretation, thus advocating resistance. I think perhaps it is time to return to Irenaeus' ordination of persons interpretation. That is the only interpretation consistent with God's ordination of Nebuchadnezzar and it makes much more sense of the context of Romans 13 as well as the principle of *lex talionis* and the avenger of blood. These powers are still accountable to the moral law that binds all people, especially the sixth and eighth commandments. They don't get special exceptions. We may remind them of that, but we are not to take up arms against them.[17]

Adams rejects the view of Rutherford and friends that the ordination is preceptive. He rejects Calvin's view that it is both as self-contradictory. He opts instead for the view that ordination is decretive.

Now the space of this article prevents me from pursuing these views in great detail. I apologize to Adams if this seems unfair to him. I hope, however, that what I say will still be cogent. Let us examine, then, the three possibilities that he raises.

There is, first, the preceptive view of Rutherford and friends. As Adams rightly recognizes, this view is very difficult because of the redemptive-historical backdrop of this passage. There are two prominent aspects to this backdrop.

There is, of course, the Roman Empire. This is the existing government of which Paul is speaking. Paul is, after all, speaking in Romans 13:1–7 of the Roman Empire that originated in wars of aggression and whose last three emperors at the time had been Caligula the Monster, Claudius the Clown, and Nero, who would shortly become the persecutor of the church.

There is also in the background of this passage the great alteration that took place when the theocratic kingdom was destroyed by Nebuchadnezzar. This was the first of the Gentile kingdoms

17 Brandon Adams, "Romans 13: Person (Decretive), Office (Preceptive), or Both?" accessed January 29, 2021, https://contrast2.wordpress.com/2020/03/20/romans-13-person-decretive-office-preceptive-or-both.

ordained of God to rule over the people of God. Nebuchadnezzar was given real authority over God's people. Jeremiah the prophet calls the Jews to fall away to Nebuchadnezzar (Jer. 21:9) and pray for and seek the welfare of Babylon (Jer. 29:7).

In neither of these two cases did either the origin or conduct of these empires meet the standards of Reformed revolutionary theory, and yet they were acknowledged as possessing genuine civil authority over the people of God. The notion that our subjection to Gentile kingdoms (which are by definition non-theocratic) is conditioned by certain standards related to their origin or conduct really strains credibility.

There is, second, the decretive view of Adams and those like Irenaeus. This says that it is the person who is exercising the power of the sword that is decretively ordained and not the office itself. While I think Adams, on other grounds, accepts the view of Rutherford, he cannot make sense of Romans 13 in light of his view. Thus, he sees Nebuchadnezzar and Rome as providentially appointed by God. Because of this, they are not to be resisted by armed force. This apparently does not apply to civil authority in general. In other cases, revolution is appropriate. It is simply forbidden in special cases of divine providence like those in view in Romans 13.

It is difficult for a couple of reasons to accept this approach to the passage. First, Babylon and Rome are simply the first and the last of the four Gentile empires prophesied in Daniel 2 and 7. These four empires represent all the civil authorities that will bear rule over the people of God during the interregnum between the destruction of the theocratic kingdom and its return in glory and power in the second coming of Christ. Second, as Adams well knows, the decretive will of God is never by itself the rule for our conduct. Yet, his view affirms that here it is. By definition, if the ordination of Romans 13 does constitute the rule for our conduct, it must have a preceptive element to it.

There is the third view mentioned by Adams: mine and, I am thankful to say, Calvin's. This view says the ordination in view here is both preceptive and decretive. God decrees certain powers into existence, and once they are in existence, they have actual authority or right to rule. Adams thinks this view is self-contradictory. I cannot agree. Why cannot some ordinations be both preceptive and decretive? In fact, we know that many ordinations are. When my children were minors in our home, I was ordained to be their fatherly authority. This ordination was both preceptive and decretive. They had a duty to obey me. That was a preceptive ordination. But that I had these children—and they had me as their father—was something decreed by God. It was decretive. It seems exegetically unavoidable to see in Romans 13 both dimensions of God's ordination. May I specify?

The decretive aspect of this ordination is clear from several things.

- It is the Roman Empire that Paul is specifying here. Its rise was certainly a matter of divine decree.

- The second half of verse 1 cannot be otherwise understood: "For there is no authority except from God, and those which exist are established by God."

- Of course, Adams himself affirms this aspect of the ordination, as noted above.

The preceptive aspect of this ordination is clear from several things.

1. This ordination creates the obligation to subordinate oneself to the powers so created (Rom. 13:1). To subordinate means to acknowledge another's right to rule. (The Greek verb is ὑποτάσσω.) God's decretive will creates no such obligation. Even if God has decreed that a drunk driver will kill me and my family, I am not obligated to acknowledge or submit to his right to kill us and do nothing to avoid it.

2. This ordination creates the obligation not to resist or oppose these powers (Rom. 13:2). Decretive will by itself creates no such obligation.

3. This ordination creates the obligation to be in subjection "for conscience sake" (Rom. 13:5). Decretive will is not the standard for our conscience. The standard for conscience is God's preceptive will.

4. This ordination creates the debts of tax, custom, fear, and honor (Rom. 13:7). Decretive will by

itself creates no such debts. That a thief has been
decretively ordained to steal my stuff creates no
obligation for me to give him my stuff!

Let me close by stating my conviction that this whole discussion
is not "a tempest in a teapot." There are important consequences to
Adams's views. Specifically, in light of the things we have discussed,
he believes that all image bearers of God have not only the right
to use the sword in self-defense, but also to take retributive justice.
Both on his internet site and in personal correspondence with me he
teaches that God has given all image bearers the power of the sword
to defend themselves and administer retributive justice. He does not
believe that God has armed a special subset of people with the sword
to rule over others and keep them in line. This is why he does not
agree with 24.1 of the confession. It teaches that God has limited this
use of the sword to the office of the civil authority.

> God, the supreme Lord and King of all the world, hath
> ordained civil magistrates to be under him, over the people,
> for his own glory and the public good and to this end hath
> armed them with the power of the sword, for defense and
> encouragement of them that do good and for the punish-
> ment of evil doers.

I hope Adams does not entirely understand the implications
of what he is saying. I, however, find such a view horrifying in its
implications. I also find it flatly unbiblical. It does not recognize the
special privileges of the civil authority. The civil authority may take
vengeance (Rom. 13:4). The ordinary Christian may not (12:19). It
may use the sword (13:4). The ordinary Christian may not. Rather,
Jesus warns the private Christian not to use such violence. Matthew
26:52 says it clearly: "Then Jesus said to him, 'Put your sword back
into its place; for all those who take the sword shall perish by the
sword.'"

14

The Ecclesiology of the Second London Confession of Faith

Thomas K. Ascol

⟶⟤⟨◦⟩⟥⟵

O NE OF THE STATED REASONS THAT the framers of the Second London Confession of 1689 followed the Westminster Confession of Faith (1646) and the Savoy Declaration and Platform of Polity (1658) so closely and employed so much of their language is because the Baptists wanted to show that they had "no itch to clogge Religion with new words."[1] In other words, they wanted to show their unity with other orthodox Protestants in those areas of primary doctrinal concern.

However, the writers of the 1689 did not simply parrot the words of their Presbyterian and Congregationalist brethren. Where necessary, they took exception to certain language in both the Westminster and the Savoy documents. Where they found deficiencies, they added statements to clarify. And where they recognized the need to address their own particular beliefs that set them apart from the Presbyterians and Congregationalists, they did so without sparing any effort to express themselves clearly and plainly.

---

1 From the preface, "To the Judicious and Impartial Reader," in William L. Lumpkin, *Baptist Confessions of Faith* (Valley Forge, Virginia: Judson, 1969), 245.

This independence of thought and conviction are clearly displayed in chapter 26, which is both the longest and most distinctively Baptist chapter in the whole confession. This is fitting since it is in the realm of ecclesiology that Baptists have made their greatest contribution to evangelical theology.

Whereas the Baptists took fifteen paragraphs to confess their convictions on the doctrine of the church, the Presbyterians took only six (chapter 25 of the Westminster Confession) and the Congregationalists only five (chapter 26 of the Savoy Declaration). However, the latter also published the Savoy Platform of Polity, which contains thirty paragraphs and from which the Baptists drew significantly.

The Greek word from which we get "ecclesiology" (the doctrine of the church) is *ekklesia*. It is found at least 115 times in the New Testament. The basic meaning of the word refers to a gathering or an assembly, often of citizens, in a specific place. As the word was used in the first century by Christians to describe themselves, it came to mean the company of people who were following Jesus Christ as their Lord.

The word is used in two primary ways in the New Testament. First, it describes Christians in a particular place who voluntarily united together into one body, who held their own meetings and managed their own affairs. This is what the New Testament means when it speaks of the churches of Galatia or the church of Ephesus. These were local congregations. Of the one-hundred-fifteen times the word appears in the New Testament, the overwhelming majority of those occurrences describe a local church.

Most of the time the word *ekklesia* is used in the New Testament to describe this kind of local assembly. Consequently, most of the teaching on the church that we have in the NT is focused on and concerned about local churches. The second way that the New Testament uses *ekklesia* is to describe the whole body of Christians who are scattered throughout the earth and across the centuries. This universal church has never gathered on earth, though one day it will in a glorious display of the eschatological reign of Christ.

The Second London Confession organizes its fifteen paragraphs in chapter 26 around these two uses of the word. The first four paragraphs deal with the universal church and the last eleven focus on the local church. Together, they provide a useful outline of Baptist ecclesiology.

The Church Universal

The confession does not defend the idea of a universal church but rather assumes it by describing its character and order. The first sentence in chapter 26 states, "The catholic or universal church, which (with respect to the internal work of the Spirit and truth of grace) may be called invisible, consists of the whole number of the elect, that have been, are, or shall be gathered into one, under Christ, the head thereof; and is the spouse, the body, the fulness of him that filleth all in all." Already the framers of the Confession show their independence from the Westminster and Savoy, which state, "The Catholic or universal Church, which is invisible...."

The Niceno-Constantinopolitan Creed of 381 teaches Christians to believe in the one, holy, catholic [universal] and apostolic church.[2] Most believers have acknowledged the universal church as that which is comprised of all Christians at all times. As the confession states, it "consists of the whole number of the elect, that have been, are, or shall be gathered into one, under Christ." Whereas the Westminster and Savoy simply identify the universal church as invisible, the Baptists speak more precisely by noting that the universal church "may be called" invisible in light of the nature of salvation. The internal, regenerating work of the Spirit and the sovereignty of God's grace remind us that we cannot infallibly know or recognize who has been, is now being, or will be in the future gathered into the church of Christ. It is because of this that the universal church "may be called invisible."[3]

Sam Waldron provides a helpful summary of the confession's meaning at this point. He writes,

> Does the Bible teach that this universal church is invisible?
> If we use the term, we must, like the Confession, use it very

2 See Philip Schaff, *The Creeds of Christendom*, 3 vol. (1931; repr., Grand Rapids: Baker Book House, 1990), 1:29.

3 Interestingly, Question 106 of *the Baptist Catechism* (commonly called, "Keach's Catechism") which was published in 1694/95, does not make this subtle distinction: "Q. 106. What is the invisible church? A. The invisible church is the whole number of the elect, that have been, are, or shall be gathered into one under Christ the head. (Eph. 1:10; 1:22, 23; John 10:16; 11:52)." (http://www.reformedreader. org/ccc/keachcat.htm, accessed September 10, 2020).

carefully, because there is no invisible church apart from the visible church. . . . The universal church is always visible, even if it is not perfectly or completely visible . . . One may not credibly profess to be a member of the invisible church while despising membership and fellowship in the visible church.[4]

Indeed, "those professing the faith of the gospel" and who are living in truth and holiness according to it "may be called visible saints; and of such ought all particular congregations to be constituted" (26.2).

It is the universal church that can lay claim to Jesus' promise to build his church such that "the gates of hell shall not prevail against it" (Matt. 16:18). Individual, local churches can apostatize by falling away from the ways of Christ and as a result experience the judgment which he threatens to carry out on the church of Ephesus—the removal of their lampstand—if they do not repent (Rev. 2:5). Despite this real prospect, the church of Christ is in no danger of disappearing from the world because "Christ always hath had, and ever shall have a kingdom in this world" (26.3).

Perhaps the most controversial statement in the confession is found in this chapter in the context of asserting the headship of Christ over the church. Since he alone has all power and authority over the church, it necessarily follows that "neither can the Pope of Rome in any sense be head thereof, but is that antichrist, that man of sin, and son of perdition, that exalteth himself in the church against Christ, and all that is called God; whom the Lord shall destroy with the brightness of his coming" (26.4).

When asked by those familiar with this statement if I believe it as written, I have occasionally replied, "It depends on which day it is ... and which pope." Ultimately, however, the specificity of the confession in identifying the pope as "that" particular "antichrist . . . man of sin, and son of perdition" (and citing 2 Thess. 2:2–9 as a proof text) is more than I can confirm without qualification. This is not to say that this line of reasoning in the confession should be completely dismissed. Scripture speaks of the "many antichrists" (1 John 2:18) that have come into the world and certainly the papacy

---

4 Samuel E. Waldron, *A Modern Exposition of the 1689 Baptist Confession of Faith*, 5th ed. (Darlington, Co. Durham, England: Evangelical Press, 2016), 368.

and individual popes can be included in that number. An institution that not only opposes but also anathematizes the doctrine of justification by grace alone through faith alone—and anyone who would ascribe to himself the title of "Vicar of Christ" while leading such an institution—certainly falls under that apostolic judgment.[5]

The confession is careful to leave no room for the structure or polity of the Roman Catholic Church by asserting that, as Head of the church, Jesus Christ is the one "in whom, by the appointment of the Father, all power for the calling, institution, order or government of the church, is invested in a supreme and sovereign manner" (26.4). Ironically, it is this point that has led some Baptists to reject the idea of an invisible, universal church altogether. If "an order and structure for it has not been set down in Scripture," can it legitimately be referred to as a church at all?[6] The confession, however, asserts the more common view (following the Westminster and Savoy at this point) that a universal church exists and the Roman Catholic Church is not it.

Local Churches

The bulk of the confession's teaching in this chapter, like the bulk of the New Testament's teaching on the church, focuses on local churches. Paragraphs 5–15 contain an excellent summary of the ownership, duties, membership, leadership, and authority of local churches.

Ownership

As the Head of the church, "all power for the calling, institution, order or government of the church" has been "invested in a supreme

---

5 In the sixth session, Canon IX of the *Council of Trent*, the Roman Catholic Church declares, "If any one saith, that by faith alone the impious is justified; in such wise as to mean, that nothing else is required to co-operate in order to the obtaining the grace of Justification, and that it is not in any way necessary, that he be prepared and disposed by the movement of his own will; let him be anathema." (http://www.traditionalcatholic.net/Tradition/Council/Trent/Sixth_Session,_Canons.html, accessed September 10, 2020).

6 See Mark Dever, *The Church: The Gospel Made Visible* (Nashville: Broadman and Holman, 2012), 93. Advocates of "Landmarkism" hold this view. Dever rightly notes that it is for this reason that the idea of a universal church is absent in the 1859 Abstract of Principles written by Basil Manly Jr. for The Southern Baptist Theological Seminary, *The Church*, 93n5.

and sovereign manner" in Jesus Christ (26.4). He is the one to whom all true local churches belong. He creates them, provides for them, and instructs them.

One of the fundamental differences between Protestantism and Roman Catholicism is the relationship between the church and the Word. Roman Catholic teaching claims that the written Word of God owes its existence to the church. Protestants insist that the exact opposite is true: it is the Word that creates churches. The confession reflects this Protestant understanding when it asserts,

> the Lord Jesus calleth out of the world unto himself, through the ministry of his word, by his Spirit, those that are given unto him by his Father, that they may walk before him in all the ways of obedience, which he prescribeth to them in his word. Those thus called, he commandeth to walk together in particular societies, or churches, for their mutual edification, and the due performance of that public worship, which he requireth of them in the world (26.5).

Every local church owes its existence to the trinitarian work of God. As the great evangelist, Jesus Christ saves elect sinners through the ministry of his Word and Spirit. Those whom he savingly calls in this way, he directs to live in obedience to his commandments. Thus, a right understanding of the Great Commission of Matthew 28:19–20 includes the recognition that God is the one who both enables and guarantees its fulfillment.

This is precisely the point Paul makes to the Corinthians when he rebukes the divisive spirit that emerged as they showed allegiance to various preachers based on personal preferences. He writes, "I planted, Apollos watered, but God gave the growth. So neither he who plants nor he who waters is anything, but only God who gives the growth" (1 Cor. 3:6–7). Christians are responsible to go and make disciples. We fulfill that responsibility in the power of the Spirit and with great care to communicate the gospel accurately as it has been revealed in the Word, knowing that only the Lord can effectually deliver people out of sin and into the kingdom of the Son of his love (see 10.1).

A significant part of the Great Commission includes teaching new disciples to observe all of Christ's commandments (Matt. 28:20), or, as the confession puts it, to "walk before him in all the ways of obedience" (26.5). Such obedience necessarily involves living in vital relationship with other believers in particular churches. How can Christians obey Christ's commandments in Matthew 18:15–20 if they are not covenanted together with other believers in a local church? At the very least the last step of church discipline—to "tell it to the church"—cannot be followed by a Christian who is trying live without belonging to a particular church.[7]

Membership

Since Christ is the one who calls sinners to faith and establishes them in local churches, it follows that churches should be comprised of a regenerate membership. This Baptist principle was widely debated among English Protestants of the seventeenth century and has been questioned and dismissed by paedobaptists to the present day. When the Westminster Assembly met in England from 1643–49 it was comprised mainly of Presbyterians with a small contingency of Independents who were called "Dissenting Brethren." The latter argued that a local church should consist of regenerate people. Their views were rejected, and they were accused of promoting spiritual pride and false assurance in their churches.[8]

Against the Presbyterian view that the visible church consists of believers "and of their children,"[9] the confession's affirmation that all particular congregations are to be constituted only of "visible saints" (26.2) follows in the train of Anabaptist and earlier Baptist statements of faith. From Peter Riedemann (an Anabaptist missionary sent out from the Hutterites of Moravia) in his 1540 *Rechenshaft Unsrer Religion, Lehre, und Glaubens* (*Account of our Religion,*

---

7 Neither can Paul's instructions to Christians in 1 Corinthians 5 be followed unless one is vitally connected to a local church. The distinction that he makes between those inside the church and those outside highlights the confession's recognition that Christ commands his people to "walk together in particular societies" (26.5).

8 William Maxwell Hetherington, *History of the Westminster Assembly of Divines* (Edmonton, AB Canada: Still Water Revival Books, 1991 reprint edition), 193–94. Hetherington, a Presbyterian historian of the Assembly writes, the "Independents held the theory of admitting none to be members of their churches except those whom they believed to have been thoroughly and in the highest sense regenerated or, in the language of the time, 'true saints'" (Hetherington, 193–94). See also Charles Hodge, *Systematic Theology*, Volume 3 (Grand Rapids: Eerdmans, 1981), 545; see also 577–79.

9 *The Westminster Confession of Faith; the Larger and Shorter Catechisms, with the Scripture Proofs at Large: Together with the Sum of Saving Knowledge* (Glasgow: Free Presbyterian Publications, 1983), 107–8.

Teaching, and Faith), to John Smyth's 1609 *Short Confession*, the
General Baptist *Propositions and Conclusions* in 1612, and the First
London Baptist Confession of 1644, the idea of regenerate church
membership has been well-documented in Baptist and pre-Baptist
life.[10]

Those whom Christ calls to salvation, he also "commandeth to
walk together in particular societies, or churches, for their mutual
edification, and the due performance of that public worship, which
he requireth of them in the world" (26.5; see p. 271). Scripture is
filled with mutual obligations that believers owe one another in the
context of committed relationships in a church. How can Christians
bear with and forgive one another, confess sins to one another, bear
with one another, outdo one another in showing honor, bear one
another's burdens, stir up one another to love and good works, and
so on, if they are not living in close enough relationship to each other
as members of a local church (Col. 3:13; James 5:16; Eph. 4:2; Rom.
12:10; Gal. 6:2; Heb. 10:24)?

The relationship between a Christian and a local church is not left
to the kind of informal arrangements that some believers advocate
("I don't have to be a member of a church in order to be a faithful
Christian"). After stating that Christ commands his followers to live
together in local churches, the confession immediately identifies
those who follow Christ in obedience as church "members."

The members of these churches are saints by calling, visibly
manifesting and evidencing (in and by their profession and walking)

---

10 Riedemann's *Rechenshaft Unsrer Religion* states in its opening article, "An assembly of children of God who have separated themselves from all unclean things
is the church. It is gathered together, has being, and is kept by the Holy Spirit.
Sinners may not be members unless they have repented of their sins." (William
L. Lumpkin, *Baptist Confessions of Faith* [Valley Forge, Virginia: Judson, 1969],
40). Smyth's *Short Confession* states, "That the church of Christ is a company of
the faithful; baptized after confession of sin and of faith, endowed with the power
of Christ." (Lumpkin, 101). Article 64 of their *Propositions and Conclusions* says,
"That the outward church visible, consists of penitent persons only, and of such
as believing in Christ, bring forth fruits worthy of amendment of life." (Lumpkin,
136). Article 33 of the *First London Baptist Confession* declares, "That Christ hath
here on earth a spirituall Kingdome, which is the Church, which he hath purchased
and redeemed to himself, as a peculiar inheritance: which Church, as it is visible to
us, is a company of visible Saints, called *&* separated from the world, by the word
and Spirit of God, to the visible profession of the faith of the Gospel, being baptized
into that faith, and joyned to the Lord, and each other, by mutuall agreement, in
the practical injoyment of the Ordinances, commanded by Christ their head and
King." (Lumpkin, 165).

their obedience unto that call of Christ; and do willingly consent to walk together, according to the appointment of Christ; giving up themselves to the Lord, and one to another, by the will of God, in professed subjection to the ordinances of the Gospel (26.6).

Membership matters. The confession employs biblical language when referring to those who "willingly consent to walk together" under the lordship of Christ as "members" of churches (see also 26.8, 13, 14, 15). Paul speaks this way to both the Romans (Rom. 12:5) and the Ephesians (Eph. 4:25) when he reminds them that, in their relationships in their respective churches they are "members (μέλος) one of another." The idea is that Christians belong to each other in a union that is so vital that it can be compared to the hands and feet—the "members"—of a human body (1 Cor. 12:14–31).

The confession removes all doubt about the importance of church membership when it states that "all believers are bound to join themselves to particular churches, when and where they have opportunity so to do" (26.12). Two of the Scripture proofs cited for paragraph 6 (26.6) also demonstrate that the framers of the confession view being a Christian (under normal circumstances) as necessarily entailing being a member of a local church. At Pentecost, those who received the message Peter preached "were baptized, and there were added that day about three thousand souls" (Acts 2:41). Luke continues in that passage to explain that this was the normal way that God dealt with those whom he saved. "And the Lord added to their number day by day those who were being saved" (v. 47).

The close connection between being in union with Christ and being in union with believers in a local church is highlighted in a second Scripture proof of paragraph 6. After the divine execution of Ananias and Sapphira in the Jerusalem church, Luke writes, "None of the rest dared join them. And more than ever believers were added to the Lord, multitudes of both men and women" (Acts 5:13, 14). Being "joined" to the Lord resulted in being "joined" to a church. Being "added" to the Lord entailed being "added" to a church.

To follow Christ faithfully, then, requires not only giving oneself up to the Lord, but also to other Christians by willingly agreeing to live together in the bonds of church membership.

Duties

Church membership has both privileges and duties. While the former are not overlooked by the confession, they tend to be subsumed under the relevant responsibilities of members to serve and care for one another and the specific responsibilities of pastors to "watching for [the] souls" in their churches (26.10). More attention is given to the duties of church members. "All that are admitted unto the privileges of a church, are also under the censures and government thereof, according to the rule of Christ" (26.12). The proof texts cited for paragraph 12 indicate that the confession is speaking here of the responsibility that every church member has to live under the discipline of the church.

The formative discipline to which church members submit is summarized in 1 Thessalonians 5:14, "And we urge you, brothers, admonish the idle, encourage the fainthearted, help the weak, be patient with them all." These activities are ordinary means of grace whereby believers, by being on both the giving and receiving end of these actions, are more deeply matured in the grace of God that is in Christ. Corrective discipline is signaled by the other proof texts. "If anyone does not obey what we say in this letter, take note of that person, and have nothing to do with him, that he may be ashamed. Do not regard him as an enemy, but warn him as a brother" (2 Thess. 3:14, 15; see also 3:6). To be a church member in a well-ordered church is to accept the corrective help (when needed) that goes with being joined together with other believers under the lordship of Christ.

Even in the best of churches, efforts to carry out corrective discipline can go awry because of remaining sin in all the members and officers. One of the ways that God conforms his children into the image of Christ is by guiding and empowering them to respond in humility and faith when mistreated and when justice is delayed or not served at all in their situation. Jesus has given his followers an example of how to bear injustices against them. "When he was reviled, he did not revile in return; when he suffered, he did not threaten, but continued entrusting himself to him who judges justly" (1 Peter 2:23).

The confession recognizes the inherent danger that goes with living in vital communion with other believers in a local church.

The closer you are to people, the more vulnerable you are to being offended by them. Such offense is too often cited as justification for leaving a church or, even worse, creating a split in the congregation. Paragraph 13 addresses this scenario directly.

No church members, upon any offence taken by them, having performed their duty required of them towards the person they are offended at, ought to disturb any church-order, or absent themselves from the assemblies of the church, or administration of any ordinances, upon the account of such offence at any of their fellow members, but to wait upon Christ, in the further proceeding of the church (26.13).

This paragraph mentions three clear duties that every church member should perform when he or she has been offended. First, an offended church member must go to the person who has created the offense and seek to work out the issue. The confession cites Matthew 18:15–17 where Jesus prescribes this very responsibility. "If your brother sins against you, go and tell him his fault, between you and him alone. If he listens to you, you have gained your brother" (v. 15). Assuming this basic responsibility has been fulfilled, the confession next gives a negative and a positive duty that offended members must perform.

Negatively, being offended is not to become an occasion for disrupting church fellowship or peace ("disturbing any church order"). This forbids any gossip or divisiveness that creates tensions in a church, including the neglecting of the regular gatherings of the church or observance of its ordinances.

Thirdly, and positively, having taken the steps prescribed by Jesus and continuing in the regular participation in the life of the church, the offended church member is to "wait upon Christ." Corrective church discipline takes time to be carried out properly. Impatience is a temptation that must be resisted. Offense does not remove the duty to live "with all humility and gentleness, with patience" and to bear "with one another in love, eager to maintain the unity of the Spirit in the bond of peace" (Eph. 4:2–3). Christ and his honor are to be uppermost in each member's mind, knowing that what most honors him will be best for those who follow him.

Along with responsibilities of individual members, the confession addresses the corporate duties which each church bears before the

Lord. Each church has an obligation "to pray continually for the good and prosperity of all the churches of Christ, in all places, and upon all occasions to further it" (26.14). This recognition of having an interest in all churches underlies the confession's admonition that "the churches (when planted by the providence of God so as they may enjoy opportunity and advantage for it) ought to hold communion among themselves, for their peace, increase of love, and mutual edification" (26.14).

Exactly what is meant by the phrase, "to hold communion," has been the subject of much discussion among confessional churches. Is this a call to informal fellowship among churches or is something more formal in view? James Renihan has argued persuasively for the latter interpretation. By examining how the phrase was used by various seventeenth-century Baptist associations and churches—including several who sent messengers to the London General Assembly in 1689 where the Second London Baptist Confession was adopted—Renihan demonstrates that what is in view is a formal, associational relationship between congregations that, in God's providence, have opportunity so to relate to each other.[11]

Such associational connections "ought" to be entered into by churches for their "mutual edification." As Renihan concludes, "There is an 'oughtness,' a duty, to this doctrine. The fullness of the Bible's teaching on visible unity could not be satisfied by pastoral friendships or conferences or minister's fraternals. They [the framers of the confession] believed that churches located in close proximity should enter into agreements for mutual benefit, and to participate together in the work of the Gospel."

What should a church do when serious problems arise, whether related to doctrine or practice? What recourse is available when there is dissension in a church, or certain members in a church have been injured by church actions or teachings? The confession teaches that in such cases it is the "communion," or associational connection, among like-minded churches that provides a God-honoring opportunity for resolution.

---

11 For Renihan's full discussion of this point see chapters 3 and 4 of *Denominations or Associations? Essays on Reformed Baptist Associations*, edited by James M. Renihan (Amityville, NY: Calvary Press, 2001). A summary of his argument is available at https://irbsseminary.org/the-confession-on-associations/#_ftnref3 (accessed September 10, 2020).

In cases of difficulties or differences, either in point of doctrine or administration, wherein either the churches in general are concerned, or any one church, in their peace, union, and edification; or any member or members of any church are injured, in or by any proceedings in censures not agreeable to truth and order: it is according to the mind of Christ, that many churches holding communion together, do, by their messengers, meet to consider, and give their advice in or about that matter in difference, to be reported to all the churches concerned (26.15).

Every church and its leaders are capable of making mistakes in complicated cases requiring correction and discipline. The confession provides guidance whereby such situations may be helped by the collective wisdom of other congregations. Messengers from other congregations "holding communion together" (in formal association with each other) can meet to consider the matter and provide counsel. Whatever advice the messengers give is to be "reported to all the churches concerned" (26.15), further highlighting the formal relationship that exists in their "communion."

The strong and biblical impulse among Baptists to protect church autonomy has sometimes led them to avoid any kind of associational connection. Baptists recognize no ecclesiastical authority above the local church. The confession honors that conviction by declaring the limitation of messengers who come to investigate and give counsel on a particular church's dispute. Such messengers "are not intrusted with any church-power properly so called; or with any jurisdiction over the churches themselves, to exercise any censures either over any churches or persons; or to impose their determination on the churches or officers" (26.15). The purpose of the messengers from other churches who are appointed to assist in a particular church's difficulties is limited to investigation and counsel. They have no authority to censure or to force their judgment on the church or its officers.

This raises an important point about the nature of the communion that churches have in formal associations. Just as each church is autonomous, so is each association. If a church is judged to be out of step with the commitments and agreements that undergird an association, then the other churches may, without violating the principle of church autonomy, remove the wayward from the association.

Being in "communion together" in this way provides wonderful opportunities for churches to establish fellowship, cooperative efforts, and methods of receiving counsel and help in times of difficulty. Many of the trials, challenges, and isolation that some churches have endured could be significantly mitigated by following the wisdom of the confession at this point.

Authority

The association that churches are to have with each other is to be engaged on a voluntary basis even though such communion is "according to the mind of Christ" (26.15). This is because each local church is vested with the authority of Christ through his apostles as provided in Scripture:

> "To each of these churches thus gathered, according to his mind declared in his word, he [Christ] hath given all that power and authority, which is in any way needful for their carrying on that order in worship and discipline, which he hath instituted for them to observe; with commands and rules for the due and right exerting, and executing of that power" (26.7).

Christ provides each church all the power and authority it needs in order to fulfill its mission. The three proof texts that are attached to paragraph 7 demonstrate this from both the words of Jesus (Matt. 18:17, 18) and the apostle Paul (1 Cor. 5:4, 5, 13; 2 Cor. 2:6–8).

In Jesus' second use of the word "church" he gives instructions for dealing with sin in a local congregation. If the first two attempts to deal with a sinning member do not result in repentance, then the next steps involve the whole church. If the wayward member refuses to hear the two or three who go to confront him over his sin, then the next step is to "tell it to the church. And if he refuses to listen even to the church," Jesus continues with a note of incredulity, "let him be to you as a Gentile and a tax collector" (Matt. 18:17). Corrective discipline is the exercise of Christ's authority by a local congregation. Furthermore, this authority extends to the very use of the keys of the kingdom, which Jesus mention in the next verse. "Truly, I say to you, whatever you bind on earth shall be bound in heaven, and whatever you loose on earth shall be loosed in heaven" (v. 18; see also Matt. 16:19).

In 1 Corinthians 5 Paul guides the church at Corinth in the proper way to exercise its Christ-given authority to deal correctively and redemptively with the flagrantly immoral member in their congregation: "When you are assembled in the name of the Lord Jesus and my spirit is present, with the power of our Lord Jesus, you are to deliver this man to Satan for the destruction of the flesh, so that his spirit may be saved in the day of the Lord" (1 Cor. 5:4–5). The linking of divine ("in the name of the Lord Jesus") and apostolic ("my spirit is present") authority demonstrates the power that belongs to a local church as it carries out its responsibilities that are written in God's Word.

Ecclesiastical authority, like all proper human authority, is not absolute but is delegated from God and can only be legitimately exercised in accordance with the instructions found in Scripture.[12] This is what the confession means when it states that the power and authority that Christ gives to a church is only for the purpose of fulfilling the work He has prescribed for them ("worship and discipline") and that such work is to be conducted according to the "commands and rules" that Christ has given "for the due and right exerting, and executing of that power" (26.7).

The authority that Christ gives to local churches results in great blessing when it is exercised properly. The church carries out its mission of proclaiming and displaying the gospel through evangelism and discipleship under the lordship of Christ, calling people to trust Christ and to live in obedience to his commandments. The message of the gospel is preserved, and its saving efficacy is manifested as the church exercises the keys of the kingdom with humility and confidence. When a church is led by elders who understand and are committed to the proper use of the power and authority granted by Christ, then the last words of King David become the testimony of its members: "When one rules justly over men, ruling in the fear of God, he dawns on them like the morning light, like the sun shining forth on a cloudless morning, like rain that makes grass to sprout from the earth" (2 Sam. 23:3–4). The proper use of God-given authority in a church brings great blessing.

---

12 For more on human authority and its limitations, see Waldron's essay in the previous chapter of this volume.

Polity

How a church wields its God-given authority largely depends on its
leadership. And how a church is led depends on its polity. The confession recognizes that Christ has authorized two types of officers for
each local church—elders and deacons.

> A particular church, gathered and completely organized
> according to the mind of Christ, consists of officers and
> members; and the officers appointed by Christ to be chosen
> and set apart by the church (so called and gathered), for
> the peculiar administration of ordinances, and execution of
> power or duty, which he intrusts them with, or calls them
> to, to be continued to the end of the world, are bishops or
> elders, and deacons. (26.8)

A well-ordered church will have both these offices. Those who
serve in them will give leadership to the congregation to fulfill the
responsibilities which Christ gives to his churches. Both offices are
to be filled "by the common suffrage of the church itself." This is
the "way appointed by Christ for the calling of any person" to be
either an elder or a deacon (26.9). Those chosen to fill these offices
are to be recognized and formally placed in their respective positions
by the congregation. Elders are to be "solemnly set apart by fasting
and prayer, with imposition of hands of the eldership of the church,
if there be any before constituted therein." Deacons, similarly, are
to be "set apart by prayer, and the like imposition of hands" (26.9).

The confession speaks specifically of the one office of "bishop
or elders" (26.9; cf. 26.8) and also calls "bishops or pastors of the
churches, to be instant in preaching the word, by way of office [sin-
gular]" (26.11). Following the pattern of the New Testament, those
three designations—bishop, elder, pastor—refer to the same office
(see Acts 20:17, 28; Titus 1:5–9; 1 Peter 5:1, 2).

Some have suggested that the confession at least opens the door
for the possibility of distinguishing between "pastors" and "elders"
(or "bishops"). The rationale for this possibility is the way that the
confession elaborates the work of "pastors" without specifically
mentioning "bishops or elders" in paragraph 10:

> The work of pastors being constantly to attend the service
> of Christ, in his churches, in the ministry of the word and
> prayer, with watching for their souls, as they that must give

an account to Him; it is incumbent on the churches to whom they minister, not only to give them all due respect, but also to communicate to them of all their good things according to their ability, so as they may have a comfortable supply, without being themselves entangled in secular affairs; and may also be capable of exercising hospitality towards others; and this is required by the law of nature, and by the express order of our Lord Jesus, who hath ordained that they that preach the Gospel should live of the Gospel. (26.10)

Waldron dismisses this view, though he does give it consideration. He rightly concludes that "There are not three offices in the church—minister or pastor, elder, and deacon. There are only two offices—overseer-elder-pastor and deacon. Pastors and elders are the same."[13]

The confession recognizes the all-encompassing nature of pastoral ministry when it states that the work of pastors involves "being *constantly* to attend the service of Christ, in his churches" (26.10, emphasis added). Based on the first division of labor among the leaders of the church in Jerusalem (Acts 6:3–4), pastors are, first of all, to give themselves to "the ministry of the word and prayer" (26.10). It was a serious problem when Hellenistic widows were being neglected in the Jerusalem church. Failure to care for those whom the Lord esteems as well as the potential for division along cultural boundaries were both worthy of the attention of the apostles who were leading the church. Yet, they wisely resisted the temptation to give themselves to the important task of directly addressing that problem. Instead, recognizing the necessity of spiritually providing for the souls of the congregation, they said, "It is not right that we should give up preaching the word of God to serve tables. . . . We will devote ourselves to prayer and to the ministry of the word" (Acts 6:2, 4). By this they established the pastoral priorities of pleading with people on behalf of God and pleading with God on behalf of people. This is a main component of pastoral oversight, for which each pastor must one day give an account to God.

These pastoral duties are stated as the basis for the obligations that churches have to their pastors. Specifically, a church owes it pastors "all due respect" and financial compensation "according to

---

13 *Waldron, A Modern Exposition, 377.*

their ability." Because a pastor should be freed from the necessity of pursuing his livelihood from "secular affairs" and is to be given to hospitality (1 Tim. 3:2), a church should seek to provide for his material needs "according to their ability" (26.10). Both nature and the Lord teach that "they that preach the Gospel should live of the Gospel" (26.10; see also 1 Cor. 9:6–14). As a general rule, when a church is blessed with godly, competent, trustworthy pastors, what the church can provide that is good for their pastors will, in turn, be good for the church.

Pastors must give themselves to the ministry of the Word and prayer, but the confession acknowledges the legitimacy of the long-standing Baptist practice of what is sometimes called "lay preaching":

> Although it be incumbent on the bishops or pastors of the churches, to be instant in preaching the word, by way of office, yet the work of preaching the word is not so peculiarly confined to them but that others also gifted and fitted by the Holy Spirit for it, and approved and called by the church, may and ought to perform it. (26.11)

This is no license for self-appointed preachers of the Word. Rather, it is a recognition that the Spirit can gift and equip others who are not yet, or perhaps never will be, pastors for the work of preaching. Where such is the case, those so empowered by the Spirit ought to engage in preaching, not, however, without being "approved and called by the church" (26.11). It is, after all, to the church corporately that Christ delegates his authority.

Conclusion

The Second London Baptist Confession of Faith served its original purpose well by showing the doctrinal agreement that the English Particular Baptists of the seventeenth century shared with their Presbyterian and Congregational brethren. During a season of persecution in England, the adoption of the confession in 1677 by the assembled messengers of many congregations meeting in the Petty France church in London marked a clear display of unity among those dissenting groups. Yet, those that adopted this revision of the Westminster Confession and the Savoy Declaration and Platform of Polity were convinced Baptists. Their agreement with the Presbyterians and Congregationalists ended at the points wherein they were convinced that they had discovered a more accurate understanding of biblical ecclesiology. Chapter 26 of the confession sets forth those convictions in unapologetic and clear terms. As such it remains a safe guide to Baptists everywhere who desire to honor the Lord of the church in their congregations.

15

The Doctrine of the Sacraments in the Second London Confession of Faith

Brian Borgman

D
URING THE REFORMATION AND Post-Reformation eras, there
was virtually no disagreement with Rome over theology
proper and Christology. There was widespread agreement
on such doctrines as the Trinity and the hypostatic union. Medieval
speculations aside, these precious biblical doctrines were truly catholic, having been codified in the ecumenical creeds and councils of
the church. However, the doctrines of Scripture and grace were wa-
tershed issues between Catholics and Protestants. The debate over
Scripture was not about the inspiration or authority of Scripture,
rather, it was about the relationship between the authority of Scripture and tradition. Furthermore, the Protestant rejection of the Catholic doctrine of grace led to a wholesale rejection of the Catholic view
that grace was conveyed through the sacraments, *ex opere operato.*[1]
The Protestants rightly rejected not only the number of sacraments

---

1 "By the work performed" is an English rendering of the Latin phrase. Richard
Muller explains the idea behind the phrase as follows: "the assumption of medieval
scholasticism and Roman Catholicism that the correct and churchly performance of
the rite conveys grace to the recipient, unless the recipient places a spiritual impedi-
ment (*obex*) in the way of grace. Sacraments themselves, therefore, have a *virtus op-
erativa*, or operative power." *Dictionary of Latin and Greek Theological Terms* (Grand
Rapids: Baker Academic, 1985), 108.

claimed by Rome, but they also rejected Rome's basic understanding of the two biblical sacraments, baptism and the Lord's Supper. Not a single Reformer retained the Catholic doctrine of transubstantiation—that is, by a miracle the bread and wine became the body and blood of Jesus, to be sacrificed in the Mass. The Reformers, by and large, also rejected baptism as the mechanism by which original sin was washed away and regeneration took place. Although there would be debate over the efficacy of baptism, the Roman Catholic doctrine of consecrated water, which brings about the death of sin and entry into the life of God, was fundamentally rejected.

The Protestants displayed unity in their rejections of the Roman Catholic doctrines. That unity was also demonstrated in the doctrines of Scripture and grace. The doctrine of the authority of God's word, above all human tradition, was a rallying point. The saving grace of God in Jesus Christ, that comes through the gospel, was also common ground. However, there were fierce intramural debates among the Reformers and their heirs over the sacraments or ordinances of the church.[2] The one point of agreement among Protestants was that there were only two sacraments, baptism and the Lord's Supper. But there were deep fragmentations among the Protestants over the doctrine of the Lord's Supper. The famous Marburg Colloquy was only the beginning of the battles over the Supper. There would be intense conflict over the Supper between the Gnesio-Lutherans and the Philippists. The *Extra Calvinisticum* was a reference, not to an extra point in TULIP, but rather to Calvin's doctrine that the Son of God retained existence outside His earthly body, so He remained infinite while becoming finite, He was omnipresent while being physically localized. Thus, Calvin rejected Luther's view of the ubiquity of Christ, that is, Christ's human nature taking on the attributes of deity. Luther's doctrine of ubiquity was the foundation of his view of the physical presence of Christ in the Supper.

The very term "crypto-Calvinist" had nothing to do with predestination and everything to do with Lutherans holding to Calvin's view of the Supper. Indeed, the debates were fierce, bubbling over, for instance, in the Palatinate at the University of Heidelberg. Robert Letham has noted, "Protestants and Roman Catholics alike

---

2 I will use term "sacrament" when referring broadly to the ordinances, respecting the term as it is used by Catholics, and especially Lutherans and the Reformed. The framers and signatories of the 2LCF sometimes used the terms interchangeably.

have spilled more ink over the Lord's Supper than over justification by faith or the authority of the Bible. . . . Yet today, the communion hardly features as a matter of significance. It is seen as an optional extra."[3]

For all the disagreement and division over the Supper, there was broad agreement among the Reformed regarding infant baptism.[4] Among the Reformed, the doctrine of infant baptism would develop along the lines of covenant theology. As the Reformed Orthodox refined their covenant theology, their position on infant baptism was solidified. However, there was a minority opinion. At the time of the Reformation, the Anabaptists, or Radical Reformers, rejected infant baptism. This rejection led to their persecution.[5] However, there would be another minority report on the proper subjects and mode of baptism that would arise from within the larger context of Reformed covenant theology. The theology of the ordinances among the Particular Baptists was strikingly similar and different from their Reformed Presbyterian and Congregational cousins. A quick glance at a tabular comparison[6] of chapter 27 of the Westminster Confession of Faith and chapter 28 of the Savoy Declaration of Faith reveals almost a verbatim expression "of the Sacraments." Both documents contain five paragraphs in the chapter. The Second London Confession of Faith, however, contains two very brief statements. The same can be said of the chapters on Baptism (WCF, chapter 28; SDF, chapter 29 and the 2LCF chapter 29). The Westminster and Savoy contain seven nearly identical chapters, while the 2LCF has four paragraphs of distinctly different content. The chapters on the Lord's Supper share much common ground.

The point of unity between the WCF and the 2LCF is that there are only two ordinances or sacraments which have been instituted by Christ, baptism and the Lord's Supper. The WCF, however, says that only "a minister of the Word, lawfully ordained" may dispense the sacraments. The 2LCF says, "These holy appointments are

---

3   Robert Letham, *The Lord's Supper: Eternal Word in Broken Bread* (Phillipsburg, NJ: Presbyterian and Reformed, 2001), 1.

4   Luther's view of infant baptism, as well as his doctrine of the Supper, were not representative of the Reformed perspectives of Calvin, Knox, Bullinger, and others.

5   Leonard Verduin, *The Reformers and Their Stepchildren* (Grand Rapids: Eerdmans, 1964).

6   James Anderson's "A Tabular Comparison of the 1646 WCF and the 1689 LBCF," accessed January 21, 2021, https://www.proginosko.com/docs/wcf_lbcf.html.

to be administered by those only who are qualified and thereunto called, according to the commission of Christ."[7] The WCF required ordained clergy to be the only administrators of the sacraments. The language of the 2LCF differs by simply saying "qualified and thereunto called." The difference in language is a bit ambiguous. On the one hand there is the avoidance of "lawfully ordained;" and on the other hand there is a tighter restriction than what would have been acceptable among many Anabaptists, namely any disciple could administer the ordinances. Waldron asserts, "Clearly, they wished to steer a middle course between the clericalism of the Presbyterians and the congregationalism of the early Baptists."[8]

Of Baptism

Although the chapter on baptism is not the only difference between the WCF and the 2LCF, it is certainly the most noticeable. The debates between Presbyterians and Baptists at times were intense. One such debate of special note was between John Flavel and Philip Cary.[9] The interesting thing to note, however, is that the debate was within the context of a generally shared covenantal perspective. Although the Particular Baptists held to covenant theology, it would be a mistake to think of the Particular Baptists simply as "deep water Presbyterians." As the Cary-Flavel debate showed, the arguments regarding baptism were based on understanding the nature of the covenants. The Baptists were robustly exegetical and theological in their covenant theology and, by extension, in their theology of the ordinances. Their convictions about baptism were not based on the simplistic notion, "well there are no babies baptized in the New Testament." Their convictions were rooted deeply in their understanding of the covenantal structure of the Bible and the new covenant. The new covenant shapes the meaning of the ordinances. "In the

---

7   2LCF 28.1 and 2.

8   Samuel E. Waldron, *A Modern Exposition of the 1689 Baptist Confession of Faith*, 5th ed. (Darlington, Co. Durham, England: Evangelical Press, 2016), 401.

9   Philip Cary, *A Just Reply to Mr. Flavell's Arguments by Way of Answer to a Discourse Lately Published, Entitled, A Solemn Call &c.* (London: J. Harris, 1690); John Flavel, *Vindiciae legis & foederis: or, A Reply to Mr. Philip Cary's Solemn Call Wherein he presents to answers all the arguments of Mr. Allen, Mr. Baxter, Mr. Sydenham, Mr. Sedgwick, Mr. Roberts, and Dr. Burthogge, for the right of believers infants to baptism, by proving the law at Sinai, and the covenant of circumcision with Abraham, were the very same with Adam's covenant of works, and that because the gospel-covenant is absolute* (London: M. Wotton, 1690).

New Covenant, baptism and the Lord's Supper make the promises of the covenant visible."[10]

The confession's treatment of baptism states that baptism is "a sign of his [the party baptized] fellowship with him [Jesus Christ], in his death and resurrection; of his being grafted into him; of remission of sins; and of giving up into God, through Jesus Christ, to live and walk in newness of life" (2LCF 29.1) There are similarities and departures with the WCF in this paragraph. The 2LCF states that baptism is a sign of union with Christ. This is not a sign and seal of the covenant of grace by being baptized into the visible church, as the WCF puts it. Rather, it is a sign of being in saving and vital union with Jesus Christ. Baptism, therefore, is not a seal of possible or promised future things, like the remission of sins and walking in newness of life, it is indeed a sign that one possesses those redemptive realities by virtue of union with Christ, as well as a testimony of authentic gospel experience. The confession, by affirming baptism as a sign, affirms that the redemptive realities spoken of belong to the party baptized. Baptism, in addition to promises made visible, expresses one's personal faith in those promises.

The 2LCF, along with the WCF, affirms that the outward element is water and the baptismal formula of "in the name of the Father, and of the Son, and of the Holy Spirit." The 2LCF parts company with the WCF over the mode of baptism. The proper administration of the ordinance of baptism is by "immersion or dipping of the person in water." The mode is no small matter, rather the mode is the symbolic expression of "his [the believer's] fellowship with him [Christ], in his death and resurrection; of his being engrafted into him." The exegetical importance of Romans 6:3–4 and Colossians 2:11–12 in being buried with Christ in baptism, is signified by immersion in water.[11]

The 2LCF continues its distinctive view by specifying that the proper subjects of baptism are *not*, in the words of the Westminster, "infants of one or both believing parents" (WCF 28.4). Instead, the 2LCF insists that "Those who do actually profess repentance

---

10 Samuel Renihan, *The Mystery of Christ: His Covenant and His Kingdom* (Cape Coral, FL: Founders, 2019), 204.

11 For a solid refutation of paedobaptist interpretations of Col. 2:11–12 and a credobaptist defense, see Richard C. Barcellos, "An Exegetical Appraisal of Colossians 2:11–12," in *Recovering a Covenantal Heritage: Essays in Baptist Covenant Theology* (Palmdale, CA: Reformed Baptist Academic Press, 2014), 449–74.

towards God, faith in, and obedience to, our Lord Jesus Christ, are the only proper subjects of this ordinance" (2LCF 29.2). This is, unashamedly, believer's or credobaptism. The confession asserts the necessity of professing a new heart and the knowledge of Christ as the basis for receiving baptism. Without equivocation, the confession affirms the proper mode of baptism as immersion and the proper subjects of baptism as those professing faith in Jesus Christ.

The affirmation of the proper mode and proper subjects of baptism were not despite the Particular Baptists' view of the covenants, but because of them. The paedobaptists saw the Abrahamic covenant as the covenant of grace. Such covenantal continuity sees the new covenant as the same covenant of grace but administered differently. If the sign and seal of the covenant was administered under the covenant of grace in the Abrahamic covenant, then it should be administered under the covenant of grace in the new covenant. Baptism replaces circumcision as the covenant sign, but the proper subjects of the sacrament remain the same, believers and their children.[12] Hercules Collins asked, in his *Orthodox Catechism*, "May the infant seed of believers under the gospel be baptized as the infant seed of Abraham under the law was circumcised?"[13] The Baptists rightly answered in the negative. "No. Abraham had a command then from God to circumcise his infant seed, but believers have no command to baptize their infant seed under the gospel."[14]

However, this rejection of infant baptism is not as a simple as "there is no command to baptize infants in the New Testament." The Particular Baptists understood the dual nature of the Abrahamic covenant, that is, the covenant had a national and physical aspect, and a spiritual aspect.[15] Collins, among a host of other Baptists, argued against the covenantal continuity between the seed of Abraham and the seed of believers precisely on the basis of the dual nature of the

12 An improvement of the new covenant administration of the covenant of grace is that girls are included in the sacrament of baptism, whereas they were excluded under circumcision.

13 Hercules Collins, *An Orthodox Catechism* (Palmdale, CA: Reformed Baptist Academic Press, 2014), 76.

14 Collins, 76.

15 See Jeffrey D. Johnson, "The Fatal Flaw of Infant Baptism: The Dichotomous Nature of the Abrahamic Covenant," in *Recovering a Covenantal Heritage: Essays in Baptist Covenant Theology* (Palmdale, CA: Reformed Baptist Academic Press, 2014), 223–256. See also, Johnson, *The Fatal Flaw of the Theology Behind Infant Baptism* (Conway, AR: Free Grace Press, 2010).

Abrahamic covenant.[16] This dual nature of the covenant is rooted in the progress of revelation and the New Testament's interpretation of the Old Testament. While paedobaptists flatline the Old and the New, and, in a sense, give a priority to the Old in interpreting the New, the Baptist perspective sees greater discontinuity between the Old and New precisely because of the interpretive priority of the New Testament.

Each element of the Abrahamic covenant has a physical, national, and temporal focus, as well as a spiritual, universal, and eternal focus. This dichotomy relates to the seed, circumcision, and the land. As important as the land promises are, they fall outside of the scope of this chapter. Nevertheless, the development of the seed of Abraham, as well as circumcision are more than enough to illustrate the dichotomy.

The promise that Abraham would have a seed had its immediate reference to the biological son of Abraham, Isaac. The seed of Abraham also has reference to the biological offspring that came through Isaac and Jacob and constituted the nation of Israel. This is the physical and national seed of Abraham. However, the promise of the seed precedes the promise to Abraham and finds its origin in Gen. 3:15, "And I will put enmity between you and the woman, and between your seed and her seed; he shall bruise you on the head, and you shall bruise him on the heel" (NASB95). This first gospel promise of the seed of the woman would develop both physically and spiritually, or both by race and grace. It would find its ultimate fulfillment in the Lord Jesus Christ, who is indeed the seed of the woman and the seed of Abraham (Matt. 1:1; Gal. 3:16). It is this Christocentric fulfillment of the seed promise, which is then understood not in its physical dimension, but rather in its spiritual dimension (Rom. 9:6–8). To be in union with the Seed of Abraham, Jesus Christ, through faith, is to be the seed of Abraham (Gal. 3:6–9).

In the Old Testament, the Messiah would have seed, or descendants, who were not physical, but spiritual, that is, of the Spirit through grace by faith (Isa. 53:10; Heb. 2:13–14). This view of the

---

16 "The covenant made with Abraham has two parts: First, a spiritual component; . . . second, this promise consisted of a temporal component" (78). Johnson lists Nehemiah Coxe, Robert Howell, John Spilsbury, Thomas Patient, Henry Lawrence, Philip Cary, and Benjamin Keach as holding to the dual nature of the Abrahamic covenant.

offspring of the Messiah is consistent with the promise that Zion herself would have children who were not biological (Isa. 49:14–21; 54:1–3; 61:8–9; 65:17–23; 66:22). The image is that fruitful Zion is apostate. The remnant, however, is barren Zion. Yahweh's suffering Servant blesses the remnant through his suffering, and through his sufferings Zion supernaturally brings forth spiritual children. This comports with the spiritual nature of the Abrahamic covenant. All the families of the earth are indeed blessed through Abraham's greater Seed, Jesus Christ.

The next consideration is the sign of the Abrahamic covenant, which was circumcision. Abraham received circumcision, which signified a salvation he had already received by faith (Rom. 4:9–12). In this sense, circumcision as a sign and seal of righteousness was unique to Abraham. However, the physical seed of Abraham were to receive the sign of the covenant on the eighth day. Failure to administer the sign was a major problem, it would result in being cut off from the people and the land.[17] The sign of the covenant was administered to all the physical descendants and those in the household of Abraham. Circumcision, then, is the physical sign of the covenant, which marked out in the flesh those who belonged to the covenant physically and nationally. This physical and national identity gave them the right to the land (Ex. 6:1–8).

However, even within the Old Testament itself, circumcision was not intended to only be a mark in the flesh, but rather symbolic of a deeper reality, that is, circumcision of the heart (Deut. 10:16; 29:4; 30:6; Jer. 4:4; 6:10; 9:25–26). Although the physical sign was administered to the children of the flesh, marking their national identity, the sign's spiritual significance was often missing in Israel (Deut. 10:16; 29:4; Rom. 2:25–29). There was always an Israel within Israel (Rom. 9:6).

Christ's spiritual seed have received circumcision of the heart through the Spirit. This brings together the true continuity between the Old and New. The spiritual seed receive spiritual circumcision (Rom. 2:25–29; Phil. 3:3; Col. 2:11–13). Now, under the new covenant, physical circumcision is altogether meaningless. Not because it was replaced with baptism for the physical seed, but because its

---

17 There is a conceptual play on words; failure to circumcise would lead to being truly "cut off" from the Lord and his people and the land.

spiritual significance is fulfilled in a renewed heart (1 Cor. 7:19; Gal. 5:6; 6:15).

The Particular Baptists made a significant contribution to the theology of baptism. It is significant to note that the background to their baptism theology was not an absence of covenant theology, but rather, a refinement of covenant theology. That refinement would emerge from a sensitivity to what is now called biblical theology. The Baptist view was not a fundamental denial of the unity of the Bible or the continuity between the Old and the New, but rather an exegetically and theologically nuanced discontinuity, driven by the New Testament's use of the Old. The confession reflects a theology of baptism that recognizes its relation to the spiritual nature of the Abrahamic covenant and its fulfillment in the new covenant newness. It is this perspective which not only properly identifies the proper subjects for baptism, but also properly identifies who belongs to the church.

Of the Lord's Supper

The Lord's Supper in the 2LCF is not nearly as controversial and when compared to the WCF it is strikingly similar. Both Confessions have eight paragraphs on the subject and are very similar in content. What the Baptist and Presbyterians lacked in agreement over baptism, they made up for in the Lord's Supper.

The confession affirms the perpetuity of the ordinance's observance as the remembrance of the Lord's sacrificial death (30.1). Again, the Supper makes the promises of the covenant visible.[18] The observance, although a memorial, is not a "mere memorial." It is designed to communicate afresh the benefits of the redemption. The Lord's Supper is a faith-strengthening ordinance. As believers eat and drink the symbols of Christ's sacrificial death, their souls are nourished, they grow in grace, and they are motivated in their duties toward God. Furthermore, the ordinance expresses both communion with God and with His people. The Supper is "to be a bond and pledge of their communion with him, and with each other."

The confession, in 30.2 denies that the Supper is a real sacrifice for the living or the dead. This is a clear denial of the Roman Catholic

---

18 Renihan, *The Mystery of Christ*, 204.

teaching, which is made explicit by saying "the popish sacrifice of the mass, as they call it, is most abominable," and "injurious to Christ's own sacrifice," which alone is the "propitiation for all the sins of the elect." The denial is matched by an affirmation, that is, the Supper is a memorial. Although the confession does not advocate a "mere memorial" position (as paragraph 7 will state), it does not shy away from the language of "memorial." For the confession, the danger is not in the word "memorial" but in the so-called sacrifice of the Mass.

The confession goes on to lay out the proper administration of the Supper, and again repudiates the Roman Catholic practice of denying the cup to the laity, lifting up the elements or carrying them for the purpose of adoration. In other words, the bread and the wine are not to be venerated in any way.[19] Furthermore, the confession sees a simple ordinance, comprised of common bread and wine, accompanied by simple prayer and simple administration.

The confession goes on to renounce the doctrine of transubstantiation in paragraphs 5–6. The bread remains bread, and the wine remains wine. They are symbols. Transubstantiation is "repugnant not to Scripture alone, but even to common sense and reason." The confession, following in the train of the Reformers, identities the Mass as superstitious, gross idolatry.

The beauty of the Supper is expressed in 30.7. This is a powerful corrective to a modern church culture which tacks on the Supper at the end of a service, with very little thought other than "this reminds us that Jesus died for us." Unfortunately, Evangelicals of all stripes have eviscerated the Supper, as if the only two options were Sacramentarianism or naked Memorialism. The confession provides a wonderful perspective on the Supper. Several things are worth noting here. First, the confession acknowledges that only "worthy partakers" can truly benefit from the Supper.[20] "Worthy partakers,"

19 This was John Knox's fundamental objection to Thomas Cranmer's 1552 *Book of Common Prayer*'s section on "The Order and Administration of the Lord's Supper." The BCP prescribed kneeling while receiving the Supper. After a sermon from John Knox on why communicants should receive the Supper while seated, the so-called "Black Rubric" was added to the BCP to clear up any possible misunderstandings on the act of kneeling while receiving the Supper. J. H. S. Burleigh, *A Church History of Scotland* (London: Oxford University Press, 1960), 162.

20 Although the Confession does not address the issue of open or closed membership to take Communion, James Renihan notes, "For the confessional churches, participating in the Lord's Supper was a privilege granted to church members, but it was not *closed communion*. They would welcome members of other churches to

derived from 1 Corinthians 11:27–28, is totally void of the notion of meriting or earning the right to the Table. Collins asks, "Who are to come to the table of the Lord?" He answers, "They only who are truly sorrowful they have offended God by their sins, and yet trust that those sins are pardoned them for Christ's sake, and what other infirmities they have, that those are covered by His passion and death, who also desire more and more to go forward in faith and integrity of life."[21]

Clearly, worthy participation is not found in the worth of the participant, but in the worth of the Savior. When the sinner saved by grace comes to the Table, he is sorry for his sins, and yet confidently trusts Christ and knows he is forgiven. The participant has no illusions of his own worthiness, but rather, he sees his deep need of the blood of Jesus and senses a deep confidence in the finished work of Christ. This confidence fuels a desire to grow in faith and holiness of life.

The participation is a visible participation, the believer needs to eat the bread and drink the wine. But the benefit is not in the physical act of eating and drinking, but in the participant's faith. The one taking the Supper is spiritually receiving Christ, spiritually feeding on Christ, who is spiritually present "to the faith of believers in that ordinance." This is the language of both the WCF and the Savoy. It is the language of Christ's spiritual presence in the Supper, but not by virtue of the elements, but by virtue of the presence of the Spirit and the promise united with faith.

The final paragraph (30.8) deals with the sin of partaking of the Supper in an unworthy manner. The "ignorant" and "ungodly" are those who are unconverted or living in scandalous sin. They not only should avoid the table, but they should also be prevented from being admitted to the table. Such unworthy eating and drinking at the

---

their observance of the Supper under some strict conditions, namely that the visitors were known in life and doctrine and in membership of a sister church; or, if not well-known, that the visitors could produce a letter from their home church indicating that they were in good standing in their church. In the church minute books it is common to find an entry stating that Brother or Sister so-and-so intended to travel (usually to London) and would like a letter from the church testifying to their membership status. The receiving church would then welcome them to what could be called "transient communion at the Lord's table." The bottom line is that known or demonstrated membership in good standing in a gospel church was the requisite." (Personal correspondence between the author and Dr. James Renihan, 10/15/2020).

21 Collins, *Orthodox Catechism*, 87.

Lord's Table would be a "great sin." The WCF even more forcefully
asserts, that it is "to their own damnation." This is the basis for pastors fencing the Table. "Out of concern for unbelievers, themselves,
we warn them not to partake of the table. We also refuse to invite
them to the table because those who reject Christ and his church
must not be admitted to the fellowship meal designed for those who
accept him and his people."[22]

There are two issues not specifically addressed in the confession.
Although "fencing the table" is implied in paragraph 8, there is no
instruction concerning how it is to be done. Those who take the
Supper seriously and want to guard its sanctity are most certainly
on the right track, but there are cautions. Pastors and Elders must
remember that the Supper is for the nourishment of poor sinners,
trusting Christ. The under-shepherds must not fence the table
in a way that leads the self-righteous to think they are worthy of
the table and the fainthearted to think they dare not touch it. The
Supper is a celebration of Christ's saving work for sinners who could
never save themselves or keep themselves. Yes, there is a place of
self-examination (1 Cor. 11:28, 31). There is a place to challenge
church members to deal with sins that have not been dealt with, or
to reconcile with other brothers or sisters (Matt. 5:23–24). But the
under-shepherds must point the sheep to the Great Shepherd of the
Sheep, who died and rose for them, and ever lives to make intercession for them (Heb. 7:25). The Lord's Table should be healing balm
for souls who know their sin. The under-shepherds can say to those
who tremble because of their sin, "The blood-sprinkled mercy-seat
is more and more indispensable and precious and you need anew the
fountain opened for sin and uncleanness."[23]

The other issue not addressed in the confession is the frequency
of the Supper. Perhaps the writers of the confession avoided this
topic for the simple reason that they saw nothing in the Scripture to
bind the consciences of churches. The result is that they may have
sought to avoid formalizing frequency in the confession on the lack
of clear biblical evidence. James Renihan observes that the Supper
was certainly observed on a regular basis, but that different churches

22 Chad Van Dixhoorn, *Confessing the Faith: A Reader's Guide to the Westminster Confession of Faith* (Edinburgh: Banner of Truth, 2014), 398.
23 John Murray, "Fencing the Table, 3" *Collected Writings of John Murray* (Edinburgh: Banner of Truth Trust, 1982), 3:279.

had different practices for how often they observed the ordinance.[24] Today, there are many who are rethinking the frequency of the Supper, and even many Baptists are choosing to observe the Supper on a weekly basis.[25] Each eldership at every local assembly ought to consider frequency and give it serious thought. But whatever the conclusion on frequency, the Supper should always be done in a way that honors the Lord Jesus Christ as the sole and exalted Mediator between God and man.

The 2LCF presents a view of the Supper that, on the one hand, maintains the element of mystery in Christ's spiritual presence at the Table and, on the other hand, avoids both the marginalization or undue exaltation of the ordinance. The language is compelling. The believer spiritually feeds on the Resurrected Christ, through the Spirit. "A taste of heaven is brought to the souls of believers by the Holy Spirit."[26] Far from the mere memorialism of today's church, the confession presents the Supper as a means of grace. There is communion with Christ in the Supper (1 Cor. 10:16–17). It is a spiritual eating and drinking (10:1–4). The believers gathered around the table share in Christ's sacrifice since they are in union with Him. "It is not by the church's administration, or merely by the activity of our memories, but through the Spirit that we enjoy communion with Christ, crucified, risen and exalted."[27] Believers also share communion with each other. "It is accordingly no accident that we have so largely come to call the Lord's Supper the 'Communion.' It is the symbol of the oneness of Christians. . . . There is but one salvation; but one Christian life; because there is but one Savior and one source of life; and all those who share it must needs stand side by side to imbibe it from the one fountain."[28]

---

24 James Renihan, *Edification and Beauty: The Practical Ecclesiology of the English Particular Baptists, 1675–1705.* Studies in Baptist History and Thought (Eugene, OR: Wipf and Stock, 2009), 144.

25 It is interesting to note that in *The First Book of Discipline* (1560), the church in Scotland determined the Supper would be observed quarterly. "Four times in the year we think sufficient to the administration of the Lord's Table, which we desire to be distinct, that the superstition of times may be avoided so far as may be" (The Ninth Head, Concerning the Policy of the Church). The Church of Scotland had an extremely high view of the Supper. This objection to weekly Communion should not be quickly dismissed.

26 Richard C. Barcellos, *The Lord's Supper as a Means of Grace: More than a Memory* (Scotland: Christian Focus, 2013), 69.

27 Sinclair Ferguson, *The Holy Spirit* (Downers Grove, IL: InterVarsity Press, 1996), 201.

28 Benjamin B. Warfield, *Faith and Life* (1916; repr., Edinburgh: Banner of

Conclusion

Robert Bruce, in his famous sermons on the Lord's Supper, said, "The Word leads us to Christ by the ear; the Sacraments lead us to Christ by the eye."[29] The confession's theology of the ordinances reflects both the unity with the broader Reformed tradition in the doctrine of the Lord's Supper and also its own distinctive covenantal understanding of the doctrine of baptism. The confession upholds the dignity and inestimable value of both ordinances and offers a serious correction to today's Baptists and broader evangelicals who reduce both ordinances to unremarkable ritual. May God use the wisdom of our confession to restore a biblical view of baptism and the Lord's Supper to the churches.

Truth, 1974), 220.
29   Robert Bruce, *The Mystery of the Lord's Supper*, ed. Thomas F. Torrance (1589; repr., Scotland: Christian Heritage, 2005, 2012), 30.

Part 5

Three Book Reviews

16

Recovering the Reformed Confession

Our Theology, Piety, and Practice

A Review

Nicolas Alford

I N *RECOVERING THE REFORMED CONFESSION*, R. Scott Clark
argues that modern Reformed churches are in the midst of an
identity crisis.[1] Like ships that have slipped their moorings and
become aimlessly adrift, they are without course, without compass,
and without captain. It is not Clark's aim, however, to point out
problems without offering solutions. Clark details what he sees as the
modern Reformed malaise but also lays out his vision for a Reformed
recovery. What he champions is a robust, historical, and exhaustive return to confessionalism. Clark's position is that the Reformed
identity is defined by the historic confession and by the manner in
which the church and its ministers subscribe to those documents.[2]

---

1 R. Scott Clark, *Recovering the Reformed Confession: Our Theology, Piety, and
Practice* (Phillipsburg, PA: Presbyterian and Reformed, 2008).
2 Clark always uses the term "confession" in the singular tense, presumably to
highlight his view of the unity of the Reformed confessions.

The first chapter is introductory, defining terms as Clark will be using them. In using the term "Reformed," Clark intends to speak of the theology, piety, and practice laid out in the six major confessions of the continental and British churches descended from John Calvin.[3] In this introduction he also begins to unveil his concerns with modern Reformed folk.[4] His charge is that the theology, piety, and practice of the modern Reformed churches include much that would be alien and even antithetical to the theology, piety, and practice of their Reformed forefathers.

The remaining chapters are divided into two parts. Part 1, which consists of chapters 2 and 3, details the current crisis of Reformed identity. This section of the book is where Clark presents his evidence to support the accusations leveled in his introduction. This evidence is presented as two illegitimate quests. Like David leering at the bathing Bathsheba, it is argued that these two quests have caught the eye of the Reformed churches and have caused them to turn from the good old paths, running headlong toward folly and mischief.

The first element of the crisis is the *Quest for Illegitimate Religious Certainty* (QIRC). Clark writes, "QIRC is the pursuit to know God in ways he has not revealed himself and to achieve epistemic and moral certainty on questions where such certainty is neither possible nor desirable" (39). In other words, having failed to maintain a robust, historic confessionalism, Reformed Christianity has been truncated. Reformed folk have sought to fill this vacuum with the QIRC, searching for some new sense of security and identity. Clark gives three examples of this QIRC: the desire to make a literal six-day/twenty-four-hour understanding of creation a Reformed *shibboleth*, the desire to claim OT theocratic and civil regulation as binding in exhaustive detail, and the desire to bring new innovations to our understanding of obedience and justification under the heading of covenant moralism. Clark dismisses each of these desires as either misguided and ill-informed (creation debates), or contrary to the confession and dangerous (theonomy and covenant moralism). In

---

3 These six major confessions are christened the "six forms of unity." Clark is referring to the Belgic Confession, Heidelberg Catechism, Cannons of Dort, Westminster Confession of Faith, Westminster Larger Catechism, and Westminster Shorter Catechism (3).

4 "Reformed folk" is Clark's preferred nomenclature. I do not know its provenance but rather like it.

each case, it is his view that preoccupation with these issues shows how untethered Reformed folk have become from their confession. Clark believes that the confession settles these matters for us, if we would but return to it as our standard and rule.

Clark titles the second half of the crisis, and his third chapter, the *Quest for Illegitimate Religious Experience* (QIRE). He now turns his critique to the spirit of revivalism as displayed in the Great Awakening, especially personified by Jonathan Edwards and his modern celebrators.[5] To Clark, revival is incompatible with Reformation. Revival seeks the immediate and extraordinary movement of God in the hearts of men, often divorced from the church and its ordinances, and as such is hopelessly infected with Pietism. Reformation, conversely, makes due use of ordinary means as prescribed in Scripture and administered weekly in the church, and in these things finds satisfaction and rest.

To Clark, a high view of revival (and the direct, relational communion with God it entails) necessitates a low view of the church (especially of its confession, and of God's appointed means of grace). This dichotomy runs throughout the book, and is evident in comments like the one found on page 330: "Perhaps attendance to the second [worship] service is actually a better indicator of spiritual maturity than are the calluses on our knees and the wear on our Bibles."[6] Clark's dichotomy between Reformation and revival (and thus between the public means of grace and private piety) is indicative of what this reviewer finds problematic in his analysis: a tendency to make enemies out of friends. Why must attendance to the second worship service be set against private prayer and Bible reading? Why must a high view of the public means of grace necessitate a low view of private piety? God's Word has a high view of both.[7] They are

5 Iain Murray and Martin Lloyd-Jones are likewise singled out as negative examples (278–82). It does not seem that Clark wrote with the intention of being elected Mr. Reformed Congeniality, as not only these men but also Abraham Kuyper, Cornelius Van Til, and John Frame are given negative attention. Clark's tone when discussing these men ranges from gently dismissive (Kuyper and Van Til) to hostile (Frame). See pp. 18n, 19, 22–25, 129–31, 233–35, 239–40, 263.

6 See also the bottom of p. 268 and the section beginning on p. 326.

7 For a high view of the means of grace, see Acts 2:41–42, Heb. 4:2, 1 Peter 3:21, and 1 Cor. 11:23–29. For a high view of private piety see Ps. 1:2, 2 Tim. 3:14–15, James 5:13–18, Col. 2:6–7, Eph. 6:10–20, and 1 Thess. 5:16–22. These two ideas are so organically linked in Scripture that many of these texts could be used under either heading. Dr. Clark publicly responded to an earlier version of this review, taking issue with this point of critique. He did not see himself as setting public and

organically related in a holistic, healthy Christianity. Shall we next set kindling against cordwood or make sunlight and soil compete for who most nourishes the plant?

Having diagnosed the crisis, Clark spends the rest of his pages detailing what a healthy recovery should look like. The remaining five chapters form part 2, titled *The Recovery*. Chapters 4 and 5 are a plea for honesty about what the confession says, what the confession means, and what the confession mandates. Chapter 6 caps this discussion by highlighting the benefits and joys of a robust and full submission to the Reformed confession. The last two chapters of the book offer a detailed survey of the exegesis, history, and confessional tradition associated with the Lord's Day and Christian worship. Clark's vision for rejuvenated Reformed worship revolves around a strict adherence to the Regulative Principle of Worship, a central view of the means of grace, and the reinstitution of a second Lord's Day worship service.

R. Scott Clark is a man of considerable academic ability who has a deep passion for the health and faithfulness of the church. He brings thorough research and a keen mind to the topics with which he interacts, and there is much value in working through his arguments and considering his conclusions, even for Baptists who are by no means his intended audience (he would not consider our confession truly Reformed, and thus it would be nonsensical from his perspective to speak of recovering a Reformed *Baptist* confession). Clark very effectively calls evangelicals searching for religion with greater substance to take up the banner of the Reformed. His invitation to resist Rome, Constantinople, and the Emergent Village in favor of Geneva is persuasive and stirring (195).[8] Reformed churches should strive for the sort of visibility and credibility that will make this a viable option for disillusioned evangelicals seeking more. Clark is correct as well when he argues for the inevitability and general benefits of confessional ecclesiology. Under his piercing analysis, the maxim "no creed but Scripture" is deflated as fallacy. Furthermore,

---

private piety against each other but rather as merely giving the public worship gathering a place of higher priority. This reviewer is sympathetic to that prioritization but had difficulty locating that more nuanced view in the book.

8 The attention given to the "Emergent Village" does feel somewhat dated. This is not a criticism of Clark for lacking clairvoyance when writing back in 2008 but rather a note of gratitude that the Emergent Church, once such an urgent threat, is now so *blasé*.

this book contains considerable amounts of very sound and helpful exegetical and historical research. Of special note is the logical and convincing exegesis of John 4:23–24 (272), and the excellent survey of the Christian Sabbath from biblical, confessional, and historical perspectives (293–326).

These positive elements are found, however, amid some problematic perspectives—and not just for Baptist readers. Even as he criticizes the QIRC and the QIRE, there is a quest which Clark himself undertakes in *Recovering the Reformed Confession*. We may call this, if some good-natured cheek may be admitted, the *Quest for Illegitimate Religious Traditionalism* (QIRT). The QIRT is an inordinate authority assigned to the confession, superseding reasonable bounds those who confess Scripture's unique and supreme authority ought not supersede. Clark writes "Not every appeal to Scripture is Reformed or reforming. Any appeal to Scripture that fundamentally overturns what it is to be Reformed cannot itself be a Reformed appeal to Scripture" (25). *Et tu, semper reformanda?* Clark goes on: "Sola scriptura [does] not teach that the Bible means what one says it does, but that the Scriptures, being God's word, form the church, and the church in subjection to the Scriptures is able to interpret them well enough to decide controversies" (25–6). While Clark's zeal for ecclesiastical authority may make some uncomfortable, this passage could be taken as nothing more than a proper condemnation of the widespread distortion of *sola Scriptura* into *solo Scriptura*. Biblicism—the habit of reading the Bible as though you are the first person to ever read it and treating that private, individual interpretation as sacrosanct—has kindled much strange fire. But it is difficult, at least for this reviewer, to find common ground with Clark's view that "the authority of the confession is . . . tantamount to that of Scripture, assuming that a given confession is biblical" (178).

This quote is taken from the context of Clark's interaction with the writings of R. B. Kuiper. Writing in 1926, Kuiper objected to the practice of the ecclesiastical courts in appealing to the confession as authoritative, without feeling the need to check the confession against Scripture. It was Kuiper's concern that this practice might give the impression that the church had adopted what we might call a form of hyper-confessionalism, wherein the confession was nearly "tantamount" to Scripture. Clark's reply, quoted above, is that the confession *is indeed* tantamount to Scripture in authority. Clark can make this assertion and stay Protestant because he qualifies that the confession must, of course, be biblical. But this seems to downplay the distinction between inherent and derivative authority. The Bible is not authoritative simply because it is true and accurate in the sort of strictly forensic way that can be reproduced in a confession, but because it is the living Word of God. The Word's authority is derived from its God-breathed, self-attesting character. The confession of our faith may be critical and urgent, even devotionally moving—but it is not like fire, nor a hammer that breaks the rock in pieces (Jer. 23:29). It is not that food that man needs beyond bread alone (Matt. 4:4). It is not living and active, sharper than a double-edged sword (Heb. 4:12).

There is no document written by man that is tantamount in authority to God's Word. The best confessions confess that clearly, as seen in the first line of the Baptist Confession of 1677/89: "The Holy Scripture is the only sufficient, certain, and infallible rule of all saving knowledge, faith, and obedience." Our Baptist forefathers thought that truth so central they inserted it at the fore of their revision to the Westminster and Savoy documents. Therein lies a faith worth confessing and a confession worth recovering. To the degree that R. Scott Clark promotes that recovery he deserves gratitude. In disagreement he deserves charity as a brother in Christ. In all things, Jesus deserves all the glory, as his church confesses him the Christ, Son of the living God. May that good confession endure, whatever other confessions be recovered.

17

The Creedal Imperative

A Review

Luke Walker

E VERY CHURCH HAS A CREED, even those who claim, "No creed but the Bible." The church has used creeds and confessions throughout its history, yet today these summaries of faith are widely considered to be outdated statements of cold, dead orthodoxy. Carl Trueman (PhD, University of Aberdeen) tackles this problem head-on in his winsome and thought-provoking *The Creedal Imperative*.[1]

Summary

In six hefty chapters, Trueman lays out a case for the right use of creedal statements in our churches. He argues that creeds and confessions are "thoroughly consistent with the belief that Scripture alone is the unique source of revelation and authority," that they are "necessary for the well-being of the church," and even posits that their existence and use "is also a biblical imperative" (20).

From the introduction onward, he engages the most common of all modern creeds: "No creed but the Bible." Trueman is careful to point out the irony of this statement: it is, in fact, itself a creed. He

---

1 Carl R. Trueman, *The Creedal Imperative* (Wheaton, IL: Crossway, 2012).

uses the introduction to set down some important principles, such as the true nature of *sola Scriptura* (16–17) and the difference between the nature of the Bible and the nature of creedal statements (*norma normata* vs. *norma normans*) (18).[2]

Chapter 1 considers powerful cultural influences that militate, directly or indirectly, against the use of creeds and confessions. Trueman makes three conscious assumptions that legitimize creeds and confessions: the relevance of the past, the validity of language itself, and the authority of the church (22–23). These, however, are the very things that modern culture denies. He takes these forces in turn. First, the past is easily set aside under the influence of science's obsession with the future, technology's rapid improvements, consumerism's constant need for new things, and the relativization of human constants through the denial of universal human nature. Second, language is no longer respected as a faithful mode of preservation and communication; in fact, "mysticism is alive and well within evangelical circles" (35). Third, authority is out of style. In today's everyone-is-a-winner mindset, we have "confused the right to speak with the right to be heard" (41). Add to this our hypersensitivity about the dangers of excluding others, and it is no wonder that dogmatic statements of faith are avoided at all costs. Trueman urges non-confessional Christians to examine whether these undetected cultural forces may be influencing them in their rejection of creeds and confessions.

Rather than answer these objections one by one, Trueman spends chapter 2 building a positive foundation for the biblical use of creeds and confessions. First, we can listen to old words because language has been endowed by God with stability and meaning. God has entrusted his truth to us in language, even his own creative language. His very presence is attached to words (56); his gospel is words (59). Therefore, words are basic and essential to our faith. They are "a normative and normal part of Christianity" (61). Second, we can listen to people from the past because all people are created in God's image: "All humans are partakers in a common human nature" (64). For instance, it is silly to dismiss something simply because it was written by an old, white male (66).

---

2 The Latin phrase *norma normata* refers to a norm that is normed. A *norma normans*, on the other hand, is a norm that norms. The former is subordinate to the latter.

Third, the church is possessed of institutional authority from God. Confessions and creeds were produced by councils of churches, not individual believers. The church has flexed its ministerial authority in the production of these documents. They give churches ecclesiastical teeth with which to govern and rule, building up members in good standing and, at times, administering church discipline. Fourth, the Bible itself contains creedal statements. Paul admonishes Timothy to protect "the form of sound words" (2 Tim 1:13), which means "a model, form, or standard, that is intended to function as a trustworthy or reliable guide" (74). When Paul's creed-like statements are considered, the true use of these forms of sound words becomes clear: they "capture in a nutshell the gospel" (77). In short, the church, through words, has produced in the creeds and confessions what are known as normed norms, while the Bible alone remains the norming norm (80).

The early church produced towering creeds. Trueman takes chapter 3 to unfold when, how, and why these ancient expressions of Christian truth came to be. A shorthand creedal expression called the Rule of Faith appeared first. The Rule is not a definite form of words, but a cohesion of content that appears in fathers such as Polycarp, Ignatius, Tertullian, and Irenaeus (83–86). A later baptismal document called the Old Roman Creed eventually became the well-known Apostles' Creed (86–87). After the Apostles' Creed came the seven ecumenical councils, the first four of which are held to by Protestants. The most famous of these is the First Council of Nicaea, which met in 325 (91). The creed produced by this council made Trinitarian advances on the Apostles' Creed, introducing the well-known expression *homoousion* (of the same substance). Constantinople, Ephesus, and Chalcedon followed, each building upon the Nicene foundation. The so-called Athanasian Creed introduced decidedly negative language, handing out anathemas to heretical hearers. Several of these creeds have been used and reverenced by the churches for hundreds of years. The modern Christian who casually dismisses these careful, faithful, time-tested productions "in favor of [their] own ideas" lacks humility (107).

A second period of major creedal endeavor is the Protestant Reformation. Here the church moved beyond simple creedal statements to produce exquisite, full-orbed confessions of faith. The Church of England led the way with its Thirty-Nine Articles;

Lutherans compiled ten confessional statements (including three ancient creeds and seven of their own productions) into the Book of Concord. The Synod of Dort (1618–1619) adopted the Three Forms of Unity to unite the Continental Reformed churches: The Belgic Confession, The Heidelberg Catechism, and the Canons of Dort. Among these the Heidelberg displays touching pastoral concern: "Indeed, anybody who thinks that Protestant confessionalism is a hard, dry creed needs to read the Heidelberg Catechism. Only the willfully stupid or deluded could possibly dismiss such a document along such lines" (125). English Puritans, under the direction of Parliament, later produced the Westminster Standards (consisting of the Confession of Faith, the Longer and Shorter Catechisms, and the Directory for Public Worship). Independents and Baptists drew from and adapted the Westminster Confession into the Savoy Declaration and 1689 Second London Baptist Confession. This is indeed "a rich confessional heritage" (130). Churches hold to these particular confessions *as churches*. To be confessional means just this: "It is an ecclesiastical term, a churchly concept, which only has real meaning in such a context" (133).

Trueman pauses to explore an under-considered aspect of creeds and confessions in chapter 5: "Confession as Praise" (135). "Historically, one could make the argument that Christian theology as a whole is one long, extended reflection upon the meaning and significance of that most basic doxological declaration, 'Jesus is Lord!' " (135). The Bible does not sever doxology from doctrine (136). The major doctrines of the Bible and of the historic creeds and confessions are the very substance of our praise. "Praise is rooted in, and expressive of, the identity of God" (139). The public nature of confessions is a matter of public praise. The early church used creeds in this way, wedding them to worship experiences like baptism. Even the Athanasian Creed (known for its strict polemics) is a matter of praise. Trueman quotes John Henry Newman to this effect: "No one can deny, looking at its whole, that it is occupied in *glorifying* Father, Son, and Holy Ghost, in declaring their infinite perfections; so much so that it has sometimes been considered what it really is in form, a Psalm or Hymn of Praise to the Blessed Trinity, rather than a Creed" (141). In fact, without doctrinal precision, God cannot be worshiped rightly. This is especially important when God's Trinitarian nature is brought into consideration. This requires "careful and clear articulation of God as Trinity" (146). Modern Christianity accuses confessions of dead formalism, as opposed to spontaneous, living worship. However, even the music that these churches sing is carefully selected and practiced ahead of time. If creeds are formal *as such*, then so are the songs celebrated by "super-spiritual" and spontaneous services. Creeds and confessions serve true doxology in three ways: they present the Bible's teaching in short, they stand squarely against unbiblical cultural influences, and they give God the worship that is his alone. These documents do more than ensure that churches *think* rightly; they ensure that churches *worship* rightly.

In his last chapter, Trueman presents the uses of creeds and confessions. Every church and every Christian in every church has a confession. In other words, they have an idea about what the Bible teaches. Most of these ideas are unwritten and private. Proper confessions, which are written and public, steward the truth well, guarding churches in the present and in the future. Creeds and confessions also keep the power of the churches in check. Hobbyhorses and heresies alike are kept out of the pulpit by these old, paper watchmen. The ministry is kept on track and focused, and the life of the body is protected from arbitrary and tyrannical leaders. Creeds and confessions also articulate the faith in short yet thorough form. These statements are short enough to be held by a team of elders, and detailed enough to bring babes in Christ to maturity over time. Confessions hit the sweet spot. In fact, they set the bar for a congregation to strive toward, bringing unity to the body. Churches possess authority from God, but that authority is ministerial, not magisterial. Confessions of faith embody this kind of authority as normed norms. In addition, they make us keenly aware that we are not the only believers who have ever existed; we are a small part of the body of Jesus Christ.

Evaluation

Thorough, thought-provoking, and timely, Trueman's work is a champion of the right use of creeds and confessions. He squarely engages objections while maintaining a winsome tone; the negatives are answered with positives. The author's sarcasm and wit are happy attendants throughout these pages. His tone confutes the most common objections to confessions: they are supposedly dry, academic, irrelevant, impractical. Trueman is anything but. He has embodied his argument in the work itself. The book, like the old creeds and confessions it treats, is very much alive. This is commendable. Confessionally winsome works are rare gifts indeed.

Taking up cultural influences first was a refreshing and unexpected way into the topic. Every believer faces these imperceptible forces, and it appears that these cultural influences have encouraged opposition to the use of confessions. Trueman does well to unmask the true culprits at hand.

The book lays a thorough foundation for understanding not only why creeds and confessions are important, but how they came about. The reader comes away with an outline of the creedal hot spots of church history, namely, the early church and the Reformation. Seeing how the documents were forged in real life conflict will warm skeptical readers to these precious deposits of our spiritual forebears. The unfolding drama that reaches its crescendo in the Westminster Standards is moving.

Trueman also displays an ecumenical spirit, including the 1689 2LCF in his historical discussions. Even though it was a mere sampling of confessions, I suspect he knew it would win favorable readers among his Reformed Baptist brethren. In this, it seems, he has succeeded.

As to weaknesses, it is difficult to be critical of irenic works of this quality. The present writer must scrape the bottom of the proverbial barrel to find much of anything. The pickings are slim. Here, we may encounter an ironic remark from a paedobaptist about church inclusion ("belonging before believing," 184), and there, what could be perceived by younger readers (and their senior John Owen) as a cynical comment about fashion as such ("the heart of fashion is the notion that by purchasing certain goods one can create an identity for oneself," 39). The latter statement may unnecessarily alienate target audience readers. The book will also find itself outdated in small, but noticeable, ways, such as its use of the term "e-zine" (40). Writers should be aware of embedding the passing trends of internet vocabulary into works that aim to be read for many years to come (in this case, perhaps "online periodical" is better).

Conclusion

Every church has a creed, or confession of faith. Some are unwritten, while others collect dust on office shelves. The common conception of creeds as cold, dead documents is simply not true. Orthodoxy is alive; it stewards the living, biblical truth among living churches and Christians. *The Creedal Imperative* addresses these issues in a thoughtful, winsome, and witty (if, at times, outdated) way. If skeptical readers sincerely engage with this book, it will inevitably win converts to the classic creeds and confessions of the Christian church.

18

The Need for Creeds Today: Confessional Faith in a Faithless Age
A Review

Vadim Chepurny

NOTHING IS MORE FRIGHTENING in the evangelical church today than religion. After all, everyone knows that Christianity is not a religion but a relationship. And any rigid system of doctrine is sure to undermine genuine Christian experience. Creeds and confessions are at the top of the list for suspicion of threatening that living relationship with Jesus. In his *The Need for Creeds Today: Confessional Faith in a Faithless Age*, J. V. Fesko thinks otherwise. Being a professor of systematic and historical theology at Reformed Theological Seminary and an ordained minister in the Orthodox Presbyterian Church, Fesko is well equipped to argue his case. From his more than twenty years of church planting and pastoral ministry experience, he is convinced that confessions of faith are not only beneficial for a living relationship with Jesus but are necessary for the well-being of the whole church (xvi). This is a short book, comprised of five chapters, with an introduction and a conclusion, totaling roughly 120 pages of content.

262 The Confessing Baptist

Summary

Chapter 1 lays out the biblical argument for confessions. Fesko examines eight passages of Scripture. However, before he goes into the particular passages, he gives a brief history of de-confessionalism. According to Fesko, the drift took place in America between the eighteenth and nineteenth centuries, as Americans reasserted their freedom of religion with the Declaration of Independence of 1776. Heading the anti-creedal movement, known as the Restoration Movement, were ex-Presbyterian ministers Barton W. Stone (d. 1844), Thomas Campbell (d. 1854) and his son Alexander (d. 1866). It was within the Stone-Campbell movement that the motto "no creed but the Bible" became popular (2). The question is then raised, What does the Bible have to say about creeds?

Fesko first examines the Passover liturgy in Exodus 13:14–15, highlighting the importance of divine tradition in reminding the people of God what he has done for them in history, and how the older generation was responsible for teaching the younger generation to reflect on the mighty works of God. Fesko calls this the "revelation-reflection-repetition" pattern (4). After God had delivered Israel out of Egypt, he had instituted the Passover and *revealed* to them its significance. The people were to then yearly *reflect* upon God's goodness to them in the Passover feast and teach future generations to *repeat* the same. Fesko then moves to Deuteronomy 6:4–6, the Shema, the most foundational confession of the Jews. While the Shema was a verbatim restatement of the inspired canonical words of God, it serves to show that certain statements of the truth of Scripture are more fundamental than others and are, therefore, to be memorized and repeated (4). The next five passages of Scripture are the apostle Paul's five trustworthy sayings (1 Tim. 1:15; 3:1; 4:7–9; 2 Tim. 2:11–13; Titus 3:4–8). Each one of the sayings touches on key doctrinal truths, such as redemption, sanctification, and church polity, providing precedent and the need to summarize these truths (7). Finally, from Jude 3, "the faith that was once for all delivered to the saints" serves to distinguish orthodoxy from heterodoxy, which has always been one of the primary functions of confessions (11).

Chapter 2 deals specifically with the Reformed confessions written between 1500–1700. Fesko is particularly interested here in showing the complementary nature of the earlier Reformed confessions with those written during the "High Orthodoxy" of the Westminster divines. He argues that those who try to pit Calvin against the Calvinists fail to see the organic development of the Reformed tradition (35). Seeing that confessions are hammered out in the crucible of controversy, the need to further revise the earlier Reformed confessions in light of new doctrinal challenges was inevitable. The First Helvetic Confession (1536) of the Swiss Reformers, for example, was revised by Heinrich Bullinger to address the Counsel of Trent and its aberrant view of justification, giving more specificity to what was meant by "justification by faith alone." The Second Helvetic Confession made clear that, properly speaking, it is not faith that justifies, but Christ who justifies, "Faith is only the instrument by which we embrace Christ, our righteousness" (26). The later generations "did not add new doctrines to the first-generation confessional foundation but elaborated on already-existing doctrinal convictions by means of lengthier explanations and sharper terminology" (27).

In chapter 3, we take a closer look at the "Causes for Deconfessionalization." Among these are skepticism, religious wars, the Enlightenment, mysticism, and individualism. While skepticism has been with us since the fall of man, Fesko considers Erasmus as one of the first great skeptics who took an anti-confessional stance, "Erasmus and Luther represent the establishment of two different Reformation-era trajectories: skepticism and confessionalism" (46). Then there were the religious wars, fought on confessional grounds. Among them, the Thirty Years' War (1618–1648) is the most notable. After the war, "population levels in the Holy Roman Empire would not return to pre-war levels until 1720" (51). Naturally, people were tired of fighting, thus the emphasis in Christendom shifted from doctrine to moral virtues such as justice, charity, and sobriety (53). Then came the Enlightenment, which was not only a reaction to theological wars, but especially the rejection of corporate thought (58). Most notable is Immanuel Kant, being a vigorous opponent of confessions of faith. He even objected to voluntary adherence to creeds and confessions, fearing that they would "keep all further enlightenment away from the human race forever" (59). From there, everything else quickly unraveled. Systematic theology gave way to higher textual criticism, since the Bible could no longer be read as book with a single divine Author. In the 1800s Schleiermacher severed theological study from the church, such that theology was no longer studied for the sake of wisdom and piety, but for the sake of scientific knowledge, as a purely intellectual exercise (63–65). Since the Bible could no longer be trusted, disillusioned Lutherans gave way to mysticism and pietism (67).[1]

Chapter 4 presents three "Benefits of Confessions." First, and most obvious, confessions distinguish orthodoxy from heterodoxy. It is not sufficient to simply assert that you believe the Bible when combating error, "The church has the responsibility of repeating, meditating on, and interpreting biblical claims in harmony with divine authorial intent" (78). Second, confessions of faith help to create a diversified orthodoxy. Here, too, Fesko considers the Westminster Confession to show how the framers added deliberate ambiguity in the chapters on the decree of God, the covenants, and assurance, to accommodate for the differing perspectives on the finer points of theology (83). Thus confessions "draw both lines and circles" (88). The lines distinguish between orthodoxy and heterodoxy, while circles encapsulate areas of doctrinal freedom. Finally, the third benefit of confessions is the codification of the church's historic witness. Fesko sets out to show that the Reformed confessions continue in the spirit of the early church and the church fathers. The citation from the preface of the Second London Baptist Confession is welcomed, "We have no itch to clog religion with new words, but do readily acquiesce in that form of sound words, which had been in consent with the holy Scriptures used by others before us" (93). And so it should be the desire of the church today to stand in line with those who have gone before us.

The final chapter, titled "Confessions and Piety," is a rehearsal and an analysis of "the duel that almost was" between Franciscus Gomarus and Matthias Martinius over a personal offense at the Synod of Dort in 1618. After recounting the story, Fesko gives a warning against anachronistically interpreting church history through the eyes of a twenty-first-century man, but still concludes that dueling is immoral in all cultures and generations (109). Christians must guard themselves against pride and arrogance when defending confessional truth (110).

---

1 Interestingly, Fesko defends Philipp Jakob Spener as someone who was not against confessions but only impious theologians (68).

Analysis

The Need for Creeds Today is most helpful on two fronts, as seen in chapters 1 and 3 of the book. It gives priority to the biblical defense of confessions and traces the historical path of de-confessionalism. If confessions of faith are not only helpful but necessary, there better be some "good and necessary" biblical warrant for them. So, in chapter 1, Fesko guards against a dead traditionalism, seeking to testify of "the living faith of the dead, not traditionalism's dead faith of the living" (13). He shows that God in his Word does advocate for a living tradition. And because certain doctrines are more foundational than others, it behooves God's people to give special care to accurately articulate and preserve them for future generations. Fesko helpfully concludes chapter 1 by pointing out that "confessions run in two directions" (13). They look back, to remind the people of God of what God has done in the past, and they look forward, to preserve the faith for future generations.

In chapter 3 we are reminded that history can be a powerful medicine. It helps to lift us up out of the spiritual mire of modernity and direct our sights to the old paths of spiritual vitality. Of course, not everything that came with modernity is to be eschewed. Much of the medical and technological developments are most welcomed. But spiritually, especially since the Enlightenment, Western civilization continues to show ever-increasing signs of decline and degeneration. This is seen in the most fundamental levels of man's thinking. Skepticism is rightly placed at the top of the list. There is no use for confessions if nothing can be said for certain (at least in the sphere of religion). If something does not make sense to man's naked reason, it is quickly disposed of as something unreasonable. True, Fesko does acknowledge that skepticism was with us in seed form even before the Enlightenment, going back as far as Cicero (d. 43 BC), and Pyrrho of Elis (d. c. 270 BC), but never before did it hold such powerful sway over the church (45).

It is also illuminating to consider how much the religious wars influenced the church's confessional stance in the seventeenth and eighteenth centuries. Wars (or lack thereof) have often had great impact on the theological outlook of a society. They also help to reveal something of the true convictions and state of the church. Interestingly, the instinctive answer to the religious wars was not to go the separation-of-church-and-state route, but to abandon confessional Christianity altogether. This goes to show that at a deeper level the people had already developed an indifference to truth.

While Fesko is helpful on multiple fronts, the whole of the book leaves something to be desired. At times it is difficult to track Fesko's arguments. For example, how exactly do Exodus 13 and Deuteronomy 6 argue for human-drafted confessions as such? The reader would be better served with a more thorough explanation of how in particular the passages are to be applied to confessions. The principles are there, but please help us see how we cross over from OT example to NT application. Certain ideas that are either assumed or vaguely hinted at could be better articulated. Fesko concludes chapter 1 by recognizing the danger of falling into mere traditionalism and the importance of subordinating tradition to Scripture, but he does not give clear direction as to how this can be accomplished (16).

At other times, Fesko takes on an overly defensive stance and ends up devoting more to defending certain narrow issues than arguing the bigger point at hand. When laying out the church's historic witness as one of the benefits of confessions, for instance, more time is invested to defending the continuity of the Reformers with earlier church history than developing a positive case for *how* confessions help codify the church's historic witness. Chapter 5 is another example. The reader would be better served if Fesko dealt more broadly with the principal relationship between confessions and how they help to foster true piety, than in retelling at length a single incident that happened at the Synod of Dort in 1618 and explaining the different attitudes that people had toward dueling.[2]

By the end, this reviewer is left wondering about the intended audience of the book. Is it mainstream evangelicals? Probably not. Anyone outside of the Calvinistic persuasion would quickly lose interest. The title of the book, *The Need for Creeds Today*, would suggest that it is written to persuade conservative evangelicals in Bible-believing churches. But even there, Fesko has much ground to make up with the conservative evangelical constituency. Gone are the days of Jonathan Edwards and *Religious Affections*, a piety cultivated within the framework of confessional Christianity. More

---

2 I do wonder if this story deserves a chapter of its own in a 120-page book.

time would need to be spent in developing things like proper biblical hermeneutics, and the application of the OT to NT times. And instead of going into the distinctions between Reformed, Early, and High Orthodoxy and whether the High Orthodoxy of the Puritans departed from the simplicity of the Reformed confessions, a broader audience would have been better served with a wider survey of confessions and creeds throughout church history.[3] Cut down on chapter 2 and expand chapter 4. If you are arguing for *historic* confessions, give more robust arguments that would appeal to those who already have their own church confessions. Many Bible-believing churches have lengthy confessions of faith which have been drafted by the leaders of their various denominations or associations. Such confessions would at least cover two of the three benefits from chapter 4, which would substantially weaken Fesko's appeal in these circles.[4]

But perhaps Fesko is writing to his own constituency, seeking to remind them and encourage them in their own Reformed heritage. This would explain chapters 2 and 5. Much of the book is an apologetic for the Westminster Confession. But the title and the introduction of the book does seem to suggest a broader audience. Be that as it may, even those who already adhere to the Westminster Confession (or the 2LCF) would be better helped with a broader survey of historic creeds and a more thorough analysis of how their own historic confessions are "necessary for both the being (*esse*) and the well-being (*bene esse*) of the church" (xvi).

Conclusion

So *The Need for Creeds Today* is left searching for a suitable audience. While helpful and insightful at certain points, as a whole, it is too specific and not specific enough at the same time. Too specific in things secondary, and not specific enough in things primary. If forced to choose just one introductory book on the need for confessions, the reader would be better helped with Carl Trueman's lengthier treatment in *The Creedal Imperative*.

---

3 Chapter 2 as a whole would probably be best moved to an appendix.
4 A similar weakness exists in Carl R. Trueman, *The Creedal Imperative* (Wheaton, IL: Crossway, 2012). Little consideration is given to the use of modern confessions.

Resources for Further Study

Below are some recommended resources for those who wish to go deeper in the study of creeds and confessions.

On the Legitimacy, Benefits, and Use of Confessions

In addition to the first two essays of this book, the works below provide good arguments for the importance and benefits of creeds, confessions, and catechisms. Of special note is Jim Renihan's little booklet *A Toolkit for Confessions*—an invaluable resource for the study of Puritan confessions, especially for the Second London Confession.

Clark, R. Scott. *Recovering the Reformed Confession: Our Theology, Piety, and Practice.* Phillipsburg: Presbyterian and Reformed, 2008.

Fesko, J. V. *The Need for Creeds Today: Confessional Faith in a Faithless Age.* Grand Rapids: Baker Academic, 2020.

Martin, Robert P. "The Legitimacy and Use of Confessions." In Samuel E. Waldron, *A Modern Exposition of the 1689 Baptist Confession of Faith.* Fifth edition. Darlington, Co. Durham, England: Evangelical Press, 2016.

Miller, Samuel. "The Utility and Importance of Creeds and Confessions." In *Doctrinal Integrity.* Presbyterian Heritage, 1989.

Renihan, James M. *A Toolkit for Confessions: Helps for the Study of English Puritan Confessions of Faith.* Palmdale, CA: Reformed Baptist Academic Press, 2017.

Trueman, Carl R. *The Creedal Imperative.* Wheaton: Crossway, 2012.

Texts and Surveys of Creeds and Confessions

Those wishing to study particular creeds and confessions and to understand their historical context and development should find the works below helpful. Additionally, the collection of essays edited by David Hall provides a historical survey and critical analysis of various views of confessional subscription among Presbyterians, which is relevant to Baptist use of confessions.

Anderson, James. "A Tabular Comparison of the 1646 WCF and the 1689 LBCF." Accessed January 21, 2021. https://www.proginosko.com/docs/wcf_lbcf.html.

Beeke, Joel R., and Sinclair Ferguson. ed. *Reformed Confessions Harmonized*. Grand Rapids: Baker Books, 1999.

Belcher, Richard P., and Anthony Mattia. *A Discussion of the Seventeenth Century Particular Baptist Confessions of Faith*. Southbridge, MA: Crowne, 1990.

Bush, L. Russ, and Tom Nettles. *Baptists and the Bible*. Revised and expanded. Nashville: Broadman & Holman, 1999.

Collins, Hercules. *An Orthodox Catechism*. Edited by Michael A. G. Haykin and G. Stephen Weaver Jr. Palmdale, CA: Reformed Baptist Academic Press, 2013.

Fairbairn, Donald, and Ryan M. Reeves. *The Story of Creeds and Confessions: Tracing the Development of the Christian Faith*. Grand Rapids: Baker Academic, 2019.

George, Timothy and Denise, ed. *Baptist Confessions, Covenants, and Catechisms*. Nashville: Broadman and Holman, 1996.

Hall, David, ed. *The Practice of Confessional Subscription*. Oak Ridge, TN: The Covenant Foundation, 1997.

Haykin, Michael A. G. *Kiffen, Knollys, and Keach: Rediscovering Our English Baptist Heritage*. Leeds, UK: Reformation Today Trust, 1996.

Kelly, J. N. D. *Early Christian Creeds*, 3rd edition. London: Longman, 1972.

Leith, John H. *Creeds of the Churches: A Reader in Christian Doctrine from the Bible to the Present*, rev. edition. Richmond, VA: John Knox, 1973.

Lumpkin, W. L. *Baptist Confessions of Faith*. Valley Forge: Judson, 1974.

Nettles, Thomas J. *Teaching Truth, Training Hearts: The Study of Catechisms in Baptist Life*. Amityville, NY: Calvary Press, 1998.

Nichols, Gregory, ed. *The Shorter Catechism: A Baptist Version*. 2nd edition. Avinger, TX: Simpson, 2003.

Noll, Mark A., ed. *Confessions and Catechisms of the Reformation*. Grand Rapids: Baker Books, 1991.

Pelikan, Jaroslav. *Credo: Historical and Theological Guide to Creeds and Confessions of Faith in the Christian Tradition*. New Haven: Yale University Press, 2003.

Reeves, Stan, ed. *Confessing the Faith: The 1689 Baptist Confession for the 21st Century*. Cape Coral, FL: Founders, 2012.

Renihan, James M., ed. *1689 Baptist Confession of Faith & the Baptist Catechism*. Vestavia Hills, AL: Solid Ground Books, 2018.

_____. *True Confessions: Baptist Documents in the Reformed Family*. Owensboro, KY: Reformed Baptist Academic Press, 2004.

Renihan, Mike. *A Confession of Faith. Printed in the Year, 1677. Facsimile Edition, 2000*. Auborn, MA: 2000.

Schaff, Philip. *The Creeds of Christendom*. 3 volumes. Edited by David S. Schaff. 1931; Reprint, Grand Rapids: Baker Books, 1990.

Warfield, Benjamin B. *The Westminster Assembly and Its Work*. 1931; reprint, Grand Rapids: Baker Book House, 1991.

Commentaries and Expositions of the 2LCF or WCF

Teaching through a confession of faith is an excellent way to present systematic theology to a Sunday school class, Bible study, or group of ministry interns. Two of the resources below include an exposition of the Second London Confession of Faith (2LCF). Since the 2LCF is based largely on the text and theology of the Westminster Confession (WCF), we have also included several analyses and expositions of the WCF.

Beddome, Benjamin. *A Scriptural Exposition of the Baptist Catechism*. Reprint, Birmingham, AL: Solid Ground Books, 2006.

DeYoung, Kevin. *The Good News We Almost Forgot: Rediscovering the Gospel in a 16th Century Catechism*. Chicago: Moody, 2020.

Duncan, Ligon, General Editor. *The Westminster Confession into the 21st Century: Essays in Remembrance of the 350th Anniversary of the Westminster Assembly*. 3 volumes. Geanies House, Fearn, Ross-shire, Scotland; Christian Focus, 2003, 2004, 2005, 2009.

Fesko, J. V. *The Theology of the Westminster Standards: Historical Context and Theological Insights*. Wheaton, IL: Crossway, 2014.

Hodge, Archibald A. *A Commentary on the Confession of Faith*. Philadelphia: Presbyterian Board of Publication and Sabbath-School Work, 1901.

Letham, Robert. *The Westminster Assembly: Reading Its Theology in Historical Context*. Phillipsburg: Presbyterian and Reformed, 2009.

Meade, Starr. *Comforting Hearts, Teaching Minds: Family Devotions Based on the Heidelberg Catechism*. Phillipsburg: Presbyterian and Reformed, 2013.

_____. *Training Hearts, Teaching Minds: Family Devotions Based on the Shorter Catechism*. Phillipsburg: Presbyterian and Reformed, 2000.

Mohler, R. Albert Jr. *The Apostles' Creed: Discovering Authentic Christianity in an Age of Counterfeits*. Nashville: Thomas Nelson, 2019.

Packer, J. I. *Affirming the Apostles' Creed*. Wheaton, IL: Crossway, 2008.

Pipa, Joseph A., Jr. *The Westminster Confession of Faith Study Book: A Study Guide for Churches*. Geanies House, Fearn, Ross-shire, Scotland: Christian Focus, 2005.

Shaw, Robert. *An Exposition of the Westminster Confession of Faith*. 1845; reprinted, Ross-shire, UK: Christian Focus, 1992.

Sproul, R. C. *Truths We Confess: A Layman's Guide to the Westminster Confession of Faith*. Phillipsburg: Presbyterian and Reformed, 2006, 2007.

Van Dixhoorn, Chad. *Confessing the Faith: A Reader's Guide to the Westminster Confession of Faith*. Edinburgh: The Banner of Truth, 2014.

_____. *The Minutes and Papers of the Westminster Assembly, 1643–1653*. 5 Volumes. Oxford: Oxford University Press, 2012.

Venema, Cornelis P. *But for the Grace of God: An Exposition of the Canons of Dort*. Middleville, MI: Reformed Fellowship, 2011.

Ventura, Rob, General Editor. *A New Exposition of The London Baptist Confession of Faith of 1689*. Forthcoming.

Vincent, Thomas. *The Shorter Catechism Explained from Scripture*. Reprint, Edinburgh: Banner of Truth, 1980.

Vos, Johannes G. *The Westminster Larger Catechism: A Commentary*. Phillipsburg: Presbyterian and Reformed, 2002.

Waldron, Samuel E. *A Modern Exposition of the 1689 Baptist Confession of Faith*. 5th edition. Durham, UK: Evangelical Press, 2016.

Watson, Thomas. *A Body of Divinity: Contained in Sermons Upon the Westminster Assembly's Catechism*. Reprint, Edinburgh: Banner of Truth, 1983.

Williamson, G. I. *The Westminster Confession of Faith for Study Classes*. 2nd edition. Phillipsburg: Presbyterian and Reformed, 2003.

Witsius, Herman. *The Apostles' Creed*, 2 volumes. Escondido, CA: The Den Dulk Foundation, 1993.

Printed in the USA
CPSIA information can be obtained
at www.ICGtesting.com
LVHW020143121123
763661LV00108B/5573

9 781952 599361